12th Workshop on Asian Language Resources 2016 (ALR 12)

Osaka, Japan
12 December 2016

ISBN: 978-1-5108-3334-0

Preface

This 12th Workshop on Asian Language Resources (ALR12) focuses on language resources in Asia, which has more than 2,200 spoken languages. There are now increasing efforts to build multi-lingual, multi-modal language resources, with varying levels of annotations, through manual, semi-automatic and automatic approaches, as the use of ICT spreads across Asia. Correspondingly, the development of practical applications of these language resources has also been rapidly advancing. The ALR workshop series aims to forge a better coordination and collaboration among researchers on these languages and in the NLP community in general, to develop common frameworks and processes for promoting these activities. ALR12 collaborates with ISO/TC 37/SC 4, which develops international standards for "Language Resources Management," and ELRA, which is campaigning LRE map, in order to integrate efforts to develop an Asian language resource map. Also, the workshop is supported by AFNLP, which has a dedicated Asian Language Resource Committee (ARLC), whose aim is to coordinate the important ALR initiatives with different NLP associations and conferences in Asia and other regions. This workshop consists of twelve oral papers and seven posters, plus a special session to introduce ISO/TC 37/SC 4 activities to the community, to stimulate further interactions between research and standardization.

ALR12 program co-chairs

Koiti Hasida
President, GSK
The University of Tokyo

Kam-Fai Wong
President, AFNLP
The Chinese University of Hong Kong

Nicoletta Calzolari
Honorary President, ELRA
ILC-CNR

Key-Sun Choi
Secretary, ISO/TC 37/SC 4
KAIST

Organisers

Koiti Hasida

Kam-Fai Wong

Nicoletta Calzolari

Key-Sun Choi

Programme Committee

Kenji Araki

Normaziah Aziz

Khalid Choukri

Kohji Dohsaka

Kentaro Inui

Hitoshi Isahara

Kai Ishikawa

Satoshi Kinoshita

Kiyoshi Kogure

Haizhou Li

Joseph Mariani

Fumihito Nishino

Win Pa Pa

Ayu Purwarianti

Lu Qin

Hammam Riza

Hiroaki Saito

Kiyoaki Shirai

Virach Sornlertlamvanich

Keh-Yih Su

Kumiko Tanaka-Ishii

Takenobu Tokunaga

Masao Utiyama

Table of Contents

Conference Program

Monday, December 12, 2016

09:00–09:05   *Opening*

09:05–10:25   **Oral Session 1: Annotation**

An extension of ISO-Space for annotating object direction
Daiki Gotou, Hitoshi Nishikawa and Takenobu Tokunaga

Annotation and Analysis of Discourse Relations, Temporal Relations and Multi-Layered Situational Relations in Japanese Texts
Kimi Kaneko, Saku Sugawara, Koji Mineshima and Daisuke Bekki

Developing Universal Dependencies for Mandarin Chinese
Herman Leung, Rafaël Poiret, Tak-sum Wong, Xinying Chen, Kim Gerdes and John Lee

Developing Corpus of Lecture Utterances Aligned to Slide Components
Ryo Minamiguchi and Masatoshi Tsuchiya

10:25–10:35   *Coffee Break*

10:35–11:55   **Oral Session 2: Data**

VSoLSCSum: Building a Vietnamese Sentence-Comment Dataset for Social Context Summarization
Minh-Tien Nguyen, Dac Viet Lai, Phong-Khac Do, Duc-Vu Tran and Minh-Le Nguyen

BCCWJ-DepPara: A Syntactic Annotation Treebank on the 'Balanced Corpus of Contemporary Written Japanese'
Masayuki Asahara and Yuji Matsumoto

SCTB: A Chinese Treebank in Scientific Domain
Chenhui Chu, Toshiaki Nakazawa, Daisuke Kawahara and Sadao Kurohashi

Big Community Data before World Wide Web Era
Tomoya Iwakura, Tetsuro Takahashi, Akihiro Ohtani and Kunio Matsui

Monday, December 12, 2016 (continued)

12:00–14:00   *Lunch Break*

14:00–14:30   **Poster session**

An Overview of BPPT's Indonesian Language Resources
Gunarso Gunarso and Hammam Riza

Creating Japanese Political Corpus from Local Assembly Minutes of 47 prefectures
Yasutomo Kimura, Keiichi Takamaru, Takuma Tanaka, Akio Kobayashi, Hiroki Sakaji, Yuzu Uchida, Hokuto Ototake and Shigeru Masuyama

Selective Annotation of Sentence Parts: Identification of Relevant Sub-sentential Units
Ge Xu, Xiaoyan Yang and Chu-Ren Huang

14:35–15:55   **Oral Session 3: Analysis**

The Kyutech corpus and topic segmentation using a combined method
Takashi Yamamura, Kazutaka Shimada and Shintaro Kawahara

Automatic Evaluation of Commonsense Knowledge for Refining Japanese Concept-Net
Seiya Shudo, Rafal Rzepka and Kenji Araki

SAMER: A Semi-Automatically Created Lexical Resource for Arabic Verbal Multiword Expressions Tokens Paradigm and their Morphosyntactic Features
Mohamed Al-Badrashiny, Abdelati Hawwari, Mahmoud Ghoneim and Mona Diab

Sentiment Analysis for Low Resource Languages: A Study on Informal Indonesian Tweets
Tuan Anh Le, David Moeljadi, Yasuhide Miura and Tomoko Ohkuma

Monday, December 12, 2016 (continued)

15:55–16:55   TC37 Session

Introducing ISO/TC 37/SC 4 Language Resources Management Activities
Nicoletta Calzolari

Towards Application of ISO-TimeML and ISOspace to Korean and other Asian Languages
Kiyong Lee

Standardization of Numerical Expression Extraction and Representations in English and Other Languages
Haitao Wang

Design of ISLRN for Asian Language Resources
Khalid Choukri

16:55–17:00   *Closing*

An extension of ISO-Space for annotating object direction

Daiki Gotou   **Hitoshi Nishikawa**   **Takenobu Tokunaga**
Department of Computer Science
Graduate School of Information Science and Engineering
Tokyo Institute of Technology
{gotou.d.aa@m, hitoshi@c, take@c}.titech.ac.jp

Abstract

In this paper, we extend an existing annotation scheme ISO-Space for annotating necessary spatial information for the task placing an specified object at a specified location with a specified direction according to a natural language instruction. We call such task *the spatial placement problem*. Our extension particularly focuses on describing the object direction, when the object is placed on the 2D plane. We conducted an annotation experiment in which a corpus of 20 situated dialogues were annotated. The annotation result showed the number of newly introduced tags by our proposal is not negligible. We also implemented an analyser that automatically assigns the proposed tags to the corpus and evaluated its performance. The result showed that the performance for entity tags was quite high ranging from 0.68 to 0.99 in F-measure, but not the case for relation tags, i.e. less than 0.4 in F-measure.

1 Introduction

Understanding spatial relations in natural language dialogue is an important issue, particularly in situated dialogues (Kruijff et al., 2007; Kelleher and Costello, 2008; Coventry et al., 2009), as in the following interaction between a worker and a client in a moving setting.

client : Place the refrigerator next to the sink.

worker: Like this? (with an appropriate action)

client : Well, turn it to this side. (with an appropriate gesture)

Assuming a computer agent as a worker being asked to put things at specified places, the agent has to be able to interpret the client's instructions through identifying the target object to move, the location at which the target object should be placed and often the direction of the target object itself. We call this kind of task *the spatial placement problem*, namely the task placing an specified object at a specified location with a specified direction according to a natural language instruction. As a necessary first step to realising a computer agent that is capable of dealing with the spatial placement problem, the present paper proposes an annotation scheme to represent spatial relations by extending an existing scheme.

In order to represent spatial relations, Mani et al. (2008) proposed an annotation scheme that annotates spatial objects and relations between them. However, their scheme does not handle object direction. In the above example, the Mani's scheme annotates the spatial relation "next to" between the two objects "the refrigerator" and "the sink", but does not annotate the direction of the refrigerator specified by "to this side". As long as using their annotation scheme, the annotated corpus lacks the information of the object direction. When taking a machine learning approach with the annotated corpus to deal with the spatial placement problem, annotating object directions in the corpus is indispensable.

To tackle this problem, we extend an existing annotation scheme so that it can describe the spatial direction of objects in addition to the spatial relations between objects. Based on the proposed scheme, we annotate an existing dialogue corpus, and construct an analyser that extracts the spatial information necessary for solving the spatial placement problem. The effectiveness of the proposed scheme is evaluated through the annotation result and the performance of the analyser.

In what follows, we briefly survey previous studies that deal with spatial information in natural language processing (section 2), then describes *the spatial placement problem* in detail which is the main

1

Proceedings of the 12th Workshop on Asian Language Resources,
pages 1–9, Osaka, Japan, December 12 2016.

objective of the present study (section 3). The rest of the paper describes the proposed annotation scheme (section 4) and its evaluation through automatic tagging using the proposed scheme (section 5). Finally we conclude the paper and argue the future work in section 6.

2   Related work

The past studies related to our proposal can be categorised into three groups in terms of their focal issues: (1) studies on the annotation scheme to annotate spatial information in corpora, (2) studies on the corpus construction including spatial information, and (3) studies on systems that can manipulate various objects according to natural language instructions in virtual or real spaces.

SpatialML proposed by Mani et al. (2008), which was mentioned in the previous section, is an annotation scheme to annotate spatial information in text corpora. SpatialML focuses on capturing geographic relations such as the distance and the relative spatial relation between two entities. For example, given the phrase "a town some 50 miles south of Salzburg in the central Austrian Alps", SpatialML annotates "town", "Salzburg", and "the central Austrian Alps" with a geographic location tag, and "some 50 miles" and "south of" with the distance and spatial relation tags between the two locations. However, SpatialML has no way to represent the direction of an object itself, i.e. which direction the object faces to.

Pustejovsky et al. (2011) introduced annotating events that cause changes in spatial relations into their annotation scheme ISO-Space. One of the significant characteristics of ISO-Space is describing changes in spatial relations according to temporal progression. For instance, changes in the object location through a motion event are annotated with the event path tag. In the sentence "The [depression $_{se1}$] was [moving $_{m1}$] westward at about 17mph (28 kph) and was expected to continue that motion for the next day or two.", the event path tag "EventPath($ep1$, source=$m1$, direction=WEST, moving_object=$se1$)" will be annotated in terms of a motion event $m1$ and a moving object $se1$ that are also annotated in the sentence. ISO-Space, however, does not have a tag for representing the direction of an object itself neither.

Since ISO-Space has an advantage over SpatialML that it can represent events and changes in spatial relations, we extend the ISO-Space scheme by introducing tags that describe object intrinsic direction, namely the direction that the object faces to. This kind of tags play an important role in the spatial placement problem as we saw in the previous section.

There have been several attempts of constructing corpora related to the spatial placement problem. The REX corpus (Tokunaga et al., 2012) and the PentoRef corpus (Zarrieß et al., 2016) are the examples of this sort. Both corpora were collected through situated dialogues in which dialogue participants jointly solved geometric puzzles such as Tangram and Pentomino. The main goal of the dialogues is placing puzzle pieces in the right places, thus, these tasks are the typical spatial placement problem.

These corpora come with the visual information that is updated during the course of dialogues, thus they include the spatial information of the objects. However, the transcribed utterances were not annotated with spatial information corresponding to the object direction. To our knowledge, there is no corpus that is linguistically annotated with spatial information including both object location and direction. Our attempt compensates for these missing information in the corpora for the spatial placement problem.

Winograd's SHRDLU is the first and seminal working system that is capable of dealing with the spatial placement problem (Winograd, 1972). SHRDLU could understand natural language questions and instructions on a virtual block world, and could manipulate various kinds of blocks to change the state of the block world. More recently, Tellex et al. (2011) realised a SHRDLU-like system in the real environment. They proposed Generalised Grounding Graphs to infer corresponding plans to linguistic instructions. They collected possible expressions of the instruction through crowdsourcing to construct a corpus which is used to train the inference model. However, SHRDLU nor the Tellex's system do not care about the direction of manipulated objects. As we saw in our moving example, understanding the object direction is crucial in some applications, which is the motivation of this study.

3   Spatial placement problem

The spatial placement problem is a task to place an specified object at a specified location with a specified direction as instructed in natural language. In this paper, we assume that there are multiple objects on the

2D plane, and *the worker* is asked to place the objects at specified locations according to instructions by *the instructor*. Therefore, the worker needs to infer the location to place the object, and it also needs to infer the direction that the object faces to. The spatial placement problem can be broken down into the following three steps.

1. Identifying the object
   The worker needs to identify the object to be manipulated in the instructional utterance. This task is regarded as the reference resolution in a multimodal setting (Iida et al., 2010; Prasov and Chai, 2010).

2. Deciding the specified location
   The worker needs to decide the location where the target object should be placed. This is also considered as resolving referring expression, but the referent is a location instead of an object. The spatial referring expressions include expressions such as "next to a triangle", "about one meter right of the bed", and "the centre of the room". Those expressions often specify the location in terms of the spatial relations between the target object and the other objects, often called *the reference object or landmark* (Coventry and Garrod, 2004).

3. Deciding the specified direction
   After identifying the target object and its location, the worker needs to decide the direction of the object. For instance, given the instruction "Turn the desk left.", the worker needs to decide the direction that the desk faces to. We assume that objects have their own intrinsic coordinate system (Levinson, 2003), namely they have a front side of their own. Thus, the worker needs to infer the object's front side and place the object so that its front side faces to the appropriate direction.

4   Extending annotation scheme

This section exemplifies annotation with ISO-Space and our extension using the following sequence of instructions.

(1) Move the small triangle under the square.

(2) Rotate it so that the right angle comes down.

4.1   Annotating the objects

Following the ISO-Space scheme, we annotate physical objects with the Spatial Entity tag. Thus expressions referring to objects in the current example are annotated as Spatial Entity as shown in Figure 1. The Spacial Entity tag can have attributes for describing information represented by modifiers in the referring expression.

Move [the small triangle $_{se1}$] under [the square $_{se2}$].
Rotate [it $_{se3}$] so that the right angle comes down.

Spatial Entity(se1, type=TRIANGLE, mod=SMALL)
Spatial Entity(se2, type=SQUARE)
Spatial Entity(se3)

Figure 1: Annotation example (objects)

4.2   Annotating the specified location

The location is annotated by the Location tag in ISO-Space as in Figure 2. The reference to the location "under the triangle", where the object "the small triangle" should be placed, is annotated as Location. In instruction (1), this location is specified in terms of the relative spatial relation "under" to the reference object "the square". The expression "under" is annotated as Spatial Signal as it implies the spatial relation between these two objects. The attribute of the Spatial Signal $sig1$ indicates its type of spatial relation, namely DIRECTIONAL in this case. Note that the DIRECTIONAL type stands for the spatial relation between two objects and it does not represent the direction of the object itself that we mainly concern in this paper. The Qualitative Spatial Link $qsl1$ represents the relation among the spatial relation (relType) with its surface string (trigger), the reference object (figure) and the location (ground).

Move [the small triangle $_{se1}$] [[under $_{sig1}$] [the square $_{se2}$] $_{loc1}$].
Rotate [it $_{se3}$] so that the right angle comes down.

Spatial Entity($se1$, type=TRIANGLE, mod=SMALL)
Spatial Entity($se2$, type=SQUARE)
Spatial Entity($se3$)
Location($loc1$)
Spatial Signal($sig1$, type=DIRECTIONAL)
Qualitative Spatial Link ($qsl1$, relType=LOWER, trigger=$sig1$, figure=$se2$, ground=$loc1$)

Figure 2: Annotation example (locations)

4.3 Annotating the specified direction

Until this moment, we annotated the current example solely with the ISO-Space scheme. To annotate the direction of objects, e.g. "it (the small triangle)" in our current example, we introduce the following new tags: *Direction Signal*, *Direction Link*, *Part* and *Part Link*, which are underlined in the current annotated example in Figure 3.

Direction Signal and Direction Link are analogous to Location Signal and Qualitative Spatial Link in ISO-Space. Expressions implying the object direction such as "so that the right angle comes down" are annotated with the Direction Signal tag, which a counterpart of the Location Signal tag for describing location. As the location is often described in terms of some spatial relation to the reference object, the object direction is often described by mentioning a part of the object. As a device for interrelating the Direction Signal tag with the reference part of the object, we introduce the Part tag and Part Link tag. The former is annotated to expressions describing a part of the object (e.g. "the right angle") with various attributes, and the latter relates the reference part to the entire object. These tags enable the Direction Link tag to describe the object direction by specifying the spatial direction of the reference part of the object. The Direction Signal tag has an attribute dirType that indicates *the frame of reference* (Levinson, 2003); The ABSOLUTE frame adopts an absolute coordinate system such as east-west-north-south, while the RELATIVE frame uses a reference object to indicate a direction.

ISO-Space uses the Motion tag to describe object movement that causes the change of object location. When an object rotates by itself, its location could remain the same even it changes its direction. Therefore we allow the Motion tag to describe movements that cause the object direction as well as the object location. The Move Link tag relates the movement and its related elements.

4.4 Annotation experiment

To argue the efficacy of our proposal, we have conducted an annotation exercise using an existing dialogue corpus. The annotation target is the REX corpus, a Japanese dialogue corpus in which two participants jointly solve the Tangram puzzle on the computer simulator (Tokunaga et al., 2012). The goal of the puzzle is arranging the seven pieces into a given goal shape. Both participants share the same working area where the puzzle pieces are arranged, but play different roles. One was given the goal shape but not a mouse to manipulate the pieces, while the other was given a mouse but not the goal shape. Due to such asymmetric task setting, the participant with the goal shape mostly played as an instructor and the other played as a worker. Thus this task can be considered as a typical spatial placement problem. The following is an excerpt of a dialogue[1] and Figure 4 shows a screenshot of the Tangram puzzle simulator in which the goal shape "bowl" is shown on the left.

---

[1] Although the corpus is a Japanese corpus, we use examples of its English translation in the rest of the paper for the convenience of readers who do not understand Japanese.

[Move $_{m1}$] [the small triangle $_{se1}$] [[under $_{sig1}$] [the square $_{se2}$] $_{loc1}$].
[Rotate $_{m2}$] [it $_{se3}$] [so that [the right angle $_{p1}$] comes down $_{ds1}$].

Spatial Entity($se1$, type=TRIANGLE, mod=SMALL)
Spatial Entity($se2$, type=SQUARE)
Spatial Entity($se3$)
Location($loc1$)
Spatial Signal($sig1$, type=DIRECTIONAL)
Qualitative Spatial Link ($qsl1$, relType=LOWER, trigger=$sig1$, figure=$se2$, ground=$loc1$)
Part($p1$, partType=APEX, mod=RIGHT_ANGLE)
Part Link($pl1$, trigger=$p1$, source=$se3$)
Direction Signal($ds1$, dirType=ABSOLUTE, direction=LOWER)
Direction Link($dl1$, trigger=$ds1$, source=$p1$)
Motion($m1$, motionClass=MOVE)
Motion($m2$, motionClass=ROTATE)
Move Link($ml1$, motion=$m1$, object=$se1$, goal=$loc1$)
Move Link($ml2$, motion=$m2$, object=$se3$, dirSignal=$ds1$)

* Our proposal elements are underlined.

Figure 3: Annotation example (directions)

instructor: *sore wo hidari ni suraido sasete hamete kudasai.*
          (Slide it leftward and fit it (to them).)
worker   : *hai.*
          (I see.)
instructor: *de, heikousihenkei wo 45 do kaiten sasete.*
          (Then, rotate the parallelogram by 45 degrees.)

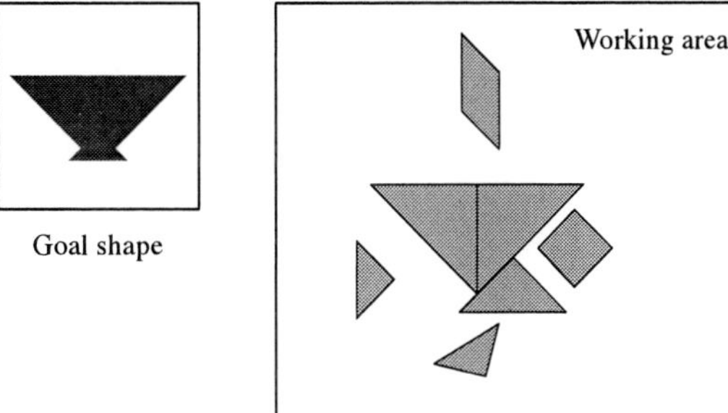

Figure 4: Screenshot of the Tangram puzzle

In this annotation experiment, we annotated the corpus with tags in Table 1 in which the underlined elements are newly introduced in our proposal. Although the ISO-Space scheme provides more than these tags, we used a minimum tag set necessary for describing the location and direction of objects for solving the spatial placement problem.

We annotated 20 dialogues with the tags listed in Table 1. The total number of utterances by the instructors was 2,020 including 360 instructional utterances. Among these 360 instructions, 60 (16.7%) of them mentioned the object direction. Table 2 shows the distribution of annotated tags in number. The table shows the number of the Directional Signal tag is comparable to that of the Spatial Signal tag, which is used for indicating spatial relations. According to this preliminary investigation, information of the object direction is not negligible in the spatial placement problem.

5   Evaluation

In order to evaluate feasibility of automatic tagging with our proposal, we implemented a system that assigns the tags shown in Table 1. Thus the goal of the system is assigning the tags to given utterances as shown in Figure 3. Given an instructional utterance, the task of the system is twofold:

entity tag	description
Spatial Entity	an entity that is not inherently a location, but one which is identified as participating in a spatial relation
Location	an inherently grounded spatial entity
Motion	an inherently spatial event, involving a change of location and direction of an object
Part	a reference to a part of an object

relation tag	description
Qualitative Spatial Link	the spatial relationship between two spatial objects
Spatial Signal	an expression representing a spatial relation
Move Link	the relation between an object changing its location or direction and its goal location or direction
Part Link	the relation between an object and its part
Direction Link	the relation between a Direction Signal instance and a reference part of an object
Direction Signal	an expression representing an object direction

* Our proposal elements are underlined.

Table 1: Annotated tags

entity tag	number	relation tag	number
Spatial Entity	357	Qualitative Spatial Link	270
Location	112	Move Link	1,420
Motion	315	Part Link	126
Part	66	Direction Link	101
		Spatial Signal	81
		Direction Signal	62
Total	850		2,060

* Our proposal elements are underlined.

Table 2: Distribution of annotated tags

1. identifying the spans to be assigned the entity tags in Table 1, and the Spatial Signal and Direction Signal tags, and

2. identifying the rest of the relations in Table 1 by linking the spans identified in step 1.

In the following subsections, each of the steps is described in more detail.

5.1 Identifying spans for entity tags

Considering the span identification for a certain tag as a sequential labelling problem, we adopt the IOB2 model (Tjong et al., 1999) to identify the tagged span. We employed the CRF++[2] implementation to conduct sequential labelling. We prepared the labelling program for each tag and ran them in parallel. Thus each tag has its own I-O-B labels. Table 3 shows correct labelling for the instruction "Rotate it so that the right angle comes down.".

tag	Rotate	it	so	that	the	right	angle	comes	down
Spatial Entity	O	B	O	O	O	O	O	O	O
Location	O	O	O	O	O	O	O	O	O
Motion	B	O	O	O	O	O	O	O	O
Part	O	O	O	O	B	I	I	O	O
Spatial Signal	O	O	O	O	O	O	O	O	O
Direction Signal	O	O	B	I	I	I	I	I	I

Table 3: Example of entity tag labelling

Given an instructional utterance for tagging, the system firstly applies the Japanese morphological analyser MeCab[3] to the input utterance to divide it into a sequence of words, then further applies the sequential labelling to the word sequence. As features for the labelling, the surface string, the part of speech, the script type (alphabet vs. digits) of the target word and its neighbouring two words in both

[2]https://taku910.github.io/crfpp/
[3]http://taku910.github.io/mecab/

sides, and the already assigned tags of the previous two words are used. Figure 5 depicts a set of features used for sequential labelling, in which the enclosed information is used for labelling the i-th word "the".

feature \ input	Rotate	it	so	that	the	right	angle	comes	down
index			$i-2$	$i-1$	i	$i+1$	$i+2$		
surface	Rotate	it	so	that	the	right	angle	comes	down
POS	verb	pron	conj	conj	det	adj	noun	verb	adv
script	alph	alph	alph	alph	alph	alph	alph	alph	alph
Spatial Entity	O	B	O	O					
Location	O	O	O	O					
Motion	B	O	O	O					
Part	O	O	O	O					
Spatial Signal	O	O	O	O					
Direction Signal	O	O	B	I					

Figure 5: Features for labelling "the"

5.2 Identifying relations

To decide the relation between tagged spans, we first constructed every pair from the set of tagged spans identified in the previous step, then we classified them into one of the relation tags listed in Table 1 except for Spatial Signal and Direction Signal since they have been already identified as the spans in the previous step. As we can see in Figure 3, the Qualitative Spatial Link and Move Link represent a trinary relation. The trinary relation is represented by two binary relations. For instance, the Move Link $ml2$ relates three spans $m1$ ("Rotate"), $se3$ ("it") and $ds1$ ("so that the right angle comes down") in Figure 3. We identify two Move Link relations between $m1$ and $se3$, and that between $m1$ and $ds1$ for this trinary relation.

Each pair is represented in terms of the features shown in Table 4 and is used for training the classifier implemented with LinearSVC[4].

feature	description
tag pair	a pair of tags assigned to two spans
distance	distance between two spans in Japanese characters
utterance length	length of the utterance in Japanese characters
number of spans	total number of spans in the utterance
pos	a quadruple of parts of speech of two adjacent word of each span
case	a pair of the case markers following each span

Table 4: Features for relation identification

5.3 Results and discussion

For both two subtasks, entity tag labelling and relation identification, we conducted the 10-fold cross validation using the corpus described in 4.4.

tag	Precision	Recall	F-measure	Total
SE	0.91	0.83	0.87	357
Motion	1.00	0.99	0.99	351
Location	0.91	0.76	0.83	112
Part	0.98	0.79	0.87	66
Spatial Signal	0.80	0.59	0.68	81
Direction Signal	0.98	1.00	0.99	62

Table 5: Result of labelling

Table 5 shows that the accuracy of the entity tag labelling is quite high. This is probably due to a very limited domain of the corpus. We should apply the proposal to corpora of broader and more complicated domains to confirm the current result.

There are two main reasons of the labelling errors: the insufficient annotation guidelines and the preprocessing errors. The number of the former is 52 and that of the latter is 138.

---

[4] http://scikit-learn.org/stable/

According to our annotation guidelines used in 4.4, only entities involved in some spatial relations were annotated. However, the analyser extracted all entities even though they had no relations with other entities. Those extracted entities were considered as the false positive instances, thus having caused errors. We should have annotated all entities regardless whether they had relations with others or not.

The errors due to the preprocessing are mainly caused by the erroneous segmentation of the Japanese morphological analyser. In this experiment, the utterances were automatically divided into a sequence of words by the Japanese morphological analyser, and thus the segmentation error causes a serious damage to the labelling phase.

Currently we apply the sequential labelling for each tag in parallel and independently. That means each labelling program does not utilise the previous two labels of other tag type. In Figure 5, for instance, when deciding the label of the Spatial Entity tag for "the", the system uses two previous Spatial Entity labels O and O but does not use labels of other tags. The performance of entity tag labelling could be further improved if the labels of other tags were also used.

Table 6 shows the result of relation identification. We calculated precision, recall and F-measure for two cases: "Gold" (using manually annotated entity tag labels) and "Estimated" (using the results of automatic labelling). The row "No Link" in the table denotes that there is no relation between the given pair of spans. Due to its dominant number of instances, the classifier might be over-tuned to the No Link class. In contrast to entity tag labelling, there is much room for improvement in relation identification. Such low performance might be attributed to the insufficient size of the corpus we used in the experiment. We need further experiments with a larger corpus.

	Gold			Estimated			
relation	P	R	F	P	R	F	Total
Qualitative Spatial Link	0.39	0.17	0.23	0.42	0.17	0.24	270
Move Link	0.41	0.39	0.40	0.43	0.27	0.33	1,420
Part Link	0.41	0.10	0.17	0.36	0.09	0.14	126
Direction Link	0.48	0.31	0.38	0.47	0.22	0.30	101
No Link	0.67	0.74	0.71	0.67	0.83	0.74	3,463

Table 6: Result of relation identification

6 Conclusion and Future Work

In this paper, we defined *the spatial placement problem* as a task placing an specified object at a specified location with a specified direction according to a natural language instruction. As a first step for tackling this problem, we proposed an extension of the existing annotation scheme ISO-Space for annotating the object direction in text corpora. To evaluate the efficacy of the proposed annotation scheme, we conducted an annotation experiment in which a corpus of 20 situated dialogues for solving the Tangram puzzle was annotated. The annotation result showed the number of newly introduced tags by our proposal is not negligible.

We implemented an analyser that automatically assigns the proposed tags to the corpus and evaluated its performance. The results showed that the performance of entity tag labelling was quite high but not the case for relation identification. The good performance of the entity tag labelling might be due to a very limited domain of the corpus. We need to conduct experiments with the corpora of broader and more complicated domains to confirm the current result. In contrast to entity tag labelling, the performance of relation identification was very poor, less than 0.4 in F-measure. This might be due to insufficient training data and over-tuning to the negative instances. We need to continue the evaluation with larger corpora of more complicated domains.

In the real setting of the spatial placement problem, the instructor uses other modalities that language, such as gesture and visuals in the instruction. The REX corpus that we used in the experiments has participant eye gaze and mouse operations on top of the transcribed utterances. Investigating the effectiveness of these kind of multimodal information in the spatial placement problem is one of the future research directions.

References

Kenny R. Coventry and Simon C. Garrod. 2004. *Saying, Seeing, and Acting*. Psychology Press.

Kenny R. Coventry, Thora Tenbrink, and John Bateman. 2009. Spatial language and dialogue: Navigating the domain. In Kenny R. Coventry, Thora Tenbrink, and John Bateman, editors, *Spatial Language and Dialogue*, pages 1–7. Oxford University Press.

Ryu Iida, Shumpei Kobayashi, and Takenobu Tokunaga. 2010. Incorporating extra-linguistic information into reference resolution in collaborative task dialogue. In *Proceedings of 48th Annual Meeting of the Association for Computational Linguistics*, pages 1259–1267.

John D. Kelleher and Fintan J. Costello. 2008. Applying computational models of spatial prepositions to visually situated dialog. *Computational Linguistics*, 35(2):271–307.

Geert-Jan M. Kruijff, Hendrik Zender, Patric Jensfelt, and Henrik I. Christensen. 2007. Situated dialogue and spatial organization: what, where and why? *International Journal of Advanced Robotic Systems*, 4(1):125–138.

Stephen C. Levinson. 2003. *Space in Language and Cognition*. Cambridge University Press.

Inderjeet Mani, Janet Hitzeman, Justin Richer, Dave Harris, Rob Quimby, and Ben Wellner. 2008. SpatialML: annotation scheme, corpora, and tools. In *Proceedings of the Sixth International Conference on Language Resources and Evaluation (LREC 2008)*, pages 410–415.

Zahar Prasov and Joyce Y. Chai. 2010. Fusing eye gaze with speech recognition hypotheses to resolve exophoric references in situated dialogue fusing eye gaze with speech recognition hypotheses to resolve exophoric references in situated dialogue. In *Proceedings of the 2010 Conference on Empirical Methods in Natural Language Processing*, pages 471–481.

James Pustejovsky, Jessica L. Moszkowicz, and Marc Verhagen. 2011. Using ISO-Space for annotating spatial information. In *Proceedings of the International Conference on Spatial Information Theory*.

Stefanie Tellex, Thomas Kollar, Steven Dickerson, Matthew R. Walter, Ashis Gopal Banerjee, Seth Teller, and Nicholas Roy. 2011. Understanding natural language commands for robotic navigation and mobile manipulation. In *Proceedings of the Twenty-Fifth AAAI Conference on Artificial Intelligence*, pages 1507–1514.

Erik F. Tjong, Kim Sang, and Jorn Veenstra. 1999. Representing text chunks. In *Proceedings of 9th Conference of the European Chapter of the Association for Computational Linguistics (EACL 1999)*, pages 173–179.

Takenobu Tokunaga, Ryu Iida, Asuka Terai, and Naoko Kuriyama. 2012. The REX corpora: A collection of multimodal corpora of referring expressions in collaborative problem solving dialogues. In *Proceedings of the Eigth International Conference on Language Resources and Evaluation (LREC 2012)*, pages 422–429.

Terry Winograd. 1972. Understanding natural language. *Cognitive Psychology*, 3(1):1–191.

Sina Zarrieß, Julian Hough, Casey Kennington, Ramesh Manuvinakurike, David DeVault, Raquel Fernandez, and David Schlangen. 2016. PentoRef: A corpus of spoken references in task-oriented dialogues. In *Proceedings of the Tenth International Conference on Language Resources and Evaluation (LREC 2016)*, pages 125–131.

Annotation and Analysis of Discourse Relations, Temporal Relations and Multi-layered Situational Relations in Japanese Texts

Kimi Kaneko
Ochanomizu University, Tokyo, Japan
`kaneko.kimi@is.ocha.ac.jp`

Saku Sugawara
University of Tokyo, Tokyo, Japan
`sakus@is.s.u-tokyo.ac.jp`

Koji Mineshima
Ochanomizu University, Tokyo, Japan
`mineshima.koji@ocha.ac.jp`

Daisuke Bekki
Ochanomizu University, Tokyo, Japan
`bekki@is.ocha.ac.jp`

Abstract

This paper proposes a methodology for building a specialized Japanese data set for recognizing temporal relations and discourse relations. In addition to temporal and discourse relations, multi-layered situational relations that distinguish generic and specific states belonging to different layers in a discourse are annotated. Our methodology has been applied to 170 text fragments taken from Wikinews articles in Japanese. The validity of our methodology is evaluated and analyzed in terms of degree of annotator agreement and frequency of errors.

1 Introduction

Understanding a structured text, such as a newspaper or a narrative, substantially involves the tasks of identifying the events described and locating them in time. Such tasks are crucial for a wide range of NLP applications, including textual entailment recognition, text summarization, and question answering. Accordingly, the task of specifying temporal information in a single text or multiple texts (cross-document event ordering) has been widely used and developed as a temporal evaluation task (Pustejovsky et al., 2009; UzZaman et al., 2012; Minard et al., 2015).

Currently, most work on temporal information processing focuses on relatively simple temporal structures, such as linear timelines. However, understanding the rich temporal content of newspapers and other similar texts often requires accounting for more complex, multi-dimensional information, including not only temporal and causal relations, but also intentional discourse relations (Asher and Lascaridas, 2003).

As an illustration, consider the mini-discourse of Figure 1:

> **(A)** The Independence Day in the United States is annually celebrated on July 4th,
> **(B) and** fireworks shows are held in various parts of the United States at night on that day.
> **(C) Because** my friend invited me to the fireworks show in New York City,
> **(D)** I saw fireworks in Brooklyn Bridge Park on the night of July 4th this year.

Figure 1: Example of discourse units A-B-C-D involving multi-dimensional temporal relations.

In this example, the temporal relation between units (A) and (B), that is, the relation of A-temporally-subsuming-B, can be specified using the temporal expressions *on July 4th* and *at night on that day*; similarly, the relations between (C) and (D), that is, C-temporally-preceding-D, and C-causally-explaining-D, can be specified by the presence of the discourse connective *because*, which explicitly indicates the causal relations.

Beyond these temporal and causal relations, however, a certain kind of temporal relation, as illustrated in the light gray and dark gray squares of Figure 2, occurs between the eventualities (i.e., events or states) described in (A)-(B), on the one hand, and those described in (C)-(D), on the other. A crucial observation is the following: Units (A) and (B) do not describe a specific eventuality (event or state) in a particular past, present or future time, but, instead, describe *general* facts of the entities mentioned (*Independence Day*, etc.); however, units (C) and (D) describe specific events occurring in a particular past time; in particular, (D) introduces an event temporally *subsumed* under the interval described in (B). We say that

10

Proceedings of the 12th Workshop on Asian Language Resources,
pages 10–19, Osaka, Japan, December 12 2016.

the (A)-(B) sequence describes a situation in the United States at the same general level, whereas the (C)-(D) sequence describes a situation at a specific level; however, (B)-(C) and (B)-(D) shift the layer of the situation from a general to a specific one. Thus, even in a single text, it is crucial to identify multiple levels of a situation described (at a general or a specific level) for a proper understanding of temporal information. We call such a (dis)continuity of a situation or a scene consisting of multiple eventualities (events or states) *a multi-layered situational relation*.

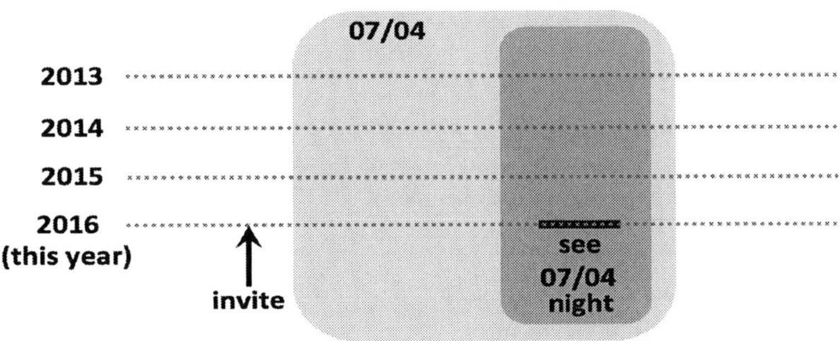

Figure 2: Multi-dimensional temporal information extracted from text in Figure 1.

The primary contribution of this paper is to introduce a new annotation schema refining and enriching previous work on temporal and discourse relation annotation schemata (Asher and Lascaridas, 2003; Kaneko and Bekki, 2014) using multi-dimensional situational relations. On the basis of the proposed method, we report a pilot annotation study of temporal and discourse relations for Japanese news texts, show an evaluation based on degree of inter-annotator agreement, and discuss the results of the annotation experiments and future work.

2 Background and Related Work

In this section, we introduce some existing studies on the annotation of temporal and discourse relations. We hypothesize that some of the difficulties in annotating temporal relations in texts stem from a failure to distinguish between two types of verbal/adjectival expressions in natural language, namely, *individual-level* predicates and *stage-level* predicates, a distinction that has been well-studied in the literature on formal semantics (Krifka et al., 1995). This distinction plays a key role in distinguishing between specific and general levels of situations described in a text. We give an overview of this distinction, which serves as necessary background for the methodology proposed in this paper.

Several specification languages for event and temporal expressions in natural language texts have been proposed, including the annotation specification language TimeML (Pustejovsky et al., 2003a); in addition, annotated corpora, such as TimeBank (Pustejovsky et al., 2003b) and the AQUAINT TimeML Corpus, have been developed. Using TimeML as a base, Asahara et al. (2013) proposed a temporal relation annotation scheme for Japanese and used it to annotate event and temporal expressions in the Balanced Corpus of Contemporary Written Japanese (BCCWJ) (Maekawa et al., 2014). More specifically, based on the framework of TempEval (Pustejovsky et al., 2009; UzZaman et al., 2012; Minard et al., 2015), Asahara et al. (2013) limited target pairs that were annotated temporal relations to the following four types of relations: (i) DCT: relations between a document creation time and an event instance, (ii) T2E: relations between temporal expressions and an event instance within one sentence, (iii) E2E: relations between two consecutive event instances, and (iv) MAT: relations between two consecutive matrix verbs of event instances. They classified event expressions into seven types, including OCCURRENCE and STATE, with respect to which the annotation agreement rates were calculated. They reported that among the seven types of event instances, those pairs containing an expression classified as STATE showed much lower degrees of inter-annotator agreement (0.424) than relations between other event instances. They argued that this difficulty was because recognition of the time interval boundaries for state expressions was relatively difficult for annotators.

We hypothesize that the difficulty in recognizing time interval boundaries of states (start and end points of states) stems from the fact that the term "state" has the following two senses: (i) permanent/stable properties of individuals and (ii) transient/episodic states applying to a particular stage of an individual. The distinction between (i) and (ii) has long been noticed in the linguistics literature; a predicate expressing a permanent/stable property of an individual is called an *individual-level predicate*, while that expressing a transient/episodic state applying to a particular stage of an individual is called a *stage-level predicate* (Carlson, 1977; Milsark, 1979; Krifka et al., 1995; Kratzer, 1995; Fernald, 2000; Ogawa, 2001). Note here that a predicate expressing a temporal and episodic event is also classified as a stage-level predicate.

For example, (1a), (1b), and (1c) are sentences containing an individual-level predicate (*being a professor of mathematics*), a stage-level predicate for an event (*gave a lecture*), and a stage-level predicate for a state (*was standing during the lecture*), respectively.

(1)   a. Susan is a professor of mathematics.   INDIVIDUAL-LEVEL/STABLE STATE

        b. Today she gave a lecture to her students on geometry.   STAGE-LEVEL/EPISODIC EVENT

        c. She was standing during the lecture.   STAGE-LEVEL/EPISODIC STATE

It seems that those examples containing an individual-level predicate cause the most difficulty in time-interval boundary recognition. For instance, it would be difficult to determine the start and end points for *being a professor of mathematics* in (1a) on the basis of the text; although it is meaningful to ask when Susan became a professor of mathematics, the information about such a temporal boundary is not the main point of statement (1a). Using the terminology introduced in Section 1, (1a) does not describe a specific eventuality (event or state), but states a general state (property) of Susan. In contrast, (1b) and (1c) introduce a temporal event or state with specific temporal boundaries. Thus, (1b) and (1c) report a continuous situation consisting of temporal events and states, while (1a) is a comment, on the individual appearing in that situation, from a different level; that is, a level that is distinguished from the level of the situation described.

It has been noticed in the literature that the distinction between individual-level predicates and stage-level predicates depends on the context of use (McNally, 1998; Jäger, 2001). In the following examples, the predicate *is an olympic swimmer* is used to deliver a temporal and transient state in (2a) extending to (2b), whereas in (3a) it expresses a stable property of John providing background information for understanding (3b).

(2)   a. John is an olympic swimmer.

        b. He will retire this spring and take up the post of head coach of the junior team.

(3)   a. John is an olympic swimmer.

        b. He participated in this olympics and was awarded a gold medal.

This means that whether a given predicate is interpreted as individual-level or stage-level often cannot be determined without reference to the surrounding context.

This example also suggests that discourse relations (rhetorical relations), such as BACKGROUND and NARRATION, play a crucial role in determining the distinction between individual-level and stage-level interpretations of predicates (that is, the layer of a situation in our terms) and, for that matter, in determining temporal relations between events/states.

With regard to discourse relations, various theories and specification languages have been proposed in the literature, including Rhetorical Structure Theory (RST) (Mann and Thompson, 1987), Segmented Discourse Representation Theory (SDRT) (Asher and Lascaridas, 2003), and many others (Carlson et al., 2001; Polanyi et al., 2004; Baldridge et al., 2007; Kaneko and Bekki, 2014). Also, annotated corpora based on them have been released, including, most notably, the Penn Discourse TreeBank (PDTB) (Prasad et al., 2005). To our knowledge, however, no label set has been proposed so far that makes a connection between discourse relations and individual/stage-level distinctions and thereby takes into account the relationship between temporal relations and discourse relations.

In fact, the difference in discourse interpretation resulting from the use of individual-level and stage-level predicates is not described by these previous theories of discourse relations. For instance, theories such as RST (Mann and Thompson, 1987) and SDRT (Asher and Lascaridas, 2003) use the discourse relation BACKGROUND to describe the relation between an event description and a state description. However, such an account fails to describe the difference exemplified in (2) and (3) because, in both cases, the first sentence describes a state in the standard sense, whereas the second sentence introduces a set of events.

PDTB (Prasad et al., 2005; Prasad et al., 2014) adopts a *lexically grounded* annotation method, in which annotators are asked to examine lexical items explicitly signaling discourse relations; when such a lexical item is absent, but a particular discourse relation is inferable for adjacent sentences, annotators are asked to find a lexical item that could serve as an explicit signal for the corresponding discourse relation. A particular label (ENTREL) is annotated when no explicit or implicit lexical item is found for adjacent sentences, but the second sentence serves to provide some further description of an entity mentioned in the first sentence (cf. *entity-based* coherence in Knott et al., 2001). This ENTREL label is the majority class label in PDTB. However, similarly to RST and SDRT, PDTB fails to capture the difference exemplified in (2) and (3), since in both examples, the second sentence provides further information about the entity (*John*) in the first sentence.

The ultimate objective of this work is to combine discourse relations, temporal relations, and multi-layered situations triggered by different types of predicates (stage-level and individual-level) in text, and, thereby, to improve existing annotation schemata for discourse and temporal information. We analyze how these different dimensions interact with one another by conducting annotation experiments.

3 Annotation Schema

We present a methodology for annotating discourse relations, temporal relations, and multi-layered situational relations. We limit target pairs for which discourse relations are annotated to (i) main and subordinate clauses in a single sentence and (ii) two consecutive sentences. For temporal relations and multi-layered situational relations, the pair of propositions in each unit is also annotated. By a proposition, we mean a tensed predicate (e.g., *hold*, *invite*, and *see* in Figure 1) denoting either an event or a (generic or specific) state. In the case of a discourse unit consisting of several propositions, such as a complex sentence, we focus on the proposition in the main clause.

The result of annotating the sample text in Figure 1 is shown below.

A-B : [NARRATION(A, B), SUBSUMPTION(A, B),
  SAME_SITU(A, B)]
B-C : [BACKGROUND(B, C), PRECEDENCE(C, B),
  SUBSUMPTION_SITU(B, C)]
B-D : [BACKGROUND(B, D), SUBSUMPTION$(B, D$
  SUBSUMPTION_SITU(B, D)]
C-D : [EXPLANATION(C, D), PRECEDENCE(C, D),
  SAME_SITU(C, D)]

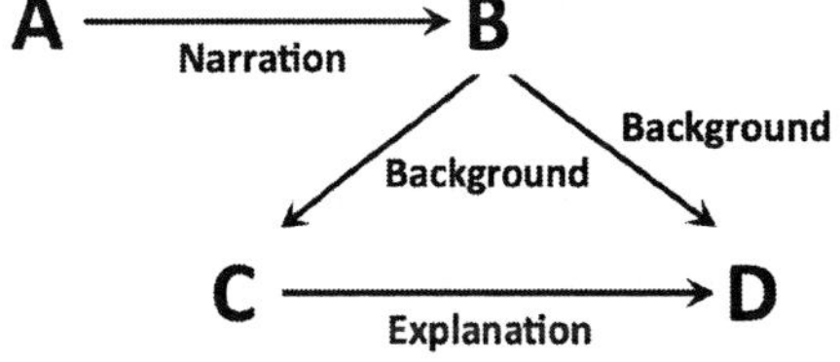

Figure 3: Result of tagging text in Figure 1.   Figure 4: Corresponding discourse graph.

In Figure 3, for each pair (X, Y) of discourse units, we annotate a triple of relations $X\text{-}Y : [D, T, S]$, where D is a discourse relation, T is a temporal relation, and S is a multi-layered situational relation between X and Y. These relations are annotated for each pair of discourse units from (A) to (D) in Figure 1. Figure 4 depicts a corresponding discourse graph that indicates the discourse relations and multi-layered situations in Figure 3. Discourse units belonging to the same layer (A-B and C-D) are positioned vertically, whereas those belonging to different layers (B-C and B-D) are positioned horizontally.

The remainder of this section is structured as follows. In Sections 3.1 and 3.2, we deal with temporal relations and multi-layered situational relations, respectively. In Section 3.3, we introduce discourse relations, and describe constraints that these three types of relations impose on one another.

Label		Description	BCCWJ-TimeBank's Labels
TEMP_REL(A, B)	PRECEDENCE(A, B)	end time (A) $<$ start time (B) In other words, eventuality A temporally precedes eventuality B.	before, after, meets, met_by
	OVERLAP(A, B)	start time (A) $<$ start time (B) $<$ end time (A) $<$ end time (B) In other words, eventuality A temporally overlaps with eventuality B.	overlapped_by, overlaps
	SUBSUMPTION(A, B)	start time (A) $<$ start time (B) & end time (B) $<$ end time (A) In other words, eventuality A temporally subsumes eventuality B. Either start times or end times between two eventualities may be simultaneous.	finishes, finished-by, during/is_included, starts, started-by, contains/includes
	SIMULTANEOUS(A, B)	Start time (A) = start time(B) & end time (B) = end time (A) In other words, eventuality A is simultaneous with eventuality B.	equal/identity
NO_TEMP_REL(A, B)		There is no temporal relation between eventuality A and eventuality B.	vague

Table 1: Temporal relations and their correspondence to temporal relations in BCCWJ-TimeBank.

Label	Description	Example
SUBSUMPTION_SITU(A, B)	The layer of situation in which A holds is more general than the one in which B holds.	**A**: The Olympic Games are held every four years. **B**: Tom participated in this Olympic Game.
SAME_SITU(A, B)	A and B hold in the same situational layer. A pair of specific eventualities, or a pair of propositions acting as individual-level predicates.	**A**: I went to the university. **B**: I took a class.

Table 2: Multi-layered situational relations.

3.1 Temporal Relations

On the basis of TimeML (Pustejovsky et al., 2003a) and BCCWJ-TimeBank (Asahara et al., 2013), we use temporal relations: PRECEDENCE, OVERLAP, SUBSUMPTION, and SIMULTANEOUS. When no temporal relations are found, NO_TEMP_REL is annotated. When any of the temporal relations (PRECEDENCE, OVERLAP, SUBSUMPTION, or SIMULTANEOUS) applies, but temporal relations are underspecified, TEMP_REL is annotated. Table 1 summarizes definitions of the temporal relations, and shows their correspondence to BCCWJ-TimeBank temporal relations. Each temporal relation can be defined as a relation between the start time and the end time of two eventualities. We assume that, for all eventualities, the start time of an eventuality e is earlier than its end time.

For each temporal relation, the order of arguments A and B can be reversed; thus, for propositions A and B with which a temporal relation is to be annotated, each temporal relation allows two possibilities; for example, PRECEDENCE(A, B) and PRECEDENCE(B, A). On the basis of these assumptions, the temporal locations of two events described by BCCWJ-TimeBank temporal relations can be reduced to the ones summarized in Table 1.

3.2 Multi-Layered Situational Relations

On the basis of the distinction between individual-level predicates and stage-level predicates as discussed in Section 2, we define multi-layered situational relations as relative differences between layers describing situations. The definition is summarized in Table 2.

For a pair of propositions A and B, multi-layered situational relations are classified into two types. First, SUBSUMPTION_SITU(A, B) indicates that A describes an individual-level, generic situation, whereas B describes a stage-level, more specific situation; hence, they belong to different layers. More specifically, we determine that the relation SUBSUMPTION_SITU(A, B) holds if (i) the main predicate in the proposition A is an individual-level predicate describing a generic state, including stable properties of individuals, and (ii) the main predicate in proposition B is a stage-level predicate describing a more specific situation (event or state). In most cases, the generic state (situation) described in A serves as background knowledge for understanding B. The multi-layered situational relations annotated in Figure 3 contain two instances of this relation, SUBSUMPTION_SITU(B, C) and SUBSUMPTION_SITU(B, D).

Secondly, the relation SAME_SITU(A, B) indicates that eventualities described in A and B belong to the same layer. There are two possibilities: Both A and B describe a stage-level, specific situation, or both A and B describe an individual-level, generic situation.

For tests distinguishing between individual-level and stage-level predicates in a given context, we use

Label	Description	Typical connectives
ALTERNATION(A, B)	"A or B": A and B denote alternative situations.	または (or)
BACKGROUND(A, B)	B describes the background situation of A.	そのとき (then)
CHANGE(A, B)	"A. By the way, B": Relation for switching a topic.	ところで、さて
CONSEQUENCE(A, B)	"If A then B": A is a condition of B.	ならば (if ∼ then ...)
CONTRAST(A, B)	"A but B": B contrasts with A.	しかし (but)
ELABORATION(A, B)	B describes a part of A in detail.	–
EXPLANATION(A, B)	A is a cause, and B is its effect.	ので、から (because)
NARRATION(A, B)	A and B occur (Alternatively, are described) in sequence, and have a common topic. A and B hold in the same situational layer.	そして、それから (and)
INSTANCE(A, B)	"A; for example, B": B describes an instance of A.	例えば (for example)
PARALLEL(A, B)	A and B have similar semantic structures, such as "It is hot in summer. It is cold in winter." Alternatively, an A is simultaneous with B.	同時に (at the same time) かつ (and)
RESTATEMENT(A, B)	B is a paraphrase of A.	つまり (namely)

Table 3: Discourse relations.

two linguistic clues/tests proposed in the literature (Kageyama, 2006). The first clue concerns the type of predicates: The following predicates (typically, appearing in the simple present tense) tend to be interpreted as individual-level predicates (Carlson, 1977).

(4)   a. Stative verbs, such as *know*, *love*, *hate*, etc. (cf. *hit*, *run*, etc.)

       b. Predicative, post-copular NPs, such as *be a professor* and *be an Olympic athlete*

       c. Adjectives, such as *intelligent*, *tall*, *blue*, etc. (cf. *drunk*, *available*, etc.)

Secondly, a stage-level predicate can be modified by an adverbial expression, such as *in a hurry*; a locative modifier, such as *in the car*; or a temporal modifier, such as *just for now* or *today*; whereas an individual predicate cannot (Kratzer, 1995). Thus, the following sentences, understood in a normal context, are anomalous:

(5)   a. *Susan is a professor {in a hurry, in the car}.

       b. *John knows Latin {in his office, today}.

In addition to the information provided by discourse relations introduced in the next subsection, these linguistic tests and clues are used to distinguish between individual-level (generic/stable) states and stage-level (specific/transient) states.

3.3   Discourse Relations

On the basis of the labels for discourse relations proposed in Kaneko and Bekki (2014), which draw on the classifications in PDTB (Prasad et al., 2005) and SDRT (Asher and Lascaridas, 2003), we use discourse relations, as summarized in Table 3. See Kaneko and Bekki (2014) and Asher and Lascaridas (2003) for more details on the definition of each discourse relation.

As mentioned in Sections 1 and 2, there is a set of discourse relations imposing constraints on temporal relations and multi-layered situational relations. Table 4 shows the manner in which temporal relations, multi-layered situational relations, and discourse relations constrain one another. By annotating discourse relations together with multi-layered situational relations, we can narrow down the range of candidates for temporal relations to be annotated. Correspondences between our labels and those presented in Kaneko and Bekki (2014) and SDRT (Asher and Lascaridas, 2003) are also shown in Table 4.

4   Results and Discussion

We applied our methodology to 90 sentences from Japanese Wikinews articles[2] in June and July 2016. The sentences were decomposed by one annotator, and labels were assigned to the decomposed segments

---

[2] https://ja.wikinews.org

Our Discourse Relation	Multi-layered Situational Relation Restriction	Temporal Restriction	Discourse Relation in Kaneko and Bekki (2014)	Discourse Relation in SDRT
ALTERNATION(A, B)	–	–	ALTERNATION(A, B)	ALTERNATION(A, B)
BACKGROUND(A, B)	SAME_SITU(A, B)	SUBSUMPTION(A, B)	BACKGROUND(A, B)	BACKGROUND(A, B)
	SUBSUMPTION_SITU(A, B)	–	COMMENTARY(A, B)	COMMENTARY(A, B)
CONSEQUENCE(A, B)	SAME_SITU(A, B)	TEMP_REL(A, B)	CONSEQUENCE(A, B)	CONSEQUENCE(A, B)
CONTRAST(A, B)	–	–	CONTRAST(A, B)	CONTRAST(A, B)
ELABORATION(A, B)	SAME_SITU(A, B)	SUBSUMPTION(A, B)	ELABORATION(A, B)	ELABORATION(A, B)
EXPLANATION(A, B)	SAME_SITU(A, B)	TEMP_REL(A, B)	EXPLANATION(A, B)	EXPLANATION(A, B) RESULT(A, B)
NARRATION(A, B)	SAME_SITU(A, B)	TEMP_REL(A, B)	NARRATION(A, B) ADDITION(A, B)	NARRATION(A, B)
CHANGE(A, B)	–	–	INTRODUCTION(A, B)	NARRATION(A, B)
INSTANCE(A, B)	SUBSUMPTION_SITU(A, B)	–	INSTANCE(A, B)	–
PARALLEL(A, B)	SAME_SITU(A, B)	–	PARALLEL(A, B)	PARALLEL(A, B)
RESTATEMENT(A, B)	SAME_SITU(A, B)	–	COMMENTARY(A, B)	COMMENTARY(A, B)

Table 4: Restrictions that types of relations impose on one another, and correspondences between our methodology, Kaneko and Bekki (2014), and SDRT.

by two annotators. We used the labels presented in Section 3, and assigned "unknown" in cases where pairs could not be labeled. The agreement for 170 pairs generated from 90 pairs and their corresponding Kappa coefficients are presented in Table 5.

Label type	Agreement	Kappa coefficient
Discourse relations	0.69	0.56
Temporal relations	0.74	0.35
Multi-layered situational relations	0.91	0.49
Mean	0.78	0.48
Total	0.89	0.86

Table 5: Agreement and Kappa coefficients in annotations.

The agreement was computed as follows:

$$Agreement = Matching\ labels/Total\ labels$$

Kaneko and Bekki (2014), which used the same set of discourse relations as ours, reported an agreement rate of 0.67 and a Kappa coefficient of 0.57 for discourse relations. Since they computed the agreement by using annotated sentence data, their results are not directly comparable with ours. Nevertheless, the similarity of the values suggests that our method is comparable to that in Kaneko and Bekki (2014) in terms of agreement.

Table 6 shows the distribution of labels for segments in our study, and compares it with that presented in Kaneko and Bekki (2014). We can see from Table 6 that NARRATION was assigned most frequently, both in our study and in Kaneko and Bekki (2014). The number of assignments of SUBSUMPTION_SITU by two annotators showed that they judged that there were some points in texts in which the situation layer had been switched.

The number of pairs for which labels tagged by two annotators were different was 52 for discourse relations, 44 for temporal relations, and 17 for multi-layered situational relations. Table 7 shows the error distribution in this annotation experiment.

Of the 52 pairs for which the two annotators assigned different discourse relations, BACKGROUND and NARRATION were assigned to 14 pairs, NARRATION and PARALLEL to 7 pairs, and NARRATION and EXPLANATION to 7 pairs. One reason that the two annotators assigned different annotations was that we did not impose constraints on BACKGROUND, NARRATION or PARALLEL with respect to assignment of temporal relations and situational relations. These three relations have been known to be difficult

---

[3]The distribution of labels in Kaneko and Bekki (2014) has been computed on the basis of Table 4.

Label	Segments	
	Kaneko and Bekki (2014)	Ours
ALTERNATION	0	$0 \cap 1 = 0$
BACKGROUND	7	$24 \cap 29 = 19$
CHANGE	8	$7 \cap 1 = 1$
CONSEQUENCE	2	$1 \cap 2 = 1$
CONTRAST	6	$12 \cap 14 = 12$
ELABORATION	23	$8 \cap 5 = 3$
EXPLANATION	10	$20 \cap 15 = 13$
NARRATION	69	$89 \cap 80 = 65$
INSTANCE	6	$0 \cap 0 = 0$
PARALLEL	0	$7 \cap 9 = 4$
RESTATEMENT	–	$0 \cap 0 = 0$
UNKNOWN	–	$0 \cap 1 = 0$
total	**128**	**170**

Annotator 1 $\cap$ Annotator 2 = Match count

Label	Segments
	Ours
TEMP_REL	$14 \cap 57 = 7$
PRECEDENCE	$88 \cap 60 = 45$
OVERLAP	$7 \cap 1 = 0$
SUBSUMPTION	$28 \cap 38 = 16$
SIMULTANEOUS	$30 \cap 3 = 3$
NO_TEMP_REL	$2 \cap 7 = 0$
UNKNOWN	$0 \cap 3 = 0$
total	**170**
SUBSUMPTION_SITU	$18 \cap 17 = 10$
SAME_SITU	$150 \cap 152 = 143$
UNKNOWN	$0 \cap 1 = 0$
total	**170**

Annotator 1 $\cap$ Annotator 2 = Match count

Table 6: Distribution of labels for segments in Kaneko and Bekki (2014) and in our study[3].

Annotator-1's label	Annotator-2's label	Frequency	Annotator-1's label	Annotator-2's label	Frequency
Discourse relation			Others		
BACKGOUND	NARRATION	14	PRECEDENCE	SUBSUMPTION	3
			SIMULTANEOUS	SUBSUMPTION	1
			SUBSUMPTION	NO_TEMP_REL	1
			SUBSUMPTION_SITU	SAME_SITU	4
PARALLEL	NARRATION	7	SIMULTANEOUS	NO_TEMP_REL	1
			PRECEDENCE	SUBSUMPTION	1
EXPLANATION	NARRATION	7		–	
BACKGOUND	ELABORATION	6	SIMULTANEOUS	SUBSUMPTION	2
			SUBSUMPTION_SITU	SAME_SITU	1
CHANGE	NARRATION	4	PRECEDENCE	SUBSUMPTION	1
			SUBSUMPTION_SITU	SAME_SITU	1
temporal relation			Others		
PRECEDENCE	SUBSUMPTION	13	BACKGOUND	NARRATION	3
			SUBSUMPTION_SITU	SAME_SITU	1
SIMULTANEOUS	SUBSUMPTION	7	BACKGOUND	ELABORATION	2
			SUBSUMPTION_SITU	SAME_SITU	2
PRECEDENCE	OVERLAP	6		–	
Multi-layered situational relation			Others		
SUBSUMPTION_SITU	SAME_SITU	15	BACKGOUND	NARRATION	4
			TEMP_REL	NO_TEMP_REL	4

Table 7: Error distribution in annotation exercise (excerpted).

to distinguish by use of a test involving insertion of a lexical item, which was used in the annotation schema of PDTB. Thus, it seems necessary to define temporal and situation constraints more precisely, or to introduce label sets for which any insertion test would be applicable.

Regarding temporal relations for which the two annotators assigned different labels, PRECEDENCE and SUBSUMPTION were assigned to 13 pairs, SIMULTANEOUS and SUBSUMPTION to 7 pairs, and PRECEDENCE and OVERLAP to 6 pairs. There are several possible reasons for these discrepancies. First, these seem to be cases in which we cannot precisely recognize time intervals, such as (B) and (D) in Figure 1; in this case, (B) and (D) only contain temporal information for *on the night of July 4th*, and therefore, SIMULTANEOUS can be assigned to this pair, as well as SUBSUMPTION. In addition, for the 6 pairs that had labeling inconsistencies between PRECEDENCE and OVERLAP, the two annotators labeled the same discourse relations and the same multi-layered situational relations. With these points in mind, our methodology should reflect partial (in)consistencies of decision, such as "we can only determine that the two eventualities temporally overlap, although their start and end point are unknown" or "we can only determine the order between the starting points of the two eventualities, although the exact time intervals of the two eventualities are ambiguous."

For multi-layered situational relations, 15 pairs were assigned SUBSUMPTION and SAME_SITU. These errors were mainly caused by ambiguity in the examples and lack of constraints imposed on discourse relations and temporal relations, as shown in Table 4. A refinement of constraints is necessary to improve the quality of annotation.

5 Conclusion

This paper proposed a methodology for building a specialized Japanese dataset for recognizing temporal relations and discourse relations. We introduced multi-layered situational relations triggered by distinctions between individual-level and stage-level predicates in text, as well as constraints imposed by each type of relation. We conducted annotation experiments in which we applied our methodology to 170 pairs of text fragments from Japanese Wikinews articles. We compared our method with that of Kaneko and Bekki (2014) in terms of agreement. In future work, we intend to address the issues discussed in Section 4. We also plan to build an inference model suited for the methodology presented in this work.

Acknowledgements

We would like to thank the anonymous reviewers at ALR12 for insightful comments. This work was supported by a Grant-in-Aid for JSPS Research Fellows, Grant Number 15J11737 and the JST CREST program, Establishment of Knowledge-Intensive Structural Natural Language Processing and Construction of Knowledge Infrastructure.

References

M. Asahara, S. Yasuda, H. Konishi, M. Imada, and K. Maekawa. 2013. BCCWJ-timebank: Temporal and event information annotation on Japanese text. In *the 27th Pacific Asia Conference of Language Information and Computation*, pages 206–214.

N. Asher and A. Lascaridas. 2003. *Logics of Conversation: Studies in Natural Language Processing*. Cambridge University Press.

Jason Baldridge, Nicholas Asher, and Julie Hunter. 2007. Annotation for and robust parsing of discourse structure on unrestricted texts. In *Zeitschrift für Sprachwissenschaft 26.2*, pages 213–239.

Lynn Carlson, John Conroy, Daniel Marcu, Dianne O'Leary, Mary Okurowski, Anthony Taylor, and William Wong. 2001. An empirical study of the relation between abstracts, extracts, and the discourse structure of texts. In *Proceedings of the DUC-2001 Workshop on Text Summarization*.

Greg N Carlson. 1977. *Reference to Kinds in English*. Garland.

Theodore Fernald. 2000. *Predicates and Temporal Arguments*. Oxford University Press.

Gerhard Jäger. 2001. Topic-comment structure and the contrast between stage level and individual level predicates. *Journal of Semantics*, pages 83–126.

Taro Kageyama. 2006. Property description as a voice phenomenon. In Masayoshi Shibatani and Taro Kageyama, editors, *Voice and Grammatical Relations: In Honor of Masayoshi Shibatani*, pages 85–114. John Benjamins.

K. Kaneko and D. Bekki. 2014. Toward a discourse theory for annotating causal relations in Japanese. In *the 28th Pacific Asia Conference of Language Information and Computation*, pages 460–469.

Angelica Kratzer. 1995. Stage-level and individual-level predicates. In Francis Jeffry Pelletier and Greg N Carlson, editors, *The Generic Book*, pages 125–175. The University of Chicago Press.

Manfred Krifka, Francis Pelletier, Greg Carlson, Alice ter Meulen, Godehard Link, and Gennaro Chierchia. 1995. Genericity: An introduction. In Francis Jeffry Pelletier and Greg N Carlson, editors, *The Generic Book*, pages 1–124. The University of Chicago Press.

Kikuo Maekawa, Makoto Yamazaki, Toshinobu Ogiso, Takehiko Maruyama, Hideki Ogura, Wakako Kashino, Hanae Koiso, Masaya Yamaguchi, Makiro Tanaka, and Yasuharu Den. 2014. Balanced corpus of contemporary written Japanese. *Language Resources and Evaluation*, 48(2):345–371.

W. C. Mann and S. Thompson. 1987. Rhetorical structure theory: A theory of text organization. Technical report, University of Southern California, Information Sciences Institute.

Luise McNally. 1998. The stage/individual distinction and (in)alienable possession. In Susan Rothstein, editor, *Events and Grammar*, pages 293–307. Springer Netherlands.

Gary Milsark. 1979. *Existential Sentences in English*. Gerland.

Anne-Lyse Minard, Manuela Speranza, Eneko Agirre, Itziar Aldabe, Marieke van Erp, Bernardo Magnini, and Ruben Urizar German Rigau. 2015. SemEval-2015 task 4: Timeline: Cross-document event ordering. In *Proceedings of the 9th International Workshop on Semantic Evaluation (SemEval 2015)*.

Yoshiki Ogawa. 2001. The stage/individual distinction and (in) alienable possession. *Language*, pages 1–25.

L. Polanyi, C. Culy, M. Van Den Berg, G. L. Thione, and D. Ahn. 2004. A rule based approach to discourse parsing. In *SIGDIAL Vol. 4*.

R. Prasad, A. Joshi, N. Dinesh, A. Lee, E. Miltsakaki, and B. Webber. 2005. The Penn discourse treebank as a resource for natural language generation. In *the Corpus Linguistics Workshop on Using Corpora for Natural Language Generation*, pages 25–32.

Rashmi Prasad, Bonnie Webber, and Aravind Joshi. 2014. Reflections on the Penn discourse treebank, comparable corpora, and complementary annotation. *Computational Linguistics*, 40(4):921–950.

James Pustejovsky, José M Castano, Robert Ingria, Roser Sauri, Robert J Gaizauskas, Andrea Setzer, Graham Katz, and Dragomir R Radev. 2003a. TimeML: Robust specification of event and temporal expressions in text. *New directions in question answering*, 3:28–34.

James Pustejovsky, David Day, Lisa Ferro, Robert Gaizauskas, Patrick Hanks, Marcia Lazo, Roser Sauri, Andrew See, Andrea Setzer, and Beth Sundheim. 2003b. The TIMEBANK corpus. In *Corpus Linguistics*, pages 647–656.

James Pustejovsky, Marc Verhagen, Xue Nianwen, Robert Gaizauskas, Mark Hepple, Frank Schilder, Graham Katz, Roser Sauri, Estela Saquete, Tommaso Caselli, Nicoletta Calzolari, Kiyong Lee, and Seohyun Im. 2009. TempEval2: Evaluating events, time expressions and temporal relations. In *SemEval-2010 Task Proposal*.

Naushad UzZaman, Hector Llorens, James Allen, Leon Derczynski, Marc Verhagen, and James Pustejovsky. 2012. TempEval-3: Evaluating events, time expressions, and temporal relations. In *SemEval-2013 Task Proposal*.

Developing Universal Dependencies for Mandarin Chinese

Herman Leung[*]   **Rafaël Poiret**[†]   **Tak-sum Wong**[*]
Xinying Chen[§]   **Kim Gerdes**[¶]   **John Lee**[*]

[*] City University of Hong Kong, [†] Zhejiang University,
[§] Xi'an Jiaotong University, [¶] Sorbonne Nouvelle, LPP (CNRS)

leung.hm@gmail.com, rafael_poiret@zju.edu.cn, tswong-c@my.cityu.edu.hk,
chenxinying@mail.xjtu.edu.cn, kim@gerdes.fr, jsylee@cityu.edu.hk

Abstract

This article proposes a Universal Dependency Annotation Scheme for Mandarin Chinese, including POS tags and dependency analysis. We identify cases of idiosyncrasy of Mandarin Chinese that are difficult to fit into the current schema which has mainly been based on the descriptions of various Indo-European languages. We discuss differences between our scheme and those of the Stanford Chinese Dependencies and the Chinese Dependency Treebank.

1   Introduction

At a time when dependency syntax is quasi-hegemonic in natural language processing (NLP), dependency treebank construction was until recently solely based on translating existing phrase-structure-based resources into dependencies (e.g., the Penn Treebank and the Stanford Dependency Parser; de Marneffe, MacCartney, & Manning, 2006), performed in the computer science departments, often in very applied perspectives. Only recently, the re-emergence of dependency-based linguistics put into question the syntactic principles underlying treebank construction. Although dependency annotation seems to be more consensual than based on phrase-structure analyses (possibly due to the lighter annotation without non-terminals or traces), different schools foster different annotation standards. For example the Prague Dependency Treebank (Böhmová, Hajič, Hajičová, & Hladká, 2003) is based on theoretical works of the Prague team (Sgall, Hajicová, & Panevová, 1986) and the Spanish MTT treebank (Mille, Vidal, Barga, & Wanner, 2009) is based on Mel'čuk's Meaning-Text Theory (1988). The annotation schemes differ mainly in the placement and number of different layers of annotation (semantics vs. deep-syntax vs. surface-syntax).

The Universal Dependencies (UD) project (de Marneffe et al., 2014; Nivre et al., 2016a) constitutes an important homogenization effort to synthesize ideas and experiences from different dependency treebanks in different languages, with the aim of facilitating multilingual research on syntax and parsing by proposing a unified annotation scheme for all languages. Up to the current version of UD (1.3)—which has released annotated data in 40 languages (Nivre et al., 2016b)—the proposed structure has been unique (no separate semantic or surface-syntactic annotation[1]). The scheme has triggered some debate on the syntactic foundation of some choices that have been made (Osborne, 2015), in particular because UD does not rely on one theoretical framework and some of the proposed goals are necessarily contradictory: syntactic correctness, applicability of the schemes for NLP tools and purposes, and above all universality (similarity of structures across languages) cannot all be fulfilled at the same time (Gerdes & Kahane, 2016). Although no separate explicit annotation scheme exists for most UD treebanks, universality seems to outweigh other considerations.

This paper describes similar choices in our adoption of UD for Mandarin Chinese, but we will try to be explicit about the advantages and disadvantages of the choices we made. The gaps and problems we describe show more generally that syntactic category and function sets that were originally created for Indo-European languages need important changes and careful balancing of criteria to foster typologically different languages, so that the distinctions become truly universal as intended. Some of

---

1   This may change in the upcoming version of the UD scheme (2.0).

Proceedings of the 12th Workshop on Asian Language Resources,
pages 20–29, Osaka, Japan, December 12 2016.

these problems can be solved by a greater universality of the vocabulary to describe the syntactic distinctions. Some idiosyncrasies simply do not have a satisfying *and* universal description.

The article starts out with a brief overview of existing dependency annotation schemes for Mandarin Chinese and how they compare overall to the UD scheme. We describe a few of the Mandarin POS tag choices of our scheme in section 3. Section 4 is devoted to the important features of our dependency annotation scheme and the sub-types of dependency relations we introduce.

2   Dependency schemes for Mandarin Chinese

Two widely used dependency schemes for Mandarin Chinese are Stanford Dependencies (SD) for Chinese (hereafter Stanford Chinese), developed by Huihsen Tseng and Pi-Chuan Chang (see Chang, 2009; Chang, Tseng, Jurafsky, & Manning, 2009), and the Chinese Dependency Treebank (CDT) developed by the Harbin Institute of Technology Research Center for Social Computing and Information Retrieval (see Che, Li, & Liu, 2012; HIT-SCIR, 2010; Zhang, Zhang, Che, & Liu, 2012). Stanford Chinese adopts its part-of-speech (POS) tagset directly from the Chinese Treebank (CTB) currently maintained at Brandeis University (Xue et al., 2013), also previously known as the Penn Chinese Treebank (hereafter Penn Chinese).

We have adapted the first version of Universal Dependencies (UD) for Mandarin Chinese (hereafter Mandarin UD) with reference to these two dependency schemes as well as the POS system of Penn Chinese. While we have taken many elements primarily from Stanford Chinese and CTB/Penn Chinese, due to their closer relation and structure to UD as well as existing SD-to-UD transformation tools, we have also made some choices that differ from some traditional Chinese linguistics analyses which Stanford Chinese and CDT follow. We will discuss these differences in detail in subsequent sections.

At the macroscopic level, our implementation of Mandarin UD differs from the other two dependency schemes in the division of labor between POS tags and relations, summarized in Table 1.

	Stanford Chinese	CDT (Harbin)	Mandarin UD
Total POS tags	**33** (rich in verbs and function words)	**26** (rich in nouns— 8 total)	**17**
Total relations	**45**	**15**	**57** (39 standard, 18 language-specific)

Table 1: Summary comparison of dependency schemes

The much smaller set of POS tags in Mandarin UD, albeit due to UD restriction, is compensated by a greater number of dependency relations, under the tenant of avoiding redundancy in annotating grammatical structures in both layers of labels. While Stanford Chinese has the highest amount of such redundancy among the three schemes, CDT takes the opposite approach of simplifying both the POS tags and dependency relations. Collapsing CDT's 8 noun POS categories into just two (nouns and proper nouns), CDT would have only three more POS tags than Mandarin UD. However, CDT differs from SD and UD in its goal of being compatible with logical semantic representation (Zhang et al., 2014). On the other hand, UD was created as a successor to SD, which was initially created to represent English syntax only (de Marneffe et al., 2014). UD was crucially created for multilingual research on syntax and parsing (Nivre et al., 2016a), hence its emphasis on cross-linguistic compatibility and rules regarding how each language should adopt it.

In the next two sections, we discuss some of the more salient examples that illustrate the issues we encountered in developing Mandarin UD.

3   Parts-of-speech annotation

Mandarin UD uses all of UD's 17 parts-of-speech (UDPOS) tags (Nivre et al., 2016a). We adopt heavily from the Penn Chinese Treebank POS system (Xia, 2000b) but differ from it in a few places, since UD's tagset is smaller and does not correspond neatly to all of Penn Chinese's tags. Since UD does not allow sub-typing of POS tags or language-specific tags, we adhere to this restriction. Below we discuss issues in adapting UDPOS for Mandarin with regard to predicate adjectives, localizers, and classifiers.

3.1 Predicate adjectives

In Chinese grammar what can be considered adjectives include two word classes, the non-predicate adjectives also known as 區別詞 *qūbiécí*, and the predicate adjectives also known as 形容詞 *xíngróngcí*. The non-predicate adjectives can only occur as prenominal modifiers. However, the predicate adjectives, despite its name, can occur both as a prenominal modifier (1a-b) and as a predicate (1c). When acting as a predicate, they are essentially intransitive stative verbs. When multisyllabic predicate adjectives act as prenominal modifiers, the particle 的 *de* is required (1b).

<table>
<tr><td>(1a)</td><td>好 花
<u>hǎo</u> huā
<u>good</u> flower
'<u>good</u> flower'</td><td>(1b)</td><td>美麗 的 花
<u>měilì</u> de huā
beautiful DE flower
'<u>beautiful</u> flower'</td><td>(1c)</td><td>那 花 很 好
nà huā hěn <u>hǎo</u>
that flower very good
'that flower <u>is good</u>'</td></tr>
</table>

While Penn Chinese treats predicate adjectives as a type of verb ('VA') separate from the nominal modifier ('JJ'), we group them together as CDT does with the non-predicate adjectives as 'ADJ', and treat the particle 的 *de* as an adjectival marker in this case (such as in (1b)). The advantage of shuffling this subclass of verbs is that we are able to separate the intransitive stative uses of the predicate verbs from other verbs, since UD does not allow one to create subcategorical POS tags. Additionally, the modifier and predicate uses of predicate verbs are easily differentiated from each other simply by looking at their head in the dependency representation. Since the decision to tag predicate adjectives as ADJ is also supported in other languages such as in the Japanese implementation of UD (Tanaka et al., 2016), we consider our categorization to be more advantageous for cross-linguistic comparison.

3.2 Localizers

This class of words is known in Chinese linguistic literature as 方位詞 *fāngwèicí*. They come after a noun and primarily indicate spatial information in relation to the noun (with grammaticized uses for temporal and other abstract concepts of location), and are often additionally paired with the preposition 在 *zài*. Examples include 上 *shàng* 'above', 中 *zhōng* 'middle', 外 *wài* 'outside', 前 *qián* 'front', 旁 *páng* 'side', among others. Both Penn Chinese and CDT give localizers a unique tag—'LC' for 'localizer' (2a) and 'nd' for 'direction noun' (2b), respectively.

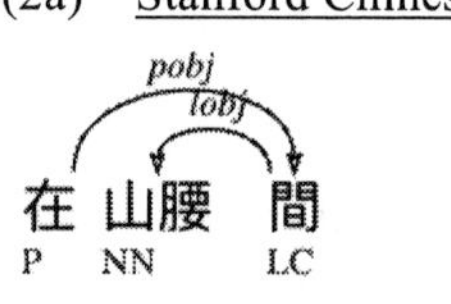
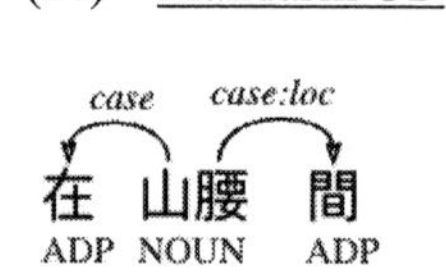

(2a) <u>Stanford Chinese</u>　(2b) <u>CDT</u>　(2c) <u>Mandarin UD</u>

zài shānyāo　　　jiān
at　mountain.waist　between
'on the mountainside'

Although localizers historically derive from nouns, they no longer have the same syntactic distribution of regular nouns and are rather limited in their usage in providing spatial information to another noun. While CDT categorizes them as nouns and Penn Chinese appears semi-agnostic in giving them a unique tag, we treat them as postpositions after early research (Peyraube, 1980; Ernst, 1988) as well as recent research (Djamouri, Waltraud, & Whitman, 2013; Waltraud, 2015), the latter of which take into account historical Chinese data as well as cross-linguistic observations, notably German which also has both prepositions and postpositions. Therefore we tag them as ADP, as adpositions (2c).

3.3 Classifiers

Classifiers are an indispensable lexical category in Mandarin as well as many East Asian and Southeast Asian languages. In Mandarin, they are often obligatorily present with a numeral modifying a noun (3)[2]. Often they are also the head of a nominal phrase when a regular noun is not present (4). They differ from nouns in that classifiers can be preceded by numerals in all syntactic contexts, but nouns can only be preceded by numerals without an intervening classifier in exceptional cases. Additionally, attributive adjectives can never immediately precede or modify a classifier, but they do so with nouns, so that a noun phrase involving all three must have the order *classifier-adjective-noun* (5). It is likely due to the unique syntactic distribution of classifiers that both Penn Chinese and CDT give them unique POS tags—'M' for 'measure word' and 'q' for 'quantity', respectively.

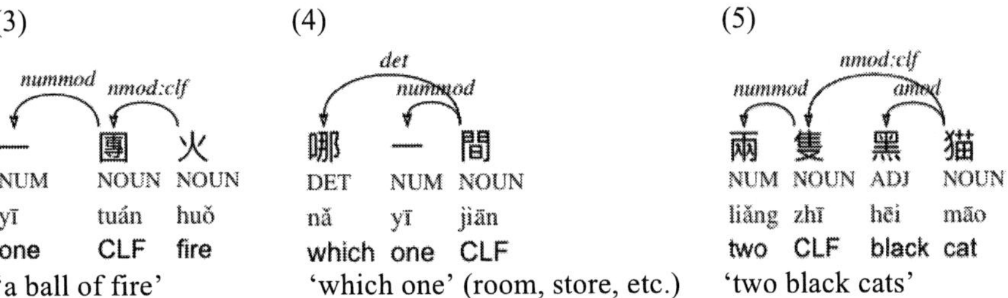

Nonetheless, due to the classifiers' partially similar syntactic distribution (when acting as the head of a noun phrase) as well as close relation to nouns—with analogy to measure words in languages such as English (e.g., *a head of cattle*) and Danish (e.g., *en kop kaffe* 'a cup of coffee')—we decided to place them under the tag NOUN, since UDPOS prohibits language-specific tags. We also considered PART ('particle'), but this would conflate classifiers with function words that cannot function as heads.

The distinction between regular nouns and classifiers is currently preserved with the dependency relation `nmod:clf`, which is used to label a classifier when it precedes a noun (3, 5). However, the distinction is lost when the classifier is the head of a noun phrase (4). We are not currently implementing features in our Mandarin UD, but a NounType feature may be a future consideration. We are also in discussion with the UD community in order to include this widely neglected category in the upcoming UD 2.0 specifications.

4   Syntax annotation

Our adoption of UD for Mandarin Chinese has presented a number of syntactic challenges, some of which are due to particular constructions whose analyses are controversial or under-researched, and some are due to what might be insufficiencies in the UD design itself. We discuss some of these issues in the subsections below.

We use 39 of the 40 dependency relations available in UD as laid out in Nivre et al. (2016), leaving out `expl` since expletives do not exist in Mandarin, and additionally propose 18 language-specific dependency relations as permitted by UD, shown in Table 2.

Label	Description	Label	Description
acl:irrealis	'irrealis descriptive clause'	**discourse:sp**	'sentence particle'
acl:realis	'realis descriptive clause'	**dobj:light**	'direct object of light verb'
advcl:purpose	'adverbial purpose clause'	**mark:dec**	'adjectival/complementizer/ nominalizer DE'
advmod:df	'duration & frequency adverbial modifiers'	**mark:dev**	'manner adverbializer DE'
aux:aspect	'aspect marker'	**nmod:agent**	'agent in long BEI phrase'
case:loc	'localizer'	**nmod:clf**	'classifier modifier'
compound:dir	'directional verb compound'	**nmod:dobj**	'direct object in BA phrase'
compound:der	'descriptive/extent DE compound'	**nmod:poss**	'possessive nominal modifier'
compound:ov	'other verb compound'	**nmod:tmod**	'temporal nominal modifier'

Table 2: Proposed language-specific relations in Mandarin UD

---

2   All tree diagrams in this paper illustrate Mandarin UD annotation unless explicitly labeled otherwise.

4.1 Adpositional phrases

One major systematic difference between UD and the previous SD (Stanford Dependencies) as well as CDT is in the treatment of adpositional phrases. Conforming to the SD system, Stanford Chinese treats all prepositions as well as postpositions as the head of adpositional phrases, with the nouns they introduce as their dependents. CDT employs the same treatment, as seen earlier in (2a-c) under the discussion of localizers in section 3.2. Since many of these adpositions also have grammaticized functions which introduce clauses instead of noun phrases, some clauses are also treated as dependents of these functions words in these schemes, illustrated in (6a-b) with a temporal adverbial clause marked by the clause-final 後 *hòu* 'after' (grammaticized from the postposition 後 *hòu* 'behind').

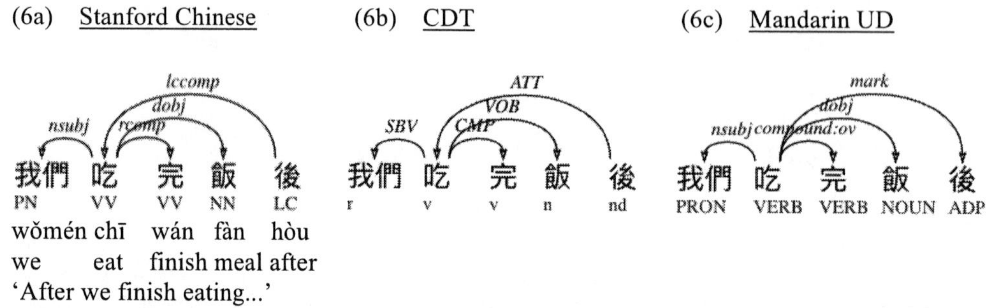

This approach of treating these function words as heads is abandoned in UD in favor of assigning heads to content words instead of function words (Nivre et al., 2016a). This not only means that the direction of the dependency relations for the above-mentioned function words are reversed in our implementation of Mandarin UD, as illustrated in (6a-c), but some of the head-child relations are also shifted, as illustrated in the earlier examples of localizers in (2a-c).

In the case of (2a-c), our implementation unfortunately loses hierarchical information between the preposition and postposition because we treat them both as direct dependents of the noun (2c), in contrast to Stanford Chinese (2a) and CDT's (2b) approaches that indicate the postpositional/localizer phrase is embedded in the prepositional phrase. However, our approach is necessary to meet the demands of the UD rubric in treating content words as governors of function words.

4.2 Aspect particles

There are three basic aspect particles in Mandarin: perfective 了 *le,* durative 着 *zhe,* and experiential 過 *guo.* Although they are written as individual characters, they can be considered suffixes since they attach immediately after verbs and have lost their original tones, making them prosodically (as well as morphosyntactically) dependent. Etymologically they likely grammaticized from verbs but no longer retain any verbal characteristics (aside from conveying aspect). We propose the language-specific `aux:aspect` to link these particles to the verb (7).

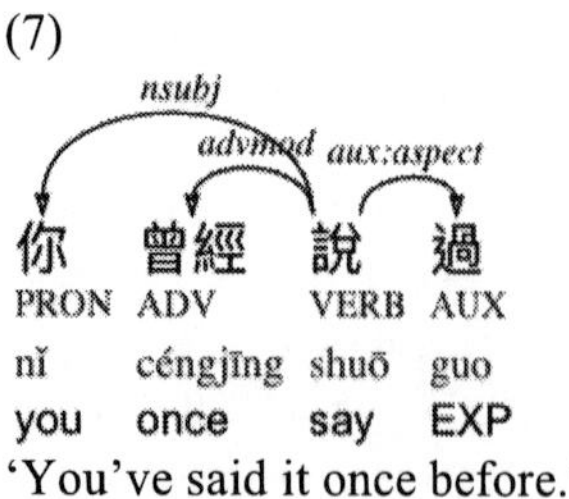

These aspect markers fit well as a subcategory of the `aux` relation because that is the only relation whose associated tag AUX has a definitional mention of verbal marking including aspect (besides tense, mood, as well as person and number marking). However, UD specifies that the `aux` relation as well as the AUX tag are used only for auxiliary *verbs,* which seems to be problematic because verbal markers are not all verbs or verbal in origin cross-linguistically. Mandarin aspect particles/suffixes are neither auxiliary verbs nor verbs, but unlike inflectional elements in morphologically rich languages, we treat them as separate tokens. Nonetheless, not all verbal markers in all languages are affixes (for example, see Bickel and Nichols, 2013), so in those languages the unbound verbal markers should be treated as individual tokens and should not be marked as part of the word token. We therefore believe there is a gap in the UD schema and that the UD definition for aux (and AUX) may benefit from revision in order to take non-affixal, non-verb verbal markers into account.

We have also considered using compound to link the aspect markers to the verb, but since this relation is used only for derivational or compositional structures rather than inflectional markers, it is not ideal, either. We tentatively annotate the aspect markers with aux:aspect, despite violation of the current UD definitions.

4.3 Sentence-final particles

Similar to classifiers, sentence-final particles are an areal feature across many East and Southeast Asian languages. They occur at the end of a sentence or utterance (8), and may have a wide variety of non-referential meanings and functions that modify the entire sentence, including modality, speech register, "speaker/hearer orientation", and other discourse and pragmatic uses. In Mandarin, these particles include 嗎 *ma* (interrogative), 了 *le* (new situation), 吧 *ba* (command/suggestion), 的 *de* (certainty), among others. They are integrated into the sentence they attach to as part of its prosodic contour with no pause in between.

(8)

'Then just let them steal.'

Although not all sentence-final particles have discourse functions, and more importantly they are very different from interjections, they seem to fit best as a sub-relation of discourse despite the fact that this relation is currently classified as a nominal dependent (of the main governor of a clause). We have also considered advmod, but the function and especially syntactic distribution of these particles are quite different from adverbs given that adverbs in Mandarin are usually preverbal and do not have a fixed syntactic position. We believe the lack of an obvious and natural space for these particles may be another possible gap in the UD schema. We tentatively propose discourse:sp for "sentence particle" to keep the name applicable cross-linguistically (for example, see Dryer, 2008, for varying positions of question particles across languages).

4.4 Light verb constructions

A number of verbs in Mandarin have semantically weakened and are used in combination with nouns to express new verbal concepts. A salient example is the verb 打 *dǎ*, which as a main verb by itself has the meaning "to hit" or "to strike." However, this meaning is no longer present, or only a vestige of it is retained, when the verb combines with nouns like 針 zhēn 'needle', 球 *qiú* 'ball', 電話 *diànhuà* 'telephone': 打針 *dǎzhēn* 'to get/give an injection', 打球 *dǎqiú* 'to play (a) ball (game)', 打電話 *dǎdiànhuà* 'to make a phone call'.

Ordinarily, UD includes light verb constructions under compound, listing Persian and Japanese as examples of languages with these constructions. However, in Mandarin the verb-noun "compound" is not a tight unit. The aspect markers still attach directly after the verb before the noun, as do duration and frequency adverbial phrases (9). The verb can further compound itself (10). For this reason we propose `dobj:light` to link the noun to the verb since the noun still behaves like a direct object, and the dependency relation will enable a distinction between the light and full verb usages of the same Chinese character.

(9)   (10)

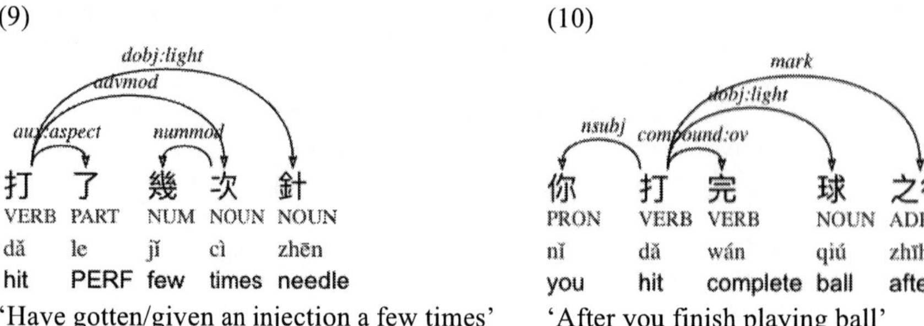

'Have gotten/given an injection a few times'   'After you finish playing ball'

4.5 Descriptive clauses

Among the most difficult structures we encountered in implementing UD for Mandarin are descriptive clauses. Li & Thompson (1981) describe two related constructions of the sequence [NP1] + <u>V1</u> + [NP2] + <u>V2</u> in which the second verb V2 (or the clause it heads) describes or comments on the second noun phrase NP2, and NP2 also serves as an object of the first verb V1. They refer to them as "realis" and "irrealis descriptive clauses" (pp. 611-620). For the *realis* kind, the clause headed by V2 describes something that is "in the here and now of the 'real world' " (p. 612)—such as 我很喜歡吃 *wǒ hén xǐhuān chī* 'I very much enjoyed eating' in (11). For the *irrealis* kind, the V2 clause describes "an unrealized event" which is "hypothetical or projected information" (p. 612), as shown by 吃 *chī* 'eat' in (12).

(11)   [他] <u>炒</u> 了 [一 個 菜] (我 很 <u>喜歡</u> 吃)   (cf. Li & Thompson, 1981: 612)
        tā chǎo le yí gè cài wǒ hén xǐhuān chī
        he fry PERF one CLF dish I very like   eat
        'He cooked a dish (that I very much enjoyed eating).'   *realis descriptive clause*

(12)   [我] <u>找</u> [東西] (<u>吃</u>)
        wǒ zhǎo dōngxǐ chī
        I   seek   thing   eat
        'I'm looking for stuff (to eat).'   *irrealis descriptive clause*

The fact that the clause headed by V2 is entirely optional in (11-12) (shown in parentheses), and that NP2 is not necessarily the subject of V2 (but an object of V2 in (12) and of a verb in an embedded clausal argument of V2 in (11)), sets these descriptive clauses apart from "pivotal constructions" (as described in Chao, 1968, and Li & Thompson, 1981). Pivotal constructions, as a type of control structure (specifically, object control), obligatorily requires the V2 clause as a clausal complement of V1, and the "pivot" NP2 must also be the subject of V2. For this reason, `xcomp`, the relation appropriate for pivotal constructions, is a bad fit for descriptive clauses.

   One possible analysis of these descriptive clauses is that they are clausal modifiers of NP2, given that they are descriptive of NP2, always involve a predicate, and are optional. This fits the definition of the relation `acl` ('clausal modifier of noun'), in which case V2 would be an `acl` dependent of NP2 (13). However, this analysis goes against the fact that Chinese is typologically regarded as a language that is strictly head-final with regards to nouns. That is, in noun phrases the noun is always last and any modifiers of that noun must precede it.

   Li & Thompson suggests that the *realis* descriptive construction such as in (11) is biclausal, where V2 heads a separate clause that has a dropped argument (an object coreferential with NP2 in these cases of (11-12)). However, this structure has received very little attention in the literature (Peng, 2016), and no study known to us to date has proposed a detailed syntactic analysis which refutes or agrees with Li & Thompson's hypothesis. Nonetheless, another option for us is to follow Li & Thompson in treating them as coordinated clauses with the `conj` relation linking V1 and V2 (14). Simplified diagrams in (13-14) illustrate the annotation differences between our two choices of `acl` and `conj` for realis descriptive clauses.

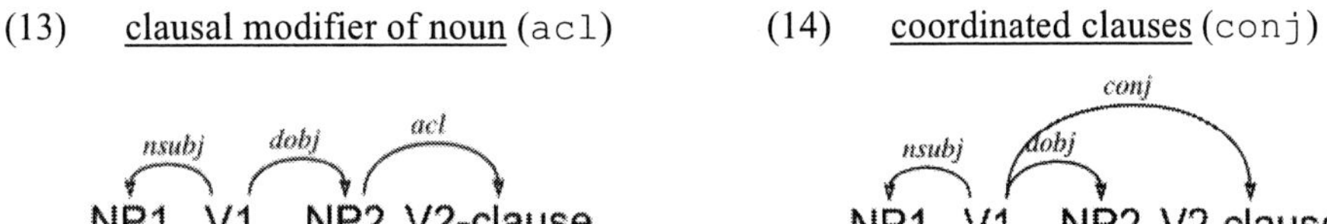

While Peng's (2016) comprehensive corpus study has brought *realis* descriptive clauses to the fore in recent years, much less research has been done on the *irrealis* ones. Li & Thompson themselves offer only several descriptive sentences on this structure, and the biclausal analysis for the *realis* constructions doesn't fit the *irrealis* ones. Sentence (15) illustrates that the subject of V2 is not coreferential with any of the noun phrases within the sentence:

(15)   [我] 有 [衣服] 要 洗   *irrealis descriptive clause*
       wǒ yǒu yīfǔ   yào xǐ
       I   have clothes need wash
       'I have clothes that need to be washed.'

In (15), the subject of the second verb is necessarily *unspecified*; whether the person who would hypothetically wash the clothes is intended to be the speaker herself or the addressee or some third party is completely arbitrary. Since subjects are only dropped in Mandarin if it can be understood pragmatically from previous context (Chao, 1968), the hypothesis that the second verb is part of an independent clause with a dropped subject is unlikely, and thus the `conj` relation would be inappropriate.

The two similar constructions above, *realis* and *irrealis* descriptive clauses, occur very frequently in Chinese, as illustrated in Peng's (2016) study of the *realis* descriptive constructions in particular, yet we have found no explicit mention in either Stanford Chinese or CDT on how to treat these structures.

Since these two types of clauses share the function of providing additional descriptive information on NP2, we propose to keep them under the same category of relations and use `acl:realis` and `acl:irrealis`, which is preferable to splitting them apart between `conj` and `acl`. Creating the two language-specific relations for these structures will also allow for easier automatic conversion in the future for either only one of the clause types or both, should new research reveal that they should be analyzed differently.

5   Conclusion and future work

We have presented our attempt to adopt Universal Dependencies (UD) to Mandarin Chinese with consideration and reference to two other dependency schemes previously created for this language, illustrating some of the challenges and solutions we have encountered and made with regard to the morphosyntactic properties of Mandarin. Through these discussions we identified possible gaps in the current UD design, especially with regards to verbal markers and sentence particles that lie beyond the purview of adverbial modifiers and discourse markers. We also identified two common structures in Mandarin, the realis and irrealis descriptive clauses, that may have eluded analysis and explicit treatment in other Chinese treebank schemes.

We are in the process of applying our proposed annotation scheme to the Mandarin Chinese text in a Cantonese-Mandarin Parallel Corpus (Lee, 2011) of over 8000 lines of text. We plan to develop Universal Dependencies for Cantonese as well, to enable comparative studies on the grammars of the two Chinese languages. Once the treebanks for Mandarin and Cantonese are finalized, we hope to release them as part of the UD project, to be made publicly available through its website (http://universaldependencies.org).

Acknowledgements

This work was supported by a grant from the PROCORE-France/Hong Kong Joint Research Scheme sponsored by the Research Grants Council and the Consulate General of France in Hong Kong (Reference No.: F-CityU107/15 and N° 35322RG); and by a Strategic Research Grant (Project No. 7004494) from City University of Hong Kong.

References

Bickel, Balthasar and Johanna Nichols. 2013. Inflectional Synthesis of the Verb. In Matthew S. Dryer and Martin Haspelmath, editors, *The World Atlas of Language Structures Online*. Max Planck Institute for Evolutionary Anthropology, Leipzig, chapter 22, http://wals.info/chapter/22.

Böhmová, Alena, Jan Hajič, Eva Hajičová, and Barbora Hladká. 2003. The Prague dependency treebank. In *Treebanks*. Springer Netherlands, pages 103-127.

Chang, Pi-Chuan. 2009. Improving Chinese-English Machine Translation through Better Source-side Linguistic Processing. Ph.D. Dissertation, Stanford University.

Chang, Pi-Chuan, Huihsin Tseng, Dan Jurafsky, and Christopher D. Manning. 2009. Discriminative Reordering with Chinese Grammatical Relations Features. *Proceedings of the Third Workshop on Syntax and Structure in Statistical Translation*: 51-59.

Chao, Yuen Ren. 1968. *A Grammar of Spoken Chinese*. University of California Press.

Che, Wanxiang, Zhenghua Li, and Ting Liu. 2012. Chinese Dependency Treebank 1.0 LDC2012T05. Linguistic Data Consortium, Philadelphia. https://catalog.ldc.upenn.edu/LDC2012T05

Djamouri, Redouane, Paul Waltraud, and John Whitman. 2013. Postpositions vs prepositions in Mandarin Chinese: The articulation of disharmony. In Theresa Biberauer and Michelle Sheehan, editors, *Theoretical Approaches to Disharmonic Word Order*. Oxford University Press, pages 4-105.

Dryer, Matthew S. 2008. Position of polar question particles. In Matthew S. Dryer and Martin Haspelmath, editors, *The World Atlas of Language Structures Online*. Max Planck Institute for Evolutionary Anthropology, Leipzig, chapter 92, http://wals.info/chapter/92.

Ernst, Thomas. 1988. Chinese postpositions—Again. *Journal of Chinese Linguistics* 16(2): 219-244.

Gerdes, Kim, and Sylvain Kahane. 2016. Dependency Annotation Choices: Assessing Theoretical and Practical Issues of Universal Dependencies. *Proceedings of the 10th Linguistic Annotation Workshop held in conjunction with ACL 2016* (LAW-X 2016): 131.

Harbin Institute of Technology Research Center for Social Computing and Information Retrieval (哈尔滨工业大学信息检索研究中心) [HIT-SCIR]. 2010. HIT-CIR Chinese Dependency Treebank Annotation Guideline (HIT-CIR 汉语依存树库标注规范).

Lee, John. 2011. Toward a Parallel Corpus of Spoken Cantonese and Written Chinese. *Proceedings of the 5th International Joint Conference on Natural Language Processing*: 1462-1466.

Li, Charles N. and Sandra A. Thompson. 1981. *Mandarin Chinese: A Functional Reference Grammar*. University of California Press.

de Marneffe, Marie-Catherine, Bill MacCartney, and Christopher D. Manning. 2006. Generating typed dependency parses from phrase structure parses. *Proceedings of the Fifth International Conference on Language Resources and Evaluation* (LREC 2006): 449-454.

de Marneffe, Marie-Catherine, Timothy Dozat, Natalia Silveira, Katri Haverinen, Filip Ginter, Joakim Nivre, and Christopher D. Manning. 2014. Universal Stanford Dependencies: A cross-linguistic typology. *Proceedings of the Ninth International Conference on Language Resources and Evaluation* (LREC 2014): 4584-4592.

Mel'čuk, Igor. 1988. *Dependency syntax: Theory and Practice*. SUNY Press.

Mille, Simon, Vanesa Vidal, Alicia Barga, and Leo Wanner. 2009. Creating an MTT Treebank of Spanish. *Proceedings of the Fourth International Conference on Meaning-Text Theory*.

Nivre, Joakim, Marie-Catherine de Marneffe, Filip Ginter, Yoav Goldberg, Jan Hajič, Christopher D. Manning, Ryan McDonald, Slav Petrov, Sampo Pyysalo, Natalia Silveira, Reut Tsarfaty, and Daniel Zeman. 2016a. Universal Dependencies v1: A Multilingual Treebank Collection. *Proceedings of the Tenth International Conference on Language Resources and Evaluation* (LREC 2016): 1659-1666.

Nivre, Joakim, Željko Agić, Lars Ahrenberg, et al., 2016, *Universal Dependencies 1.3*, LINDAT/CLARIN digital library at the Institute of Formal and Applied Linguistics, Charles University in Prague, http://hdl.handle.net/11234/1-1699.

Osborne, Timothy. 2015. Diagnostics for Constituents: Dependency, Constituency, and the Status of Function Words. *Proceedings of the Third International Conference on Dependency Linguistics* (Depling 2015): 251-260.

Peng, Rui. 2016. Chinese Descriptive Pivotal Construction: Taxonomy and Prototypicality. *Language and Linguistics* 17(4): 529-573.

Peyraube, Alain. 1980. *Les constructions locatives en chinois moderne*. Editions Langages croisés, Paris.

Sgall, Petr, Eva Hajicová, and Jarmila Panevová. 1986. *The meaning of the sentence in its semantic and pragmatic aspects*. Kluwer, Dordrecht.

Tanaka, Takaaki, Yusuke Miyao, Masayuki Asahara, Sumire Uematsu, Hiroshi Kanayama, Shinsuke Mori, and Yuji Matsumoto. 2016. Universal Dependencies for Japanese. *Proceedings of the Tenth International Conference on Language Resources and Evaluation* (LREC 2016): 1651-1658.

Waltraud, Paul. 2015. *New Perspectives on Chinese Syntax*. De Gruyter, Berlin.

Xia, Fei. 2000a. The Segmentation Guideliens for the Penn Chinese Treebank (3.0). University of Pennsylvania Institute for Research in Cognitive Science Technical Report No. IRCS-00-06, http://repository.upenn.edu/ircs_reports/37/

Xia, Fei. 2000b. The Part-of-Speech Tagging Guidelines for the Penn Chinese Treebank (3.0). University of Pennsylvania Institute for Research in Cognitive Science Technical Report No. IRCS-00-07, http://repository.upenn.edu/ircs_reports/38/

Xue, Nianwen, Xiuhong Zhang, Zixin Jiang, Martha Palmer, Fei Xia, Fu-Dong Chiou, and Meiyu Chang. 2013. Chinese Treebank 8.0 LDC2013T21. Linguistic Data Consortium, Philadelphia, https://catalog.ldc.upenn.edu/ldc2013t21

Zhang, Meishan, Yue Zhang, Wanxiang Che, and Ting Liu. 2014. A Semantics Oriented Grammar for Chinese Treebanking. *CICLing 2014, Part I:* LNCS 8403: 366-378.

Developing Corpus of Lecture Utterances Aligned to Slide Components

Ryo Minamiguchi and **Masatoshi Tsuchiya**
Department of Computer Science and Engineering
Toyohashi University of Technology
1–1 Hibarigaoka, Tempaku-cho, Toyohashi, Aichi, Japan
`minamiguchi@is.cs.tut.ac.jp` and `tsuchiya@cs.tut.ac.jp`

Abstract

The approach which formulates the automatic text summarization as a maximum coverage problem with knapsack constraint over a set of textual units and a set of weighted conceptual units is promising. However, it is quite important and difficult to determine the appropriate granularity of conceptual units for this formulation. In order to resolve this problem, we are examining to use components of presentation slides as conceptual units to generate a summary of lecture utterances, instead of other possible conceptual units like base noun phrases or important nouns. This paper explains our developing corpus designed to evaluate our proposing approach, which consists of presentation slides and lecture utterances aligned to presentation slide components.

1 Introduction

Automatic text summarization is one of the tasks that have long been studied in natural language processing area. One of well-known approaches for automatic text summarization is an extractive method which picks important textual units (e.g. sentences) from given documents (Kupiec et al., 1995; Goldstein et al., 2000; Radev et al., 2000).

(Filatova and Hatzivassiloglou, 2004) introduced *conceptual units* to represent meaning components, and formulated the extractive method of text summarization as a maximum coverage problem with knapsack constraint (henceforth, denoted as MCKP). Suppose a finite set T of textual units which means whole given documents, and a finite set C of conceptual units which represents whole information described by T. In this representation, a textual unit may describe one or more conceptual units, and an information overlap between picked textual units is considered as a redundant conceptual unit(s) which is described by plural textual units. In other words, the meaning of each textual unit is regarded as a subset of C, and the extractive method of text summarization is defined as a problem to find a subset of T which satisfies the constraint of its total length and describes as many conceptual units as possible. Various methods including greedy algorithm (Filatova and Hatzivassiloglou, 2004), stack decoding (Yih et al., 2007) and linear programming solver (Takamura and Okumura, 2009) were employed to solve text summarization in this representation.

This representation provides a concrete and concise formulation of text summarization, however, a big problem still remains: the appropriate granularity of conceptual units. (Hovy et al., 2006) proposed to use basic elements as conceptual units, which are dependency subtrees obtained by trimming dependency trees. (Takamura and Okumura, 2009) proposed to use weighted content words as conceptual units, whose weights reflect their importance. Although these possible conceptual units treat linguistic clues of original documents, they do not represent the intuition of the writer (or the speaker) of the original documents.

In order to resolve this problem, we are examining to extract dependency structure between primitive objects such as texts, pictures, lines and basic diagrams, and to use these objects as conceptual units when generating a summary of lecture utterances. We think that this approach has two advantages than the previous approach of conceptual units. The first is that terminology and character formatting of these objects may reflect the intuition of the lecturer about his/her talk, because these objects are selected

Place license statement here for the camera-ready version, see Section **??** of the instructions for preparing a manuscript.

Proceedings of the 12th Workshop on Asian Language Resources,
pages 30–37, Osaka, Japan, December 12 2016.

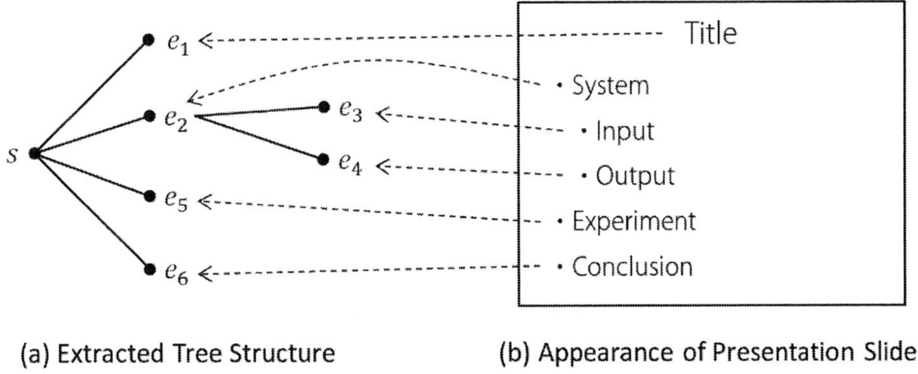

Figure 1: A presentation slide example

and located by him/herself. For example, he/she will use either a larger point font or a bold style font, to represent an important part of his/her talk. The second is that this approach naturally introduces multi-level granularity of conceptual units because our using method proposed by (Hayama et al., 2008) extracts relationship between objects as a tree structure. When multi-level granularity of conceptual units is available, the remaining problem to decide appropriate granularity of conceptual units can be considered as a simple optimization problem.

This paper explains our developing corpus which consists of lecture utterances, presentation slides, and their alignment information. We think that this corpus will give a foundation to evaluate our assumption about conceptual units.

2 Structure of Presentation Slide

Generally speaking, a presentation slide consists of one or more primitive objects, such as texts, pictures, lines and basic diagrams. We call these primitive objects as *slide components* in this paper. Slide components are carefully located in a presentation slide by its author, taking his/her presentation speech procedure into consideration. Thus, from the human view point, a dependency structure between slide components represented by either their relative positional relationship or basic diagrams including an arrow sign emerges.

Unfortunately, it is necessary to extract the dependency structure between slide components, because it is not explicitly represented in the slide data itself. We employ the method proposed by (Hayama et al., 2008), which uses relative positional relationship between slide components to extract dependency structure. Figure 1 shows an example of presentation slide designed in the traditional style and the dependency structure extracted from it. The root node represents the slide s itself. The root node has children including the headline e_1 of the slide, the first-layer bulleted ed text snippets e_2, e_5, and e_6. And more, the node e_2 has the second-layer bulleted text snippets e_3 and e_4 as the children of e_2.

It is true that our using method cannot extract structures from all styles of presentation slides. In the modernized style introduced in (Alley et al., 2005), basic diagrams play more important role to represent relationships between slide components than ones in the traditional style. Because our using method uses relative positional relationship between slide components as key clues and does not handle basic diagrams, it faces limitation against the modernized style slides. However, the dependency structure between slide components still exists in the modernized style, and an improved structure extraction method will resolve this limitation.

3 Alignment between Slide Components and Lecture Utterances

This section describes the detail of our corpus design.

Table 1: Statistics of CJLC

# of speakers	15
# of courses	26
# of lectures	89
Duration	3,780 min.

Table 2: Age of Speakers, their teaching history and number of their courses

	minimum	average	maximum
Age of speakers	31	41.5	58
Teaching history	2	14.2	30
# of courses	2	4.2	7

3.1 Corpus

Corpus of spoken Japanese Lecture Contents (henceforth, denoted as CJLC) developed by (Tsuchiya et al., 2008) is used as the main target of this research. It is designed as the fundamental basis of researches including large vocabulary continuous speech recognition and extraction of important sentences against lecture contents, and consists of speech, transcriptions, and presentation slides that were collected in real university classroom lectures. Thus, we think that the design objective of CJLC matches well our research.

CJLC is formally defined as a set of classroom lecture data, and each data consists of following 5 items:

1. a lecture speech recorded with several microphones,

2. its synchronized transcription,

3. a presentation slide data (Microsoft PowerPoint formed),

4. a timetable of slide show, and

5. a list of important utterances.

Table 1 shows the statistics of CJLC. Generally speaking, a course of CJLC is a series of one or more lectures. All speeches of CJLC were transcribed by human annotators. Table 2 shows the distribution of 15 speakers recorded in CJLC. A lecture speech data and its synchronized transcriptions are provided for all lectures, but a presentation slide data, a timetable of slide show and a list of important utterances are not attached to all lectures.

Note that each speech of CJLC was automatically segmented into utterances using the amplitude of the speech signal described in (Kitaoka et al., 2006; Otsu, 1979), and that their segmentation do not match to sentence boundaries for spontaneous speech proposed by (Takanashi et al., 2003). Although it means that automatically segmented utterances of CJLC are not sentential units from the view point of their senses, automatically segmented ones are referred as textual units, for two reasons. The first reason is that automatic detection methods of sentence boundary against spontaneous speech were proposed by (Shitaoka et al., 2004; Akita et al., 2006), however, they do not achieve sufficient performance when results of automatic speech recognition contain many errors. The second reason is to keep compatibility with important utterance extraction information of CJLC.

3.2 Alignment Labels

Four labels are introduced to represent alignment information between textual units and slide components. First of all, Label **I** and Label **O** are introduced to distinguish whether textual units correspond

	Content of utterance	Aligned slide component
t_a	Generally, a computer system has two kinds of operation devices, such as an input device, an output device.	e_2
	$\vdots$	
t_b	Typical input devices are a keyboard and a mouse, and typical output devices are a monitor and a speaker.	e_2
	$\vdots$	
t_c	In this stage, the monitor displayed the photos and the videos for the experiment.	e_4/e_5

Figure 2: Example of alignment label with slide components

to any slide components or not. Label **B** and Label **E** are introduced to resolve mismatch between automatic power-based boundary and sentence boundary. The following is more detailed descriptions of these labels.

- Label **I** means that its labeled textual unit is either an utterance or a part of an utterance to explain a slide component. An explanation may be carried by either a same content word, a synonym, a hypernym, a hyponym, a paraphrase, an expression to instantiate a general case shown by the slide component into a specific case, or an expression to abstract a specific case shown by the slide component into a general case. When the textual unit t_i explains the slide component c_j, a pair of Label **I** and the sequence number j is assigned to t_i.

- Label **B** means that its labeled textual unit belongs to the succeeding textual unit from the view point of sentence boundary, only when the succeeding unit has either Label **I** or Label **B**. In other words, the textual unit which has Label **B** is a former part of a sentence, which must contain one or more textual units which have Label **I**.

- Label **E** is the opposite label of Label **B**, and means that its labeled textual unit belongs to the preceding textual unit from the view point of sentence boundary only when the preceding unit has either Label **I** or Label **E**. In other words, the textual unit which has Label **E** is a latter part of a sentence, which must contain one or more textual units which have Label **I**.

- Label **O** means that its labeled textual unit are not related to any slide components.

The alignment label system described in the above can represent the case that one or more textual units explain a slide component. It, however, involves difficulty for the case that a single textual unit explains multiple slide components.

In order to conquer this difficulty, this case is divided into three sub cases, and procedures to select an appropriate slide component are prepared. Figure 2 shows example of alignment label with slide components in three sub cases.

The first sub case is that a parent-child relationship exists between the two slide components explained by a single textual unit. Suppose that the slide component e_2 and the slide component e_3 of Figure 1 are explained by the single textual unit t_a. In this corpus, the parent node e_2 is selected as the label of the textual unit t_a. The second sub case is that a sibling relationship exists between the two slide components explained by a single textual unit, and that two slide components share the same parent node. The example of the second sub case is that the slide component e_3 and the slide component e_4 of Figure 1 are explained by the single textual unit t_b. In this corpus, the parent node e_2 shared by the explained nodes e_3 and e_4 is selected as the label of the textual unit t_b. The last sub case is the rest of the above sub cases. For example, suppose that the slide component e_4 and the slide component e_5 are explained by the single textual unit t_c. In order to resolve the last sub case, both e_4 and e_5 are recorded in parallel as the label of t_c while annotation work. Because the last sub case is rare, for the following analysis of this paper, the preceding node e_4 is referred as the label of t_c and the succeeding node e_5 is ignored.

The alignment manual for annotators reflects the descriptions of labels explained in the above. The following is the abstract of the manual.

1. The supervisor supplies a set of textual units and a set slide components to the annotator.

2. The annotator is requested to find all kind of explanations and to assign all Label **I** in the given set. When a single textual unit explains multiple slide components, the annotator must select an appropriate node in compliance with the procedures described in the above.

3. After assignment of Label **I**, the annotator is requested to find all Label **B** and Label **E** in the given set. In other words, the annotator must find sentence boundaries around textual units labeled as Label **I**.

4. After that, Label **O** is assigned to all remaining textual units.

3.3 Annotation Results

Two annotators[1], who are master course students of the department of computer science, are employed for the annotation work of the corpus. Table 3 shows their annotation results. Each lecture has a lecture ID (for example, *L11M0011*) which is composed of four parts: its first part is a letter *L* which means a first letter of lecture, its second part is a two didit number *11* which identifies a anonymized speaker, its third part is a letter *M* which means a gender of a speaker, and its last part is a four digit number *0011* which distinguishes a lecture. Furthermore, the last four digit number is composed of two sub parts: its first sub part is a three digit number *001* which means a course, and its second sub part is a one digit number *1* means the sequence number of the specified lecture in the course. In order to measure agreement of two human annotators' results, the following κ statistics (Chklovski and Mihalcea, 2003; Ng et al., 1999) is widely used.

$$\kappa = \frac{P_a - P_e}{1 - P_e} \tag{1}$$

Here, P_a denotes the empirical agreement ratio between two human annotators, while P_e denotes the probability of agreement by chance.

The annotation label system of our corpus is two layered: the first layer labels, such as Label I, Label B, Label E and Label O, represent whether their labeled textual units are related to slide components or not, and the second layer, which consists of sequence numbers of Label I, represents explanation relationships between textual units and slide components. In order to measure fairly agreements of this two layered label system, two kinds of granularity are introduced when computing κ statistics. When computing κ statistics for coarse granularity to measure the agreement of the first layer labels, the empirical agreement ratio P_a is defined as the following equation.

$$P_a = \frac{\sum_{X=\{I,B,E,O\}} a(X)}{|T|} \tag{2}$$

$a(X)$ is the number of textual units which two human annotators give the same label X, and $|T|$ is the number of textual units. The probability of agreement by chance P_e is calculated as follows:

$$P_e = \sum_{X=\{I,B,E,O\}} P^2(X), \tag{3}$$

where $P(X)$ is the label occurrence probability. When maximum likelihood estimation is employed, $P(X)$ is defined as follows:

$$P(X) = \frac{f(X)}{|T|}, \tag{4}$$

---

[1]An annotators is one of the authors.

Table 3: Result of Manual Annotation

Lecture ID	# of slides	# of slide components	# of utterances	# of labels				κ statistics	
				I	B	E	O	coarse	fine
L11M0010	21	370	742	578	4	26	134	0.68	0.61
L11M0011	29	431	704	584	11	14	95	0.58	0.72
L11M0012	12	276	811	546	2	5	258	0.83	0.65
L11M0030	58	822	680	414	41	57	168	0.92	0.75
L11M0050	22	159	2362	1280	39	81	962	0.68	0.6
L11M0064	27	469	1110	559	51	58	442	0.69	0.72

where $f(X)$ is the number of textual units to which Label X is assigned.

When computing κ statistics for fine granularity to measure the agreement of the second layer labels, which means the agreement of sequence numbers, the empirical agreement ratio P'_a is defined as the following equation.

$$P'_a = \frac{\sum_{j=1}^{|C|} a(c_j)}{f(\text{I})}, \tag{5}$$

where $|C|$ is the number of slide components, and $a(c_j)$ is the number of textual units which are associated to the same slide component c_j. When the probability of agreement by chance is calculated for fine granularity, as already described in Equation 3, the probability which a slide component c is assigned to textual units by a human annotator is required. When uniform distribution is assumed in order to avoid zero frequency problem, it is defined as follows:

$$P(c) = \frac{1}{|C|} \tag{6}$$

The larger the κ statistics, the more reliable the results of the human annotators. (Carletta, 1996) reported that $\kappa > 0.8$ means good reliability, while $0.67 < \kappa < 0.8$ means that tentative conclusions can be drawn. According to his criteria, when measuring the agreement of two human annotators for coarse granularity, the reliability level of 2 lectures is good, the reliability level of three lectures is tentative, and the rest lecture, L11M0011, is not reliable. Its presentation slide contains many figures, and our using method to extract slide components from the presentation slide has the limitation to handle figures as already described in Section 2. We think that this limitation causes the inagreement of L11M0011. When measuring the agreement of two human annotators for fine granularity, the reliability level of all lectures are tentative.

4 Automatic Alignment between Slide Components and Lecture Utterances

Automatic alignment between slide components and lecture utterances will be required to realize automatic text summarization using slide components as conceptual units. This section explains our preliminary result of automatic alignment.

First of all, we formulate the automatic alignment problem between slide components and lecture utterances as the problem to find the mapping set M. A member of M is a single mapping m from a lecture utterance u to a slide component e ($u \rightarrow e$). Although there are many possible mapping sets, the eligible mapping set M must maximize the following objective function

$$f(M) = \lambda \sum_{m \in M} f_w(m) + (1 - \lambda) \sum_{m \in M} f_c(m, M), \tag{7}$$

where $f_w(m)$ represents the content-based agreement between the utterance u and the slide component e which are specified by the mapping m, and $f_c(m)$ represents the consistency score.

The content-based agreement score function $f_w(m)$ of the mapping m is defined as follows

$$f_w(m) = \frac{|N_u \cup N_e|}{|N_u \cap N_e|}, \tag{8}$$

Table 4: Result of Automatic Alignment (L11M0030)

λ	Accuracy		Recall		Overall accuracy
	I	O	I	O	
0	0.0896	0.656	0.113	0.734	0.247
0.25	0.329	0.693	0.424	0.734	0.425
0.5	0.335	0.693	0.432	0.734	0.429
0.75	0.341	0.697	0.440	0.734	0.434
1	0.248	0.699	0.321	0.728	0.365

where N_u is a set of nouns included in the utterance u specified by the mapping m, and N_e is a set of nouns included in the slide component e specified the mapping m. In this paper, the simplest agreement score function is employed as preliminary experiments, and it is future work to employ more sophisticated score function like (Guo and Diab, 2012).

Generally speaking, a common lecturer has a tendency to explain slide components in their appearance order. The latter member of the objective function $f(M)$ is designed to capture this tendency, and the consistency score function $f_c(m_i, M)$ is defined as follows:

$$f_c(m_i, M) = \begin{cases} -\sum_{j=0}^{i-1} \delta(e_i < e_j) & f_w(m_i) = 0 \\ 0 & otherwise \end{cases} \qquad (9)$$

Suppose a mapping m_j which appears former than the certain mapping m_i in the utterance sequence. In other words, the utterance u_j specified by the mapping m_j precedes the utterance u_i specified by the mapping m_i. When the lecturer explains slide components in their appearance order, the slide component e_j specified by the mapping m_j precedes the slide component e_i specified by the mapping m_i consistently. The above function counts the number of mappings which do not meet this condition.

Table 4 shows the preliminary result of automatic alignment. λ is allowed to vary with the result of experiments, f_c has been found to not contribute significantly to the accuracy of the automatic alignment. Therefore, to further improve accuracy of the automatic alignment is needed improvements f_w.

5 Conclusion

This paper describes our developing corpus of lecture utterances aligned to slide components, which contains two contributions. The first contribution is to design the label system which represents alignment between textual units and slide components even when there are boundary mismatches between textual units and sentential boundaries. It is crucial inevitable problem to handle spontaneous speeches. The second contribution is to show the agreements between human annotators when the label system is employed. As a future work, we are going to investigate automatic decision of granularity level of slide components.

Acknowledgements

This work was supported by JSPS KAKENHI Grant No. 15K12097 and No. 25280062.

References

Yuya Akita, Masahiro Saikou, Hiroaki Nanjo, and Tatsuya Kawahara. 2006. Sentence boundary detection of spontaneous Japanese using statistical language model and support vector machines. In *Proceedings of INTERSPEECH*, pages 1033–1036.

M. Alley, M. Schreiber, and J. Muffo. 2005. Pilot testing of a new design for presentation slides to teach science and engineering. In *Frontiers in Education, 2005. FIE '05. Proceedings 35th Annual Conference*, pages S3G–7, Oct.

Jean Carletta. 1996. Assessing Agreement on Classification Tasks: The Kappa Statistic. *Computational Linguistics*, 22(2):249–254, 6.

Timothy Chklovski and Rada Mihalcea. 2003. Exploiting agreement and disagreement of human annotators for word sense disambiguation. In *Proceedings of the Conference on Recent Advances in Natural Language Processing (RANLP2003)*.

Elena Filatova and Vasileios Hatzivassiloglou. 2004. A formal model for information selection in multi-sentence text extraction. In *Proceedings of Coling 2004*, pages 397–403, Geneva, Switzerland, Aug 23–Aug 27. COLING.

Jade Goldstein, Vibhu Mittal, Jaime Carbonell, and Mark Kantrowitz. 2000. Multi-document summarization by sentence extraction. In *Proceedings of the 2000 NAACL-ANLPWorkshop on Automatic summarization-Volume 4*, pages 40–48. Association for Computational Linguistics.

Weiwei Guo and Mona Diab. 2012. Modeling sentences in the latent space. In *Proceedings of the 50th Annual Meeting of the Association for Computational Linguistics (Volume 1: Long Papers)*, pages 864–872, Jeju Island, Korea, July. Association for Computational Linguistics.

Tessai Hayama, Hidetsugu Nanba, and Susumu Kunifuji, 2008. *PRICAI 2008: Trends in Artificial Intelligence: 10th Pacific Rim International Conference on Artificial Intelligence, Hanoi, V ietnam, December 15-19, 2008. Proceedings*, chapter Structure Extraction from Presentation Slide Information, pages 678–687. Springer Berlin Heidelberg, Berlin, Heidelberg.

Eduard Hovy, Chin-Yew Lin, Liang Zhou, and Junichi Fukumoto. 2006. Automated summarization evaluation with basic elements. In *Proceedings of the Fifth Conference on Language Resources and Evaluation (LREC 2006)*, pages 604–611.

N. Kitaoka, T. Yamada, S. Tsuge, C. Miyajima, T. Nishiura, M.Nakayama, Y. Denda, M. Fujimoto, K. Yamamoto, T. Takiguchi, S.Kuroiwa, K. Takeda, and S. Nakamura. 2006. CENSREC-1-C: Development of evaluation framework for voice activity detection under noisy environment. In *IPSJ technical report, Spoken Language Processing (SIG-SLP), Vol.2006, No.107*, pages 1–6.

Julian Kupiec, Jan Pedersen, and Francine Chen. 1995. A trainable document summarizer. In *Proceedings of the 18th annual international ACM SIGIR conference on Research and development in information retrieval*, pages 68–73. ACM.

Hwee Tou Ng, Chung Yong Lim, and Shou King Foo. 1999. A case study on inter-annotator agreement for word sense disambiguation. In *Proceedings of the ACL SIGLEX Workshop on Standadizing Lexical Resource (SIGLEX99)*, pages 9–13.

N. Otsu. 1979. A threshold selection method from gray-level histograms. *IEEE Transactions on Systems, Man and Cybernetics*, SMC-9(1):62–66.

Dragomir R Radev, Hongyan Jing, and Malgorzata Budzikowska. 2000. Centroid-based summarization of multiple documents: sentence extraction, utility-based evaluation, and user studies. In *Proceedings of the 2000 NAACL-ANLP Workshop on Automatic summarization*, pages 21–30. Association for Computational Linguistics.

Kazuya Shitaoka, Kiyotaka Uchimoto, Tatsuya Kawahara, and Hitoshi Isahara. 2004. Dependency structure analysis and sentence boundary detection in spontaneous japanese. In *Proceedings of the 20th International Conference on Computational Linguistics*, COLING '04, Stroudsburg, PA, USA. Association for Computational Linguistics.

Hiroya Takamura and Manabu Okumura. 2009. Text summarization model based on maximum coverage problem and its variant. In *Proceedings of the 12th Conference of the European Chapter of the Association for Computational Linguistics*, pages 781–789. Association for Computational Linguistics.

Katsuya Takanashi, Takehiko Maruyama, Kiyotaka Uchimoto, and Hitoshi Isahara. 2003. Identification of "sentences" in spontaneous Japanese - detection and modification of clause boundaries. In *ISCA & IEEE Workshop on Spontaneous Speech Processing and Recognition*, pages 183–186.

Masatoshi Tsuchiya, Satoru Kogure, Hiromitsu Nishizaki, Kengo Ohta, and Seiichi Nakagawa. 2008. Developing corpus of Japanese classroom lecture speech contents. In European Language Resources Association (ELRA), editor, *Proceedings of the Sixth International Language Resources and Evaluation (LREC'08)*.

Wen-tau Yih, Joshua Goodman, Lucy Vanderwende, and Hisami Suzuki. 2007. Multi-document summarization by maximizing informative content-words. In *IJCAI*, volume 7, pages 1776–1782.

VSoLSCSum: Building a Vietnamese Sentence-Comment Dataset for Social Context Summarization

Minh-Tien Nguyen[1,2], Viet Dac Lai[1], Phong-Khac Do[1], Duc-Vu Tran[1], and Minh-Le Nguyen[1]
[1] School of Information Science,
Japan Advanced Institute of Science and Technology (JAIST), Japan.
[2] Hung Yen University of Technology and Education, Vietnam.
{tiennm, vietld, phongdk, vu.tran, nguyenml}@jaist.ac.jp

Abstract

This paper presents *VSoLSCSum*, a Vietnamese linked sentence-comment dataset, which was manually created to treat the lack of standard corpora for social context summarization in Vietnamese. The dataset was collected through the keywords of 141 Web documents in 12 special events, which were mentioned on Vietnamese Web pages. Social users were asked to involve in creating standard references and the label of each sentence or comment. The inter-agreement calculated by Cohen's Kappa among raters after validating is 0.685. To illustrate the potential use of our dataset, a learning to rank method was trained by using a set of local and cross features. Experimental results indicate that the summary model trained on our dataset outperforms state-of-the-art baselines in both ROUGE-1 and ROUGE-2 in social context summarization.

1 Introduction

In the context of social media, users can freely discuss the content of an event mentioned in a Web document in the form of comments. For example, after reading an event, e.g. CASA rescue airplane explosion from Dan Tri[1], readers can write their comments on the interface of Dan Tri. These comments, one form of social information (Amitay and Paris, 2000; Delort et al., 2003; Sun et al., 2005; Hu et al., 2008; Lu et al., 2009; Yang et al., 2011; Wei and Gao, 2014; Nguyen and Nguyen, 2016), have two critical characteristics: (i) reflecting the content and sharing the topic of a Web document, and (ii) revealing the opinions of readers with respect to that event. This observation inspires a novel summarization task, which utilizes the social information of a Web document to support sentences for generating summaries.

Automatic summarization was first studied by (Luhn, 1958; Edmundson, 1969). Until now, extractive summarization methods usually focus on plain-text documents and select salient sentences by using statistical or linguistic information in the form of binary classification (Kupiec et al., 1995; Conroy and O'Leary, 2001; Osborne, 2002; Yeh et al., 2005; Shen et al., 2007; Yang et al., 2011; Cao et al., 2015b). These methods, however, only consider internal information of a Web document, e.g. sentences while ignoring its social information.

Social context summarization is a task which selects both important sentences and representative comments from readers of a Web document. It has been studied by using different kind of social information such as hyperlinks (Amitay and Paris, 2000; Delort et al., 2003), click-through data (Sun et al., 2005), comments (Delort, 2006; Hu et al., 2007; Hu et al., 2008; Lu et al., 2009), opinionated text (Kim and Zhai, 2009; Ganesan et al., 2010; Paul et al., 2010), or tweets (Yang et al., 2011; Gao et al., 2012; Wei and Gao, 2014; Wei and Gao, 2015; Nguyen and Nguyen, 2016). (Yang et al., 2011) proposed a dual wing factor graph model for incorporating tweets into the summarization and used Support Vector Machines (SVM) (Cortes and Vapnik, 1995) and Conditional Random Fields (CRF) (Lafferty et al., 2001) as preliminary steps in calculating the weight of edges for building the graph. (Wei and Gao, 2014) used a learning to rank (L2R) approach with 35 features trained by RankBoost for news highlight extraction. (Nguyen et al., 2016c) extended the work of (Wei and Gao, 2014) by proposing entailment and

---

[1]http://dantri.com.vn

Proceedings of the 12th Workshop on Asian Language Resources,
pages 38–48, Osaka, Japan, December 12 2016.

semantic features for summarizing Web documents and their comments. In contrast, (Gao et al., 2012) proposed a cross-collection topic-aspect modeling (cc-TAM) as a preliminary step to generate a bipartite graph, which was used by a co-ranking method to select sentences and tweets for multi-document summarization. (Wei and Gao, 2015) proposed a variation of LexRank, which used auxiliary tweets for building a heterogeneous graph random walk (HGRW) to summarize single documents. (Nguyen and Nguyen, 2016) proposed SoRTESum, a ranking method using a set of recognizing textual entailment features (Nguyen et al., 2015) for single-document summarization. However, these methods were applied for English. To the best our knowledge, no existing method studies social context summarization for Vietnamese due to the lack of a standard corpora.

The objective of this study is to create a standard corpus for social context summarization in Vietnamese. This paper makes the following contributions:

- We create and release a Vietnamese dataset[2] which can be used to evaluate summary methods in social context and traditional summarization. The dataset includes 141 Web documents with their comments in 12 special events. The gold-standard references are selected by social users.

- We investigate social context summarization by state-of-the-art summary approaches. This investigation helps to point out the best summarization method in this task. Our demo system can be also accessed[3].

In the following sections, we first introduce the creation of our dataset with detail observation. Next, we show the formulation of summarization in the form of a learning to rank task. After training a summary model, we compare our results with various summary methods, along with discussion and analysis. We finish by drawing important conclusions.

2 VSoLSCSum for Summarization

This section shows the creation of our dataset in three steps: annotation framework introduction, data collection and data annotation with deep observation, and summarization.

2.1 Annotation Framework

The dataset was created by using a framework shown in Figure 1. The framework contains two main modules: data collection and data annotation. The data collection receives a keyword corresponding to an event, then collects a bunch of Web documents related to this event. Afterward, the pre-processing step eliminates unnecessary information, e.g. HTML, and tokenizes sentences. In the annotation module, raw texts were shown on an annotation website where social users were asked to annotate each document and its comments based on an instruction.

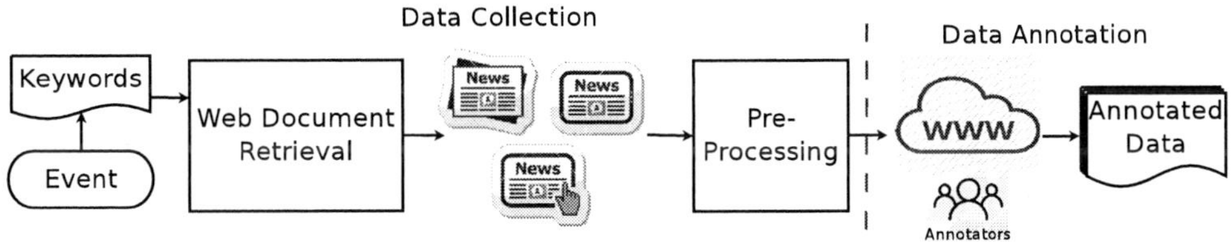

Figure 1: The overview of annotation framework

2.2 Data Collection

To create the dataset, 12 special events appearing on Vietnamese Web pages in September 2016 were first identified. Each event was empirically assigned by a noun phrase keyword which reflects the major object of the event. The noun phrase is a major entity which appears in an event. For example, in CASA rescue airplane explosion, the keyword is *"casa"*. It is possible to define a list of keywords for each

---

[2]Download at: https://github.com/nguyenlab/VSoLSCSum-Dataset
[3]http://150.65.242.101:9293/?paper=coling_alr

event. However, we collect the Web documents of an event from several news providers (non-duplicate); therefore, creating a set of keywords is unnecessary. All keywords are shown in Table 1.

Table 1: The events and corresponding keywords

Event	Keyword	Event	Keyword
CASA rescue airplane explosion	*"casa"*	Michael Phelps golden medal	*"michael phelps"*
American president election	*"donald trump"*	Pokemon Go game	*"pokemon go"*
Formosa pollution	*"formosa"*	Tan Son Nhat airport	*"tan son nhat"*
Vietnamese Olympic godel medal	*"hoang xuan vinh"*	Trinh Xuan Thanh	*"trinh xuan thanh"*
IS Islamic State	*"is"*	Vu Quang Hai	*"vu quang hai"*
Murder in Yen Bai	*"yen bai"*	Huynh Van Nen	*"huynh van nen"*

After defining keywords, a set of relevant Web documents was retrieved by using HTMLUnit library[4]. Subsequently, raw data was collected by parsing the Web documents using JSOUP parser[5]. The information of each document contains six elements shown in Table 2. In parsing, sentences and comments were also tokenized[6].

Table 2: The elements of a Web document

Element	Description
Title	The title of a Web document
Abstract	A short summary of a Web document written by writer
Content	The content of a Web document
Writer	The writer of a Web document
Comment	A set of comments showing the opinions from readers
Tag	A set of keywords which indicate the topic of a Wed document

The dataset consists of 141 open-domain articles along with 3,760 sentences, 2,448 gold-standard references, and 6,926 comments in 12 events. Note that the gold-standard references also include comments. Table 3 shows the statistics of the dataset.

Table 3: Statistical observation; s: sentences, c: comments.

Documents	Sentences	Summaries	Comments	Observation	Sentences	Comments
141	3,760	2,448	6,926	# positive examples	1,343	964
# Tokens	83,010	60,953	93,733	# negative examples	2,417	5,962
# Avg-sentences/article	26.666	17.361	49.120	% positive examples	35.718	13.918
# Avg-tokens/article	588.723	432.290	664.773	—	—	—
# Avg-tokens/sentence	22.077	24.899	13.533	% Token overlapping	s/c: 37.712	c/s: 44.820

2.3 Data Annotation

Data creation was conducted in two steps: annotation and validation. In the annotation, to ask social users, an annotation website was created for annotating this data[7]. Five native Vietnamese speakers involved to annotate the dataset. Each annotator read a complete document and its comments to select summary sentences and comments (called instances) which reflect the content of each document. Each sentence or comment was assigned a Cosine score calculated by bag-of-words model, which measures the similarity of the abstract and the current sentence or comment. The Cosine score indicates that a summary sentence or comment should include salient information of a Web document mentioned in the abstract. Note that the score is only used to calculate the similarity between sentences with the abstract (or comments with the abstract). In selection stage, annotators have to consider the following constraints to select a summary sentence or comment:

---

[4] http://htmlunit.sourceforge.net/
[5] https://jsoup.org
[6] http://mim.hus.vnu.edu.vn/phuonglh/softwares/vnTokenizer
[7] http://150.65.242.91:9080/vn-news-sum-annotator/annotate

- Each chosen sentence or comment has to reflect the content of a document.

- The Cosine score of each sentence or comment affects the selection. The higher Cosine score of a sentence or comment is, the higher probability of this sentence or comment should be selected.

- The selected instances are no less than four sentences and six comments (less than 30% of average sentences per document, see Table 3). The total selected instances are no more than 30, including both sentences and comments.

The label of a sentence or comment was generated based on majority voting among social annotators. For example, given a sentence, each annotator makes a binary decision in order to indicate whether this sentence is a summary candidate (YES) or not (NO). If three annotators agree yes, this sentence is labeled by 3. Therefore, the label of each sentence or comment ranges from 1 to 5 (1: very poor, 2: poor, 3: fair, 4: good; 5: perfect). The gold-standard references are those which receive at least three agreements from annotators (3/5).

Table 4: A translated example of label from five annotators, taken from Pokemon Go event.

Sentence	Label
This game requires the move of users to search the virtual pet, collect balls and eggs (S)	1:0:1:1:1
The idea of Pokemon Go is a significant improvement (C)	0:1:0:0:0

Table 4 shows a translated example from Vietnamese texts of Pokemon Go event. The sentence (S) receives four agreements over five annotators, so its final label is 4 and it becomes a standard reference. The label of comment (C) is 1 due to only one agreement, then it is non-standard reference.

In the validation, to ensure the quality of the dataset, two other native Vietnamese raters were asked to vote each sentence or comment, which were already labeled. The inter-agreement was calculated based on the voting of the two users. The agreement was computed by Cohen's Kappa[8] between the two annotators is 0.685 with 95% confidence interval. The strength of agreement is considered to be good.

2.4 Data Observation

Table 3 (right table) illustrates two primary points: (i) there exists common words or phrases between sentences and comments (the last right row) and (ii) readers tend to use words or phrases appearing in sentences to create their comments (44.820% of word overlapping of comments on sentences).

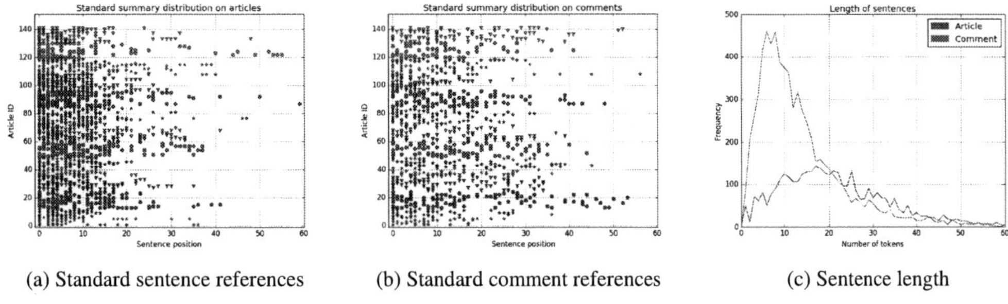

(a) Standard sentence references (b) Standard comment references (c) Sentence length

Figure 2: The position of standard summaries over 12 events and sentence length distribution.

The position of gold-standard references and sentence length over the corpus were also observed, in which color points in Figures 2a and 2b represent gold-standard sentences and comments. Figures 2a and 2b show that: (i) gold-standard references locate within first 10 sentences and top 20 comments, and (ii) standard-comment references tend to appear in a wider range compared to sentences. Figure 2c indicates that the length distribution of almost sentences ranges from five to 40 and of almost comments are from three to 40. The average sentence length and comment length is 22.077 and 13.533 respectively (see Table 3).

---

[8]https://graphpad.com/quickcalcs/kappa1/

Table 5: The statistics of six datasets

Dataset	# Docs	# Sentences	# References	# Comments	Abstraction	Label
DUC 01	309	10,639	60	0	Yes	Yes
DUC 02	567	15,188	116	0	Yes	Yes
DUC 04	500	13,129	200	0	Yes	Yes
TGSum (Cao et al., 2015a)	1,114	33,968	4,658	—	No	No
WG (Wei and Gao, 2014)	121	6,413	455	78,419 (tweets)	Yes	No
SoLSCSum (Nguyen et al., 2016b)	157	3,462	5,858	25,633	No	Yes
VSoLSCSum	141	3,760	2,448	6,926	No	Yes

Table 5 represents the comparison of our dataset with previous datasets in English. Compared results indicate that the number of sentences and comments in our dataset is sufficient for the summarization. In addition, our dataset includes both social information and labels annotated by human, which are not available in other datasets in Vietnamese.

2.5 Summary Generation

The summarization was formulated in the form of a learning to rank suggested by (Svore et al., 2007; Wei and Gao, 2014). To train a learning to rank model (L2R), Ranking SVM[9] (Joachims, 2006), a powerful method for information retrieval (Liu, 2011; Nguyen et al., 2016a), was adopted. Ranking SVM applies the characteristics of SVM (Cortes and Vapnik, 1995) to perform pairwise classification. Given n training queries $\{q_i\}_{i=1}^n$, their associated document pairs $(x_u^{(i)}, x_v^{(i)})$ and corresponding ground truth label $y_{(u,v)}^{(i)}$, Ranking SVM optimizes the objective function shown in Eq. (1):

$$\min \frac{1}{2}\|w\|^2 + \lambda \sum_{i=1}^n \sum_{u,v:y_{u,v}^{(i)}} \xi_{u,v}^{(i)} \tag{1}$$

$$\text{s.t. } w^T(x_u^{(i)} - x_v^{(i)}) \geqslant 1 - \xi_{u,v}^{(i)}, \text{ if } y_{u,v}^{(i)} = 1 \tag{2}$$

$$\xi_{u,v}^{(i)} \geqslant 0, i = 1, ..., n \tag{3}$$

where: $f(x) = w^T x$ is a linear scoring function, (x_u, x_v) is a pairwise and $\xi_{u,v}^{(i)}$ is the loss. The document pair-wise is sentence-sentence or comment-comment and the pair-wise order is determined by the agreement of each sentence or comment (the total label 1 over five annotators). After training, the summarization was generated by selecting top m ranked sentences and comments.

3 Results and Discussion

3.1 Experimental Setup

Comments with less than five tokens were eliminated since they are fairly short for summarization. 5-fold cross validation with $m = 6$ (less than 30% average sentences, see Table 3) was used.

Support Vector Machines (SVM)[10] (Cortes and Vapnik, 1995) was selected for the classification because it has shown as a competitive method for summarization. Uni-gram and bi-gram taken from KenLM[11] trained from Vietnamese data[12],[13] were used as language models for learning to rank (L2R).

3.2 Summary Systems

We validated the potential usage of our dataset on several social context summarization methods. The methods are listed as below:

- **SentenceLead:** chooses the first x sentences as the summarization (Nenkova, 2005).

[9]https://www.cs.cornell.edu/people/tj/svm_light/svm_rank.html
[10]http://www.csie.ntu.edu.tw/~cjlin/libsvm/
[11]https://kheafield.com/code/kenlm/
[12]http://www.ted.com/talks
[13]http://vlsp.hpda.vn:8080/demo/?page=about&lang=en

- **SociVote**: selects sentences based on the voting of Cosine similarity suggested in (Wei and Gao, 2015); the threshold = 0.65.

- **LexRank**: algorithm[14] (Erkan and Radev, 2004); tokenization and stemming[15] were used.

- **cc-TAM**: built a cross-collection topic-aspect modeling (cc-TAM) as a preliminary step to generate a bipartite graph for co-ranking algorithm (Gao et al., 2012).

- **HGRW**: is a variation of LexRank named Heterogeneous Graph Random Walk (Wei and Gao, 2015); the threshold was 0.7.

- **SVM:** was used in (Yang et al., 2011; Kupiec et al., 1995; Osborne, 2002; Yeh et al., 2005). RBF kernel was used with scaling in [-1, 1].

- **RT-One Wing**: uses the features from (Nguyen and Nguyen, 2016), but only using one wing (sentences or comments) when generating the summarization. For example, when modeling a sentence, the remaining ones in the same side was utilized.

- **SoRTESum:** was proposed by (Nguyen and Nguyen, 2016) using a set of RTE similarity features (Nguyen et al., 2015). This method includes two models: SoRTESum-Inter Wing and Dual Wing.

3.3 Evaluation Metric

Gold-standard references were used for the evaluation of summary methods. Evaluation metric is F-1 of ROUGE-N[16] (N=1, 2) (Lin and Hovy, 2003).

3.4 Results and Discussion

Table 6 shows the results of summary methods on our dataset. The results indicate that: (i) our dataset benefits social context summarization in Vietnamese and (ii) social information accelerates the performance of summary methods, e.g. RTE-One Wing vs. RTE Inter Wing and Dual Wing.

Ranking SVM with local and cross features is the best in Table 6. This is because, firstly, SVMRank inherits powerful properties of SVM. For example, it can create correct margins for classification based on the help of margin maximization. In training, these properties help SVMRank to avoid an overfitting problem, which often appears in other methods, e.g. AdaBoost or RankBoost. The results of L2R using RankBoost in Table 7 support this statement. Secondly, SVMRank integrates social information leading to significant improvements compared to SVM which only uses local features, e.g. sentence length, sentence position. This also shows the efficiency of local and cross features proposed in (Wei and Gao, 2014). Finally, formulating the summarization in the form of learning to rank may be more appropriate than sentence classification, i.e. SVM.

Table 6: Summary performance on our dataset; * is supervised method; **bold** is the best value; *italic* is the second best; SentenceLead was not used in summarizing comments. Methods with *S* use social information.

System	Document						Comment					
	ROUGE-1			ROUGE-2			ROUGE-1			ROUGE-2		
	P	R	F-1	P	R	F-1	P	R	F-1	P	R	F-1
SentenceLead	0.838	0.295	0.437	0.751	0.266	0.393	—	—	—	—	—	—
SociVote (S)	0.804	0.290	0.427	0.699	0.256	0.375	0.638	0.148	0.241	0.454	0.103	0.169
LexRank	0.784	0.336	0.471	0.629	0.272	0.381	0.671	0.231	0.344	0.496	0.163	0.246
HGRW (S)	0.816	0.375	*0.514*	0.691	0.320	*0.438*	0.697	0.244	*0.362*	0.525	0.177	*0.265*
cc-TAM (S)	0.798	0.271	0.405	0.653	0.226	0.336	0.682	0.116	0.199	0.427	0.073	0.125
SVM*	0.793	0.370	0.505	0.689	0.321	*0.438*	0.511	0.237	0.324	0.309	0.127	0.181
RTE-One Wing	0.786	0.364	0.498	0.670	0.309	0.423	0.613	0.219	0.324	0.420	0.143	0.214
SoRTESum IW (S)	0.774	0.338	0.471	0.629	0.275	0.383	0.669	0.224	0.336	0.482	0.153	0.233
SoRTESum DW (S)	0.819	0.345	0.486	0.718	0.304	0.427	0.652	0.191	0.296	0.469	0.129	0.203
SVMRank* (S)	0.846	0.380	**0.525**	0.769	0.346	**0.478**	0.655	0.251	**0.364**	0.490	0.182	**0.266**

---

[14] https://code.google.com/p/louie-nlp/source/browse/trunk/louie-ml/src/main/java/org/louie/ml/lexrank/?r=10
[15] http://nlp.stanford.edu/software/corenlp.shtml
[16] http://kavita-ganesan.com/content/rouge-2.0-documentation

Results in Table 6 also indicate that HGRW is a competitive method, which achieves a second best result compared to Ranking SVM. This is because HGRW exploits the support of social information for the summarization. It also notes that HGRW is an unsupervised method. SVM obtains competitive results even social information was not integrated. This shows the efficiency of features for summarization in (Yang et al., 2011; Nguyen and Nguyen, 2016). SoRTESum with the support from social information obtains significant improvements as opposed to a strong method Sentence Lead, which simulates the summarization by picking up some first sentences (Nenkova, 2005). Interestingly, cc-TAM achieves the lowest result even though this method is competitive in English (Gao et al., 2012). The reason is that cc-TAM was developed for multi-document summarization but our dataset was created for single-document summarization.

3.5 The Performance of L2R Methods

The performance of Ranking SVM was compared to other L2R methods by using the same feature set (local and social features) in (Wei and Gao, 2014). The L2R methods include RankBoost (Freund et al., 2003) (*iteration* = 300, *metric* is ERR10), RankNet (Burges et al., 2005) (*epoch* = 100, *the number of layers* = 1, *the number of hidden nodes* per layer = 10 and *learning rate* = 0.00005), Coordinate Ascent (Metzler and Croft, 2007) (random restart = 2, iteration = 25, tolerance = 0.001 with non-regularization), and Radom Forest (Breiman, 2001) (*the number of bags* = 300, *sub-sampling rate* = 1.0, *feature sampling rate* = 0.3, *ranker to bag with MART*, *the number of trees* in each bag = 100, *learning rate* = 0.1, and *the min leaf support* = 1) implemented in RankLib[17].

Table 7: The performance of L2R methods.

System	Document						Comment					
	ROUGE-1			ROUGE-2			ROUGE-1			ROUGE-2		
	P	R	F-1	P	R	F-1	P	R	F-1	P	R	F-1
RankBoost	0.820	0.366	0.507	0.717	0.324	0.447	0.663	0.242	0.355	0.498	0.175	0.259
RankNet	0.788	0.401	**0.532**	0.685	0.351	0.465	0.595	0.253	0.355	0.437	0.179	0.255
Coordinate Ascent	0.811	0.349	0.489	0.712	0.308	0.431	0.643	0.244	0.354	0.472	0.173	0.254
Random Forrest	0.847	0.374	0.520	0.771	0.343	0.475	0.649	0.252	**0.364**	0.486	0.182	0.265
SVMRank	0.846	0.380	0.525	0.769	0.346	**0.478**	0.655	0.251	**0.364**	0.490	0.182	**0.266**

Results in Table 7 illustrate that Ranking SVM (Joachims, 2006) ($C = 3$ with *linear kernel*) is the best except for ROUGE-1 in document summarization due to nice properties which Ranking SVM inherits from SVM. RankNet obtains the best result in ROUGE-1 because neural networks used in RankNet may positively affect the summarization. The remaining methods are competitive compared to results in Table 6. This concludes that formulating sentence selection as a L2R task benefits the summarization.

3.6 Summary Sentence Position Observation

The position of summary sentences and comments generated from Ranking SVM was observed. Figures 3a and 3b indicate that extracted sentences are within top 10 for sentences and 20 for comments. This supports the observation in Section 2.4. There also are outlier points, e.g. 52 in Figure 3a and 180 in Figure 3b. Results from Section 2.4, Figures 3a and 3b show that: (i) Sentence Lead is a competitive method (see Table 6) because Sentence Lead formulates the summarization by selecting several first sentences and (ii) this method is inefficient for comments because representative comments usually appear in a wider range in contrast to sentences. Considering Figures 2a, 2b, 3a, and 3b, we conclude that sentence position is an important feature for document summarization, not for comments.

3.7 Summary Sentence Length Observation

The average sentence length of extracted summaries generated from summary methods was also analyzed. As can be seen from Figures 4a and 4b, long sentences belong to competitive methods, e.g. SVMRank, HGRW while poor methods generate shorter sentence, e.g. cc-TAM or Sentence Lead. SVMRank obtains the longest sentences and comments, e.g. 31 in sentence and 27 in comment supporting results

---

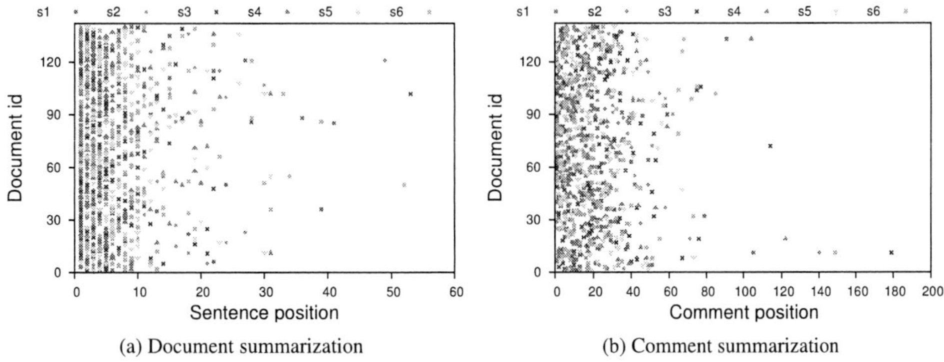

(a) Document summarization   (b) Comment summarization

Figure 3: The sentence position of extracted summaries.

in Table 6. The trend of extracted comments in Figure 3b shares the same property with sentences in Figure 3a. Considering results in Figures 4a and 4b, we conclude that sentence length is one of the most important features for the summarization.

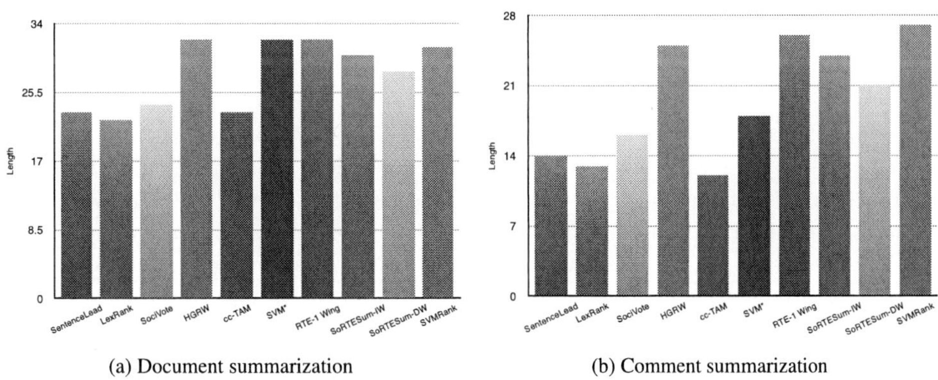

(a) Document summarization   (b) Comment summarization

Figure 4: The sentence length of extracted summaries.

4   Error Analysis

Table 8 shows the output of Ranking SVM and gold-standard references (six summary sentences and comments are shown with seven references). Ranking SVM selects three correct (denoted by [+]) and three incorrect sentences (represented by [-]) compared to the references. This is because summary sentences include vital words, e.g. *"Pokemon"*, *"driver"* and they are long sentences; as the result, local features can capture these sentences. In addition, summary sentences also share critical words with comments, e.g. *"police"*, *"Pokemon"*. In this case, cross features from comments also help to enrich information in these sentences. Nevertheless, there are several sophisticated sentences so that our model made incorrect decisions. For instance, a long non-summary sentence *S3* shares important words, e.g. *"game"* with comments.

For comment summarization, it is interesting that two comments (*C1* and *C2*) are derived from sentences. This supports the data observation in Section 2.4, which indicates that readers tend to use words or phrases appearing in article to build their comments. Since *C6* contains salient information, with local features and cross features, Ranking SVM selected this sentence correctly. Meanwhile, *C3*, *C4*, and *C5* mention readers' opinions rather than the content of the event. In this view, these comments also contribute to enrich the summarization.

45

Table 8: A summary example of 6th Pokemon Go event document generated by Ranking SVM.

Gold-standard references
A Vietnamese woman died on August 25 by a car accident relating to Pokemon Go game in Japan
Daily news Mainichi announces that the victim is a 29-year-old Vietnamese woman living in Kasugai city, Aichi, Japan
On August 11 evening, when crossing the road by bicycle, the woman was crashed by a car
While charging his phone, he could not see the woman and the accident happened
Playing game while driving, the driver should be suspended his driver license
I am a game player and I really expect this game to be removed from online stores
Addiction games are dangerous for health and money

Summary	
Sentences	**Comments**
[+]S1: Daily news Mainichi of Japan announces that the victim is a 29-year-old Vietnamese woman living in Kasugai city, Aichi, Japan	[+]C1: The driver was released immediately after he was arrested
[+]S2: On August 11 evening, when crossing the road by her bicycle, the woman was hit by a car	[+]C2: The police is investigating the accident
[-]S3: The driver said that his phone had been out of battery due to playing the game	[-]C3: We prohibit what we cannot control, I often play this game but in a park, so there's no negative effects to other people
[+]S4: Despite driving his car, the 26-year-old driver still played Pokemon Go	[-]C4: If you don't like, you should not play because you can not give up.
[-]S5: The driver was released immediately after he was arrested	[-]C5: It depends on the responsibility of players, we can not conclude that people playing Pokemon are bad guys.
[-]S6: The police is investigating the accident	[+]C6: Driving a car while playing Pokemon, suspend their driver license rather than let get involved in a crash.

5   Conclusion

This paper presents a Vietnamese dataset named VSoLSCSum for social context summarization. The dataset is created by collecting Web documents via keywords from Vietnamese online news providers. It contains 141 documents in 12 special events. Gold-standard references are manually annotated by social users. The inter-agreement among annotators after validating calculated by Cohen's Kappa is 0.685. VSoLSCSum has two essential characteristics: (i) it includes comments as social information to support sentences for generating a high-quality summarization and (ii) it includes labels, which can be used to train supervised summary methods, e.g. SVM or L2R. Experimental results show the potential utilization of our dataset in Vietnamese social context summarization and conclude that formulating sentence selection as a L2R task benefits the summarization.

For future directions, abstractive summaries of each event should be generated. Human evaluation should also be conducted to ensure summary quality.

Acknowledgements

We would like to thank Chien-Xuan Tran for creating demo website, Gao and Li for sharing the code of (Gao et al., 2012). We also would like to thank anonymous reviewers for their detailed comments for improving our paper. This work was supported by JSPS KAKENHI Grant number 15K16048, JSPS KAKENHI Grant Number JP15K12094, and CREST, JST.

References

[Amitay and Paris2000] Einat Amitay and Ce'cile Paris. 2000. Automatically summarising web sites: is there a way around it?. In *CIKM: 173-179.*

[Breiman2001] Leo Breiman. 2001. Random forests. *Machine Learning 45(1): 5-32.*

[Burges et al.2005] Christopher J. C. Burges, Tal Shaked, Erin Renshaw, Ari Lazier, Matt Deeds, Nicole Hamilton, and Gregory N. Hullender. 2005. Learning to rank using gradient descent. In *ICML: 89-96.*

[Cao et al.2015a] Ziqiang Cao, Chengyao Chen, Wenjie Li, Sujian Li, Furu Wei, and Ming Zhou. 2015a. Tgsum: Build tweet guided multi-document summarization dataset. In *arXiv preprint arXiv:1511.08417.*

[Cao et al.2015b] Ziqiang Cao, Furu Wei, Li Dong, Sujian Li, and Ming Zhou. 2015b. Ranking with recursive neural networks and its application to multi-document summarization. In *AAAI: 2153-2159.*

[Conroy and O'Leary2001] John M. Conroy and Dianne P. O'Leary. 2001. Text summarization via hidden markov models. In *SIGIR: 406-407*.

[Cortes and Vapnik1995] Corinna Cortes and Vladimir Vapnik. 1995. Support-vector networks. *Machine Learning 20(3): 273-297*.

[Delort et al.2003] J.-Y. Delort, B. Bouchon-Meunier, and M. Rifqi. 2003. Enhanced web document summarization using hyperlinks. In *Hypertext'03: 208-215*.

[Delort2006] Jean-Yves Delort. 2006. Identifying commented passages of documents using implicit hyperlinks. In *Hypertext: 89-98*.

[Edmundson1969] Harold P. Edmundson. 1969. New methods in automatic extracting. *Journal of the Association for Computing Machinery, 16(2): 264-285*.

[Erkan and Radev2004] Gunes Erkan and Dragomir R. Radev. 2004. Lexrank: Graph-based lexical centrality as salience in text summarization. *Journal of Artificial Intelligence Research, 22: 457-479*.

[Freund et al.2003] Yoav Freund, Raj D. Lyeryer, Robert E. Schapire, and Yoram Singer. 2003. An efficient boosting algorithm for combining preferences. *Journal of Machine Learning Research 4: 933-969*.

[Ganesan et al.2010] Kavita Ganesan, ChengXiang Zhai, and Jiawei Han. 2010. Opinosis: a graph-based approach to abstractive summarization of highly redundant opinions. In *COLLING: 340-348*.

[Gao et al.2012] Wei Gao, Peng Li, and Kareem Darwish. 2012. Joint topic modeling for event summarization across news and social media streams. In *CIKM:1173-1182*.

[Hu et al.2007] Meishan Hu, Aixin Sun, and Ee-Peng Lim. 2007. Comments-oriented blog summarization by sentence extraction. In *CIKM: 901-904*.

[Hu et al.2008] Meishan Hu, Aixin Sun, and Ee-Peng Lim. 2008. Comments-oriented document summarization: Understanding document with readers' feedback. In *SIGIR: 291-298*.

[Joachims2006] Thorsten Joachims. 2006. Training linear svms in linear time. In *KDD: 217-226*.

[Kim and Zhai2009] Hyun Duk Kim and ChengXiang Zhai. 2009. Generating comparative summaries of contradictory opinions in text. In *CIKM: 385-394*.

[Kupiec et al.1995] Julian Kupiec, Jan O. Pedersen, and Francine Chen. 1995. A trainable document summarizer. In *SIGIR: 68-73*.

[Lafferty et al.2001] John D. Lafferty, Andrew McCallum, and Fernando C. N. Pereira. 2001. Conditional random fields: Probabilistic models for segmenting and labeling sequence data. In *ICML: 282-289*.

[Lin and Hovy2003] Chin-Yew Lin and Eduard H. Hovy. 2003. Automatic evaluation of summaries using n-gram co-occurrence statistics. In *HLT-NAACL: 71-78*.

[Liu2011] Tie-Yan Liu. 2011. *Learning to Rank for Information Retrieval*. Springer, ISBN 978-3-642-14266-6, pp. I-XVII, 1-285.

[Lu et al.2009] Yue Lu, ChengXiang Zhai, and Neel Sundaresan. 2009. Rated aspect summarization of short comments. In *WWW: 131-140*.

[Luhn1958] Hans P. Luhn. 1958. The automatic creation of literature abstracts. *IBM Journal of Research Development, 2(2): 159-165*.

[Metzler and Croft2007] Donald Metzler and W. Bruce Croft. 2007. Linear feature-based models for information retrieval. *Inf. Retr. 10(3): 257-274*.

[Nenkova2005] Ani Nenkova. 2005. Automatic text summarization of newswire: lessons learned from the document understanding conference. In *AAAI: 1436-1441*.

[Nguyen and Nguyen2016] Minh-Tien Nguyen and Minh-Le Nguyen. 2016. Sortesum: A social context framework for single-document summarization. In *ECIR: 3-14*.

[Nguyen et al.2015] Minh-Tien Nguyen, Quang-Thuy Ha, Thi-Dung Nguyen, Tri-Thanh Nguyen, and Le-Minh Nguyen. 2015. Recognizing textual entailment in vietnamese text: An experimental study. In *KSE: 108-113*.

[Nguyen et al.2016a] Minh-Tien Nguyen, Viet-Anh Phan, Truong-Son Nguyen, and Minh-Le Nguyen. 2016a. Learning to rank questions for community question answering with ranking svm. In *CoRR abs/1608.04185*.

[Nguyen et al.2016b] Minh-Tien Nguyen, Chien-Xuan Tran, Duc-Vu Tran, and Minh-Le Nguyen. 2016b. Solscsum: A linked sentence-comment dataset for social context summarization. In *CIKM: 2409-2412*.

[Nguyen et al.2016c] Minh-Tien Nguyen, Duc-Vu Tran, Chien-Xuan Tran, and Minh-Le Nguyen. 2016c. Learning to summarize web documents using social information. In *ICTAI*.

[Osborne2002] Miles Osborne. 2002. Using maximum entropy for sentence extraction. In *ACL Workshop on Automatic Summarization: 1-8*.

[Paul et al.2010] Michael J. Paul, ChengXiang Zhai, and Roxana Girju. 2010. Summarizing contrastive viewpoints in opinionated text. In *EMNLP: 66-76*.

[Shen et al.2007] Dou Shen, Jian-Tao Sun, Hua Li, Qiang Yang, and Zheng Chen. 2007. Document summarization using conditional random fields. In *IJCAI: 2862-2867*.

[Sun et al.2005] Jian-Tao Sun, Dou Shen, Hua-Jun Zeng, Qiang Yang, Yuchang Lu, and Zheng Chen. 2005. Webpage summarization using clickthrough data. In *SIGIR: 194-201*.

[Svore et al.2007] Krysta Marie Svore, Lucy Vanderwende, and Christopher J. C. Burges. 2007. Enhancing single-document summarization by combining ranknet and third-party sources. In *EMNLP-CoNLL: 448-457*.

[Wei and Gao2014] Zhongyu Wei and Wei Gao. 2014. Utilizing microblogs for automatic news highlights extraction. In *COLING: 872-883*.

[Wei and Gao2015] Zhongyu Wei and Wei Gao. 2015. Gibberish, assistant, or master?: Using tweets linking to news for extractive single-document summarization. In *SIGIR: 1003-1006*.

[Yang et al.2011] Zi Yang, Keke Cai, Jie Tang, Li Zhang, Zhong Su, and Juanzi Li. 2011. Social context summarization. In *SIGIR: 255-264*.

[Yeh et al.2005] Jen-Yuan Yeh, Hao-Ren Ke, Wei-Pang Yang, and I-Heng Meng. 2005. Text summarization using a trainable summarizer and latent semantic analysis. *Inf. Process. Manage. 41(1): 75-95*.

BCCWJ-DepPara: A Syntactic Annotation Treebank on the 'Balanced Corpus of Contemporary Written Japanese'

Masayuki ASAHARA◇   **Yuji MATSUMOTO**♣
◇ **National Institute for Japanese Language and Linguistics,**
National Institutes for the Humanities, Japan
♣ **Nara Institute of Science and Technology, Japan.**

Abstract

Paratactic syntactic structures are difficult to represent in syntactic dependency tree structures. As such, we propose an annotation schema for syntactic dependency annotation of Japanese, in which coordinate structures are separated from and overlaid on *bunsetsu*(base phrase unit)-based dependency. The schema represents nested coordinate structures, non-constituent conjuncts, and forward sharing as the set of regions. The annotation was performed on the core data of 'Balanced Corpus of Contemporary Written Japanese', which comprised about one million words and 1980 samples from six registers, such as newspapers, books, magazines, and web texts.

1 Introduction

Researchers have focused much attention on syntactic dependency parsing, as evidenced in the development of treebanks of many languages and dependency parsers on these treebanks. Most of the developed dependency treebanks have been word-based. However, treebanking based on *bunsetsu* (base phrase unit) has been adopted by the Japanese NLP community, due to the nature of the Japanese *bunsetsu* dependency structure, such as strictly being head-final and projective on the *bunsetsu* units.

Several annotation schemas for the *bunsetsu*-based treebanks are accessible in selected Japanese corpora. First is the Kyoto Text Corpus Schema(hereafter $\boxed{\text{KC}}$)(Kurohashi and Nagao, 1998), which is used for newspaper articles. Second is the Corpus of Spontaneous Japanese (Maekawa, 2003) Schema (hereafter $\boxed{\text{CSJ}}$)(Uchimoto et al., 2006).

We propose a novel annotation schema for the Japanese *bunsetsu* dependency structure, in which we also annotate coordinate and apposition structure scopes as segments. In this standard, we define the detailed inter-clause attachment guideline based on (Minami, 1974) and also introduce some labels to resolve errors or discrepancies in the upper process of *bunsetsu* and sentence boundary annotation.

We applied the annotation schema for the core data of 'Balanced Corpus of Contemporary Written Japanese' (Maekawa et al., 2014) which comprised data from newspaper(PN), books(PB),magazines(PM), white paper(OW), Yahoo! Answers(OC), and Yahoo! Blogs(OY). The core data includes 1.2 million words. We manually checked the annotation three times in seven years. This annotation schema is, thus, named BCCWJ-dependency parallel structure annotation (hereafter $\boxed{\text{BCCWJ}}$). Contributions of the paper are summarised in the following:

- We developed a one-million-word *bunsetsu*-based dependency annotations on a balanced corpus that is comprised of newspaper, books, magazines, whitepapers, and web texts.

- We introduced a new annotation schema for coordinate structures and appositions.

- We defined inter-clause attachments by the clause type.

- We resolved the errors of the upper process (word-segmentation and POS tagging layer) in the annotation schema, such as *bunsetsu* and sentence boundaries.

Proceedings of the 12th Workshop on Asian Language Resources,
pages 49–58, Osaka, Japan, December 12 2016.

In this article, we focus on the annotation schema of coordination and apposition structures in the dependency treebank. Section 2 presents an overview of the annotation schema. Section 3 describes the details of the annotation schema on the coordination and apposition structures. Section 4 shows the inter-clause attachment annotation schema. Section 5 illustrates the basic statistics of the annotation data. Section 6 discusses the conclusion of this article.

2 Overview of the Annotation Schema

Table 1: Comparison of *bunsetsu*-based dependency structure annotation schema

Label	BCCWJ	(group)	CSJ	KC
Normal	D	-	no label	D
Parallel	D	(Parallel)	P	P
Parallel (non-constitutent conjunct)	D	(Parallel)	I	I
Apposition	D	(Apposition)	A	A
Apposition (Generic)	D	(Generic)	A2	A
Right to Left	D	-	R	undef
No attachment	F	-	undef	undef
(for *Bunsetsu*)	BCCWJ	-	CSJ	KC
Concatenate *Bunsetsu*	B	-	B+	undef
(Misc)	BCCWJ	(segment)	CSJ	KC
Filler	F	-	F	undef
Smiley	F	-	undef	undef
Sentence conjunction	F or D		C	D
Interjection	F or D	-	E	D
Vocative	Z	-	Y	undef
Disfluency/Self-correction				
(one *bunsetsu*)	D	-	D	undef
(more than one *bunsetsu*)	D	-	S(S:S1, S:E1)	undef
Non speech sound	F	-	no label	undef
Whitespace, URL	F	-	undef	undef
Inversion/non-projective	D	-	X	undef
Foreign word	D	(Foreign)	undef	undef
Archaic word	D	(Foreign)	K(K:S1,K:E1)	undef
Sentence end	Z	-	undef	undef
Grammatical error	undef	-	S	undef

We present the overview of the annotation schema of the BCCWJ by establishing a comparison with two other linguistics annotation schemas using *bunsetsu*-based dependency structure. Table 1 illustrates the comparative differences of the BCCWJ annotation schema from those in the KC and CSJ.

The BCCWJ schema defines four labels on the dependency relations: 'D' for normal dependency relation, 'B' for the concatenation to make a longer *bunsetsu*, 'F' for no dependency relation, and 'Z' marks the end of sentence (EOS).

We introduce 'segment' and 'group' to express coordination and apposition structures: Figure 1 demonstrates examples of these expressions. Segment is a region of the subsequence of words in the sentences. Group is a set of segments. Group is used for equivalence class by equivalance relations such as coordinate structures and coreference relations.

In the first example, the rounded corner squares are the conjuncts of a coordinate structure defined by the group 'Parallel'. The conjuncts are defined by the short unit word sequences in the BCCWJ, which is the smallest morpheme unit in the corpus. Therefore, the conjunct boundary can be defined within a *bunsetsu*. In that case, the hyphenation is used to indicate NOT *bunsetsu* boundary. As illustrated in the second example in Figure 1, the dotted rounded corner squares represent the conjuncts of an appositional structure in the narrow sense defined by the group 'Apposition'. We also define other segment and group in 'Generic', which stands for an apposition structure in the broad sense.

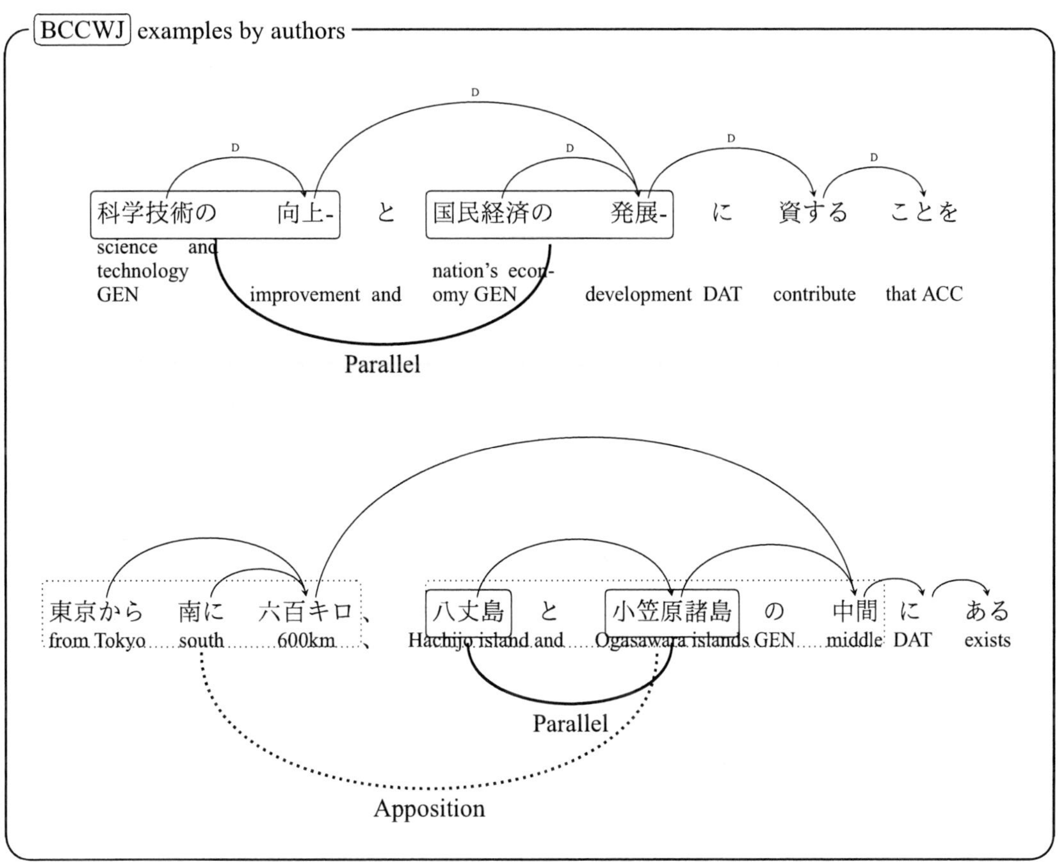

Figure 1: The assignment of 'segment' and 'group' to express coordinate and apposition structure

First, we present the differences of coordination and apposition structures among the annotation standards. In the KC standard, the label 'P' is defined for coordinate structure relation, and the label 'A' is defined for apposition structure relation. For non-constituent conjuncts, the label 'I' is used to avoid non-projective arcs in the dependency structure. The CSJ standard is based on KC, but it further defined apposition structures. The CSJ divide the apposition structure into a narrow sense with label 'A' and a broad sense with the label 'A2': The label 'A2' represents the generic name for the part-of relation or the numerical expression for the attribute-value relation in an apposition structure. In the BCCWJ standard, we avoid expressing coordination and apposition structures by their dependency relation, because these structures in dependency would make the dependency tree structure skewed. As presented above, we assign 'segment' and 'group' to each of the labels, namely, 'Parallel', 'Apposition', and 'Generic'. The subsequent section 3 provides in-depth explanation on this.

Second, we present the labels for the case to violate the projective or strictly head final constraints. The KC standard does not define special labels for such violation, because KC analyses texts that are derived from newspaper articles; therefore the dependency structures do not tend to violate these constraints. In the CSJ standard, the label 'X' is defined for the inversion of a non-projective arc, whereas the label 'R' represents the relation from right to left. In the BCCWJ standard, though both non-projective structure and right-to-left relation are permitted, we use the label 'D' to define a normal dependency relation.

Third, we present the labels to resolve errors or discrepancies in the upper process. In the $\boxed{\text{KC}}$ standard, all annotations are performed in the same research group. Hence, they do not define any special labels for these errors or discrepancies. However, in the $\boxed{\text{CSJ}}$ standard, the discrepancy of *bunsetsu* boundaries is inherent to the original $\boxed{\text{CSJ}}$ source, namely, speech. As such, the *bunsetsu* boundaries can be inserted by a speech pause or an interval. In the syntactic layer, we sometimes need to concatenate more than one item into one *bunsetsu*. In that case, the label 'B+' is introduced. In the $\boxed{\text{BCCWJ}}$ standard, the *bunsetsu* and sentence boundaries are annotated by other research group based on morphology. As a result of some discrepancies between the morphology and syntactic layer research group, we have decided to introduce the labels 'B' for the *bunsetsu* and 'Z' for sentence boundaries. Note that, we permit nested sentence in the $\boxed{\text{BCCWJ}}$ standard.

Fourth, we present the labels to avoid annotating the dependency relation. In the $\boxed{\text{KC}}$ standard, the target data is from newspaper articles and tends to be normative. Therefore, no special label is assigned to syntactic dependency relation. In contrast, the $\boxed{\text{CSJ}}$ standard defines the label 'D' for disfluency, 'F' for filler, 'C' for conjunction, 'E' for interjection, 'Y' for call, 'N' for no dependency attachment, and 'K' for archaic words. In the $\boxed{\text{BCCWJ}}$ standard, we define the label 'F' for filler or no dependency attachment and 'Z' for sentence end or call. We also define the segments of 'Foreign' for the foreign language region and 'Disfluency' for the disfluency region. In the segments, the dependency attachment is to the neighbouring right *bunsetsu*.

3 Examples of Coordination and Apposition Structures

In this section, we exemplify the dependency annotation standards of coordination and apposition.

3.1 Coordination of nominal phrases

In the $\boxed{\text{BCCWJ}}$ standard, coordinate structures of nominal phrases are represented by segments with the label 'Parallel' with grouping. The dependency arc is labelled 'D'. However, in the case of $\boxed{\text{CSJ}}$ and $\boxed{\text{KC}}$, the coordination of nominal phrases is expressed by the dependency arc labelled 'P'.

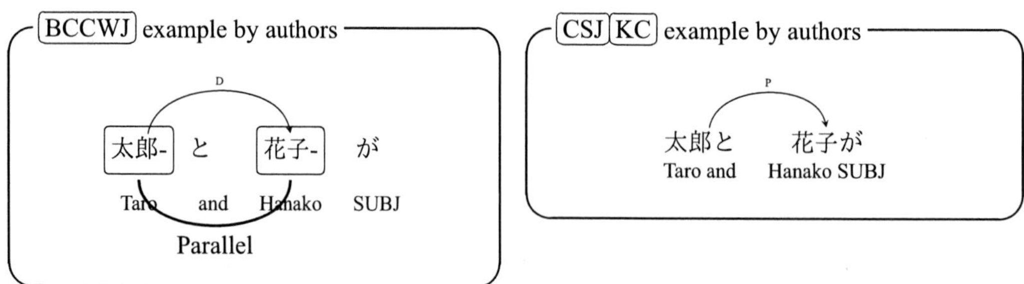

3.2 Predicate coordination

Since the identification of a predicate coordination is difficult, the $\boxed{\text{BCCWJ}}$ standard does not focus on using labels or segments to define these structures. We regard a predicate coordination as a normal dependency attachment (labelled 'D'). As a comparison, the $\boxed{\text{CSJ}}\boxed{\text{KC}}$ standards label 'P' for predicate coordination.

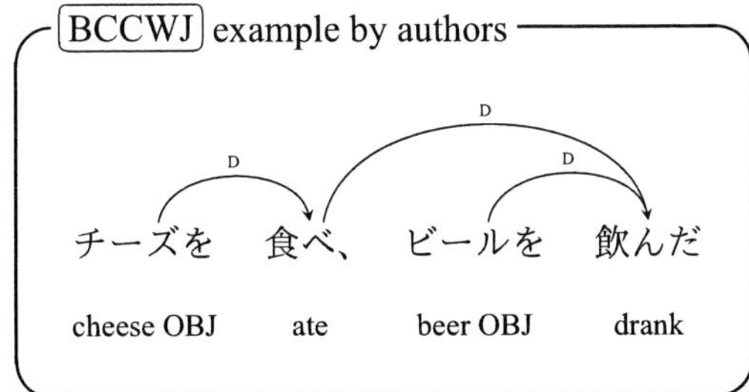

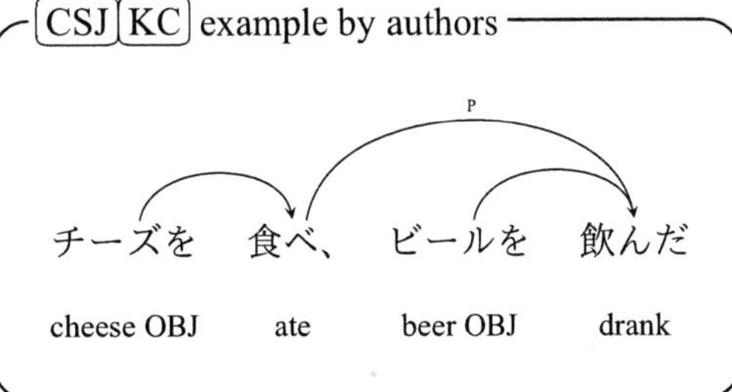

3.3 Non-constituent coordination

The non-constituent coordinate structure may violate projective or double 'を (wo: object marker)' constraints. The CSJ KC standards define the label 'I' to show the scope of such coordination and to maintain projective constraints. However, in the BCCWJ standard, we only define the segments on non-constituent coordination and normal dependency attachment with the label 'D'.

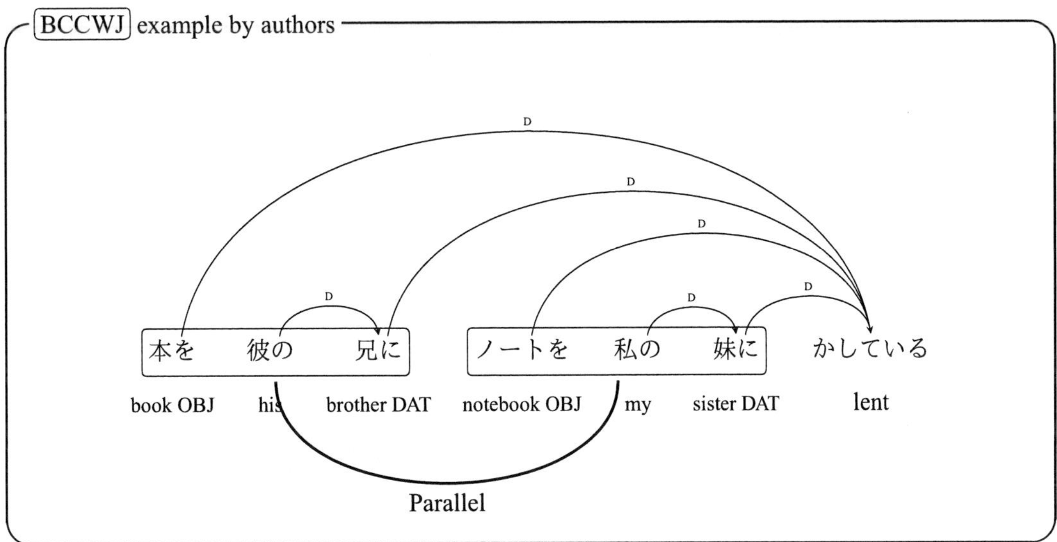

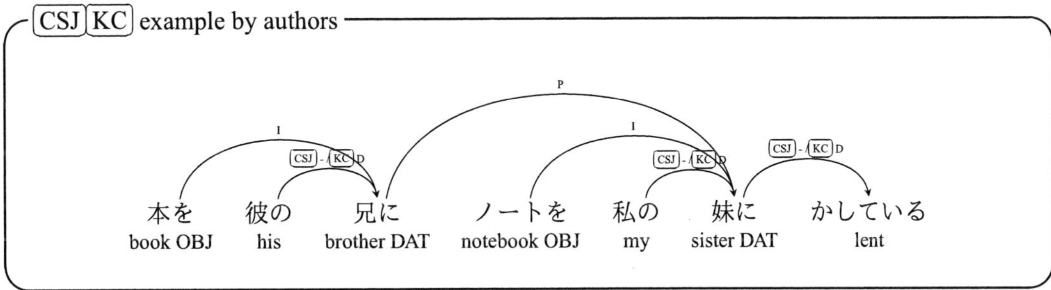

3.4 Coordination with more than two constituents

In the BCCWJ standard, coordination with more than two constituents is expressed by segments which are attached to the rightmost *bunsetsu* within the right adjacent coordinate constituent with the label 'D'. In the example, '風合い (texture)', '風格 (dignity)', and '高級感あふれる質感 (high-grade quality)' are expressed by grouping the segments. The conjunction 'そして (and)' (underlined in the below figure) attaches the rightmost *bunsetsu* within the rightmost coordinate constituent with the label 'D'.

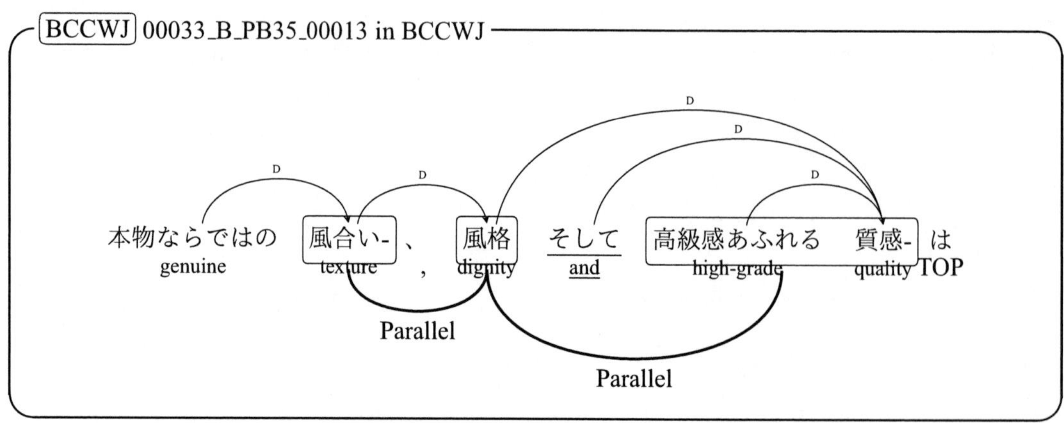

In contrast, the CSJ standard labels 'C' for the conjunction. However, the illustration is omitted due to space limitation.

3.5 Forward sharing

Forward sharing is a unique trait of a coordinate structure, in which one *bunsetsu* attaches all constituents in the coordination.

In the example below, 'オ（リックス）は (Orix TOP)' attaches both 'オーストリア (Austria)' and 'オーストラリア (Australia)'. Attaching the leftmost constituent of the coordination means forward sharing. Note that since Japanese language is essentially a strictly final language, we are not concerned about backward sharing.

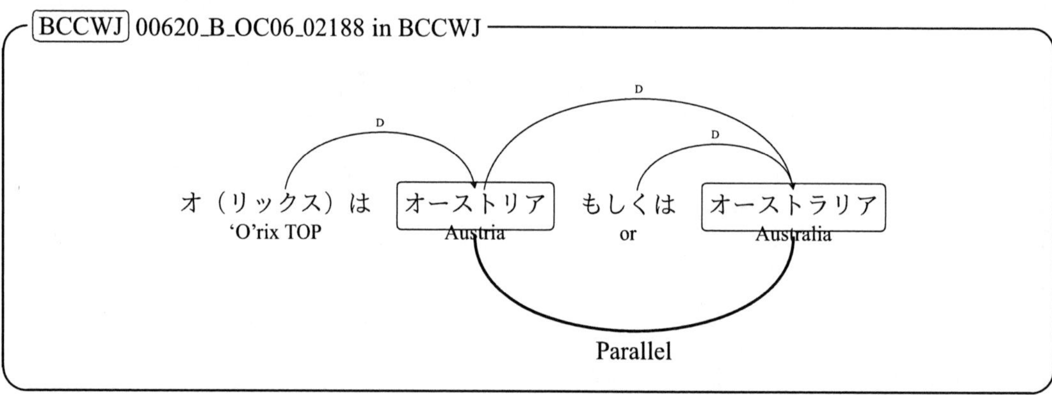

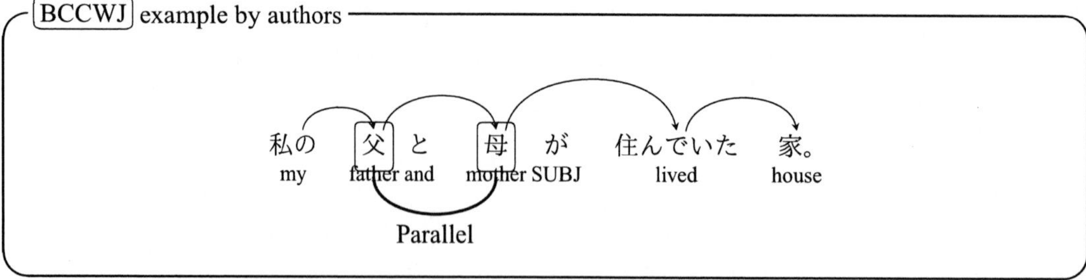

3.6 Apposition in the narrow sense

In the BCCWJ standard, apposition structures are also expressed by segments and groups. The example below illustrates that the appositive noun phrases, namely, '米国大統領 (US president)' and 'ジョン・F・ケネディ(John F. Kennedy)' are grouped and labelled 'Apposition'. However, in the KC CSJ standards, these appositive noun phrases are expressed by the dependency arc with the label 'A'.

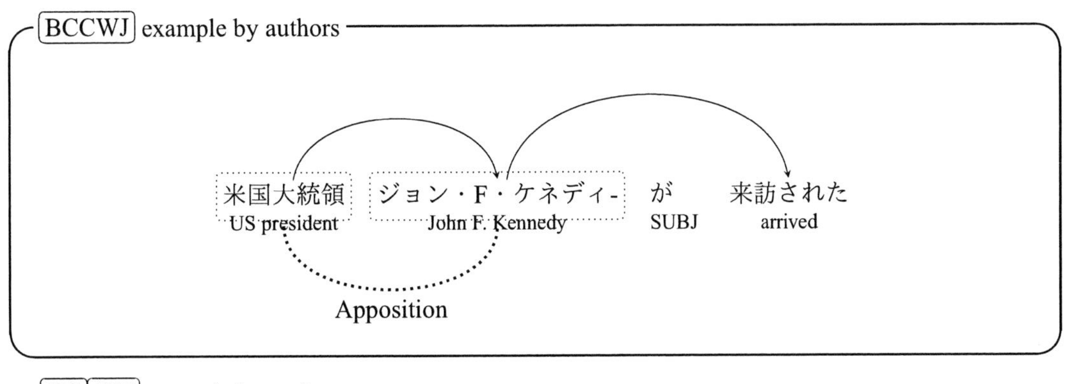

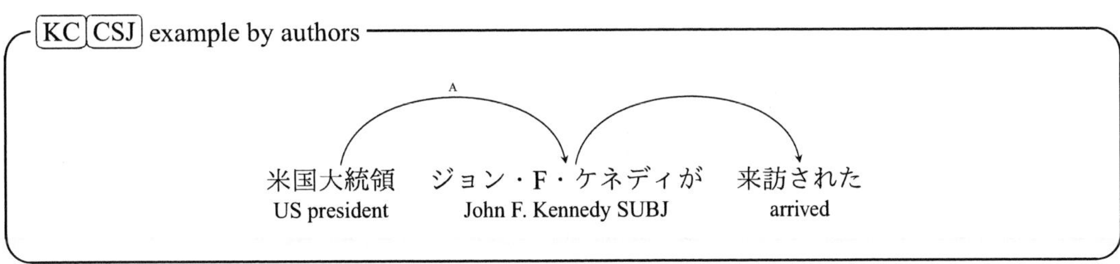

3.7 Generic – Apposition in a broad sense

In the KC standard, the apposition label 'A' is defined in the broad sense, which includes the apposition between examples and generic expressions, and between examples and numeral expressions (attribute-value relation). In comparison, the CSJ standard restricts the label 'A' to the narrow sense of apposition, whereas the label 'A2' represents apposition in the broad sense.

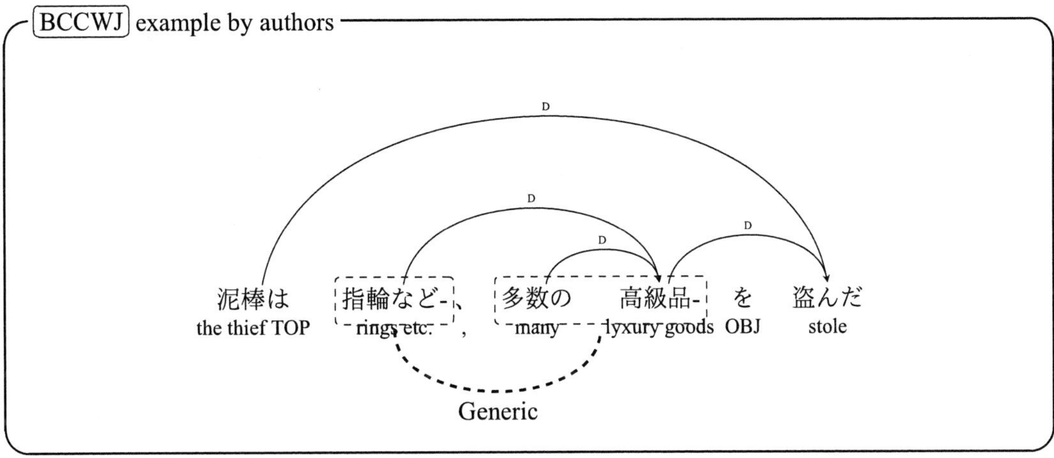

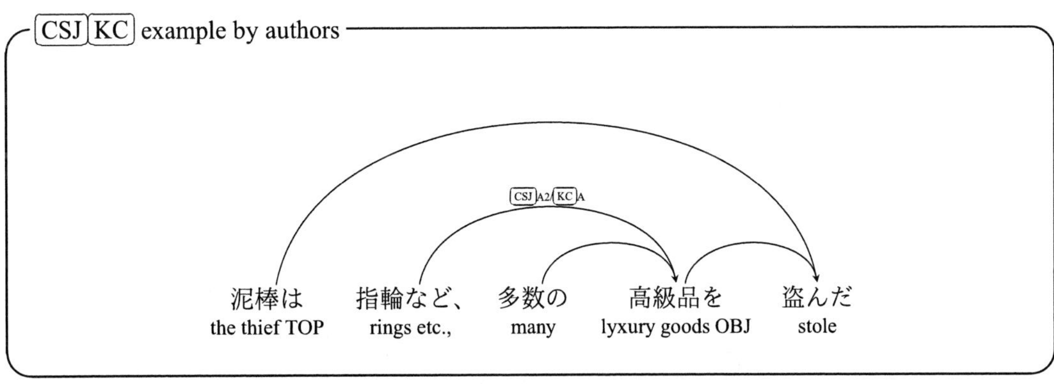

4 Inter-clause attachment

Inter-clause attachment is one of issues of annotation consistency among the annotators. We use subordinate clause classes (Minami, 1974) to determine the inter clause attachments. Table 2 shows the annotation schema. The subordinate clause is classified into three classes (i.e. A, B, C). The classes define the scope of the constituents.

The most frequent inconsistency is the attachment of case markers. Whereas the subjective *"-ga"* can attach to class B and C, the topicalization *"-ha"* can attach only to class C. Other case markers such as the objectives *"-wo"* and *"-ni"* can attach to all classes.

In the definition, the annotators need to judge the usages of *"-te"* and the conjunctive form. However, we did not record the judgment. In our future work, we will annotate the class of clauses.

5 Basic Statistics of the BCCWJ-DepPara

In this section, we present the basic statistics of the BCCWJ-DepPara data. Table 3 shows the number of sample files, short unit words (SUW), long unit words (LUW), *bunsetsus*, the dependency arc labels of 'D', 'B', 'F', 'Z', and end of sentences ('EOS'). The label 'F' in both OW and OY registers tends to be larger than of those in the other registers. The OW register includes many item markers, whereas the OY register includes many smiley strings, all labelled 'F'. Since we permit nested sentences, the number of the label 'Z' is more than the number of 'EOS'[1].

Table 4 shows the basic statistics of the coordination and apposition structures. The register 'OW' tends to include many 'Parallel' annotations. Because coordinate structures permit more than two constituents, the average number of constituents (seg/grp) of coordinate structures ranges from 2.19-2.35. However, since the 'Apposition' and 'General' labels are paired constituent structures, the average number of the constituents of these labels is nearly 2.00. Some exceptions of apposition expressions are caused by paraphrasing more than one time in several forms.

6 Conclusion

This article presents the annotation standard of dependency and coordination structures in the BCCWJ-DepPara. In the standard, the coordinate structure was taken out of the dependency structure, and it was, then, expressed by segments and groups.

Due to space limitation, we have omitted the annotation standard related to the inter-clause attachment, in which the scopes of phrases or clauses are defined by Minami's clause classes(Minami, 1974). Though the annotator used the clause classes for judgement, we did not annotate the clause classes on the corpus. Our current work is to annotate the clause classes based on the standard of 'Japanese Semantic Pattern Dictionary – Compound and Complex Sentence Eds.' (Ikehara, 2007).

The data of the BCCWJ-DepPara are accessible at `http://bccwj-data.ninjal.ac.jp/mdl/` for any purchaser of the BCCWJ DVD edition.

Parsing models should be adopted for the BCCWJ standard. (Iwatate, 2012) proposed a model that involves the BCCWJ standard, in which the dependency attachments and coordinate structures are estimated by a dual decomposition method.

Acknowledgements

This work was supported by JSPS KAKENHI Grant Numbers JP18061005, JP23240020, JP25284083, and JP15K12888. The work was also supported by the NINJAL collaborative research project 'Basic Research on Corpus Annotation'. We also appreciate the annotators and contributors of the BCCWJ-DepPara.

---

[1] Whereas the label 'Z' defines both inner and outer sentence ends, the label 'EOS' defines only the outer sentence ends.

Table 2: Minami's clause classes and their attachments

Non-predicative constituents:

Clause class	Subordinate clause form	Noun + Case Particle other than subjective (-ga)	Stative adverb	Degree adverb	Class A clauses	Subjective (-ga)	Temporal modifier	Locative modifier	jitsuni, tonikaku, yahari, etc.	Evaluative modifier	Class B clause	Topicalization -ha	osoraku, tabun, masaka, etc.	Class C clause
class C	‡conjunctive form (coordination)	+	+	+	+	+	+	+	+	+	+	+	+	+
class C	†*-te* (citation)	+	+	+	+	+	+	+	+	+	+	+	+	+
class C	*-shi* (coordination)	+	+	+	+	+	+	+	+	+	+	+	+	+
class C	*-keredo* (coordination)	+	+	+	+	+	+	+	+	+	+	+	+	+
class C	*-kara* (reason)	+	+	+	+	+	+	+	+	+	+	+	+	+
class C	*-ga*	+	+	+	+	+	+	+	+	+	+	+	+	+
class B	*-naide*	+	+	+	+	+	+	+	+	+	+	·	·	·
class B	*-zu* or *zuni*	+	+	+	+	+	+	+	+	+	+	·	·	·
class B	‡conjunctive forms (sequence)	+	+	+	+	+	+	+	+	+	+	·	·	·
class B	†*-te* (sequence)	+	+	+	+	+	+	+	+	+	+	·	·	·
class B	*-temo* (assumption)	+	+	+	+	+	+	+	+	+	+	·	·	·
class B	*-nara* (assumption)	+	+	+	+	+	+	+	+	+	+	·	·	·
class B	*-tara* (assumption)	+	+	+	+	+	+	+	+	+	+	·	·	·
class B	*-ba* (assumption)	+	+	+	+	+	+	+	+	+	+	·	·	·
class B	*-noni* (reason or focus)	+	+	+	+	+	+	+	+	+	+	·	·	·
class B	*-node* (reason or focus)	+	+	+	+	+	+	+	+	+	+	·	·	·
class B	*-nagara* (contradictory)	+	+	+	+	+	+	+	+	+	+	·	·	·
class B	*-to* (assumption)	+	+	+	+	+	+	+	+	+	+	·	·	·
class B	†*-te* (other than collateral, sequence or citation)	+	+	+	+	+	+	+	+	+	+	·	·	·
class A	‡conjunctive forms of adjective)	+	+	+	+	+	·	·	·	·	·	·	·	·
class A	‡repetition of conjunctive forms	+	+	+	+	·	·	·	·	·	·	·	·	·
class A	†*-te* (collateral circumstance)	+	+	+	+	·	·	·	·	·	·	·	·	·
class A	*-tsutsu* (collateral circumstance)	+	+	+	+	·	·	·	·	·	·	·	·	·
class A	*-nagara* (collateral circumstance)	+	+	+	+	·	·	·	·	·	·	·	·	·

Predicative constituents:

Clause class	Subordinate clause form	Declinable word without dummy noun	Causative form	Passive form	Receiving form	Respect form	Polite form	Negation form	Past form	Declinable word with dummy noun	Volition form	Conjecture form
class C	‡conjunctive form (coordination)	+	+	+	+	+	+	·	·	·	·	·
class C	†*-te* (citation)	+	+	+	+	+	+	+	·	·	·	·
class C	*-shi* (coordination)	+	+	+	+	+	+	+	+	+	+	+
class C	*-keredo* (coordination)	+	+	+	+	+	+	+	+	+	+	+
class C	*-kara* (reason)	+	+	+	+	+	+	+	+	+	+	+
class C	*-ga*	+	+	+	+	+	+	+	+	+	+	+
class B	*-naide*	+	+	+	+	+	+	+	·	·	·	·
class B	*-zu* or *zuni*	+	+	+	+	+	+	+	·	·	·	·
class B	‡conjunctive forms (sequence)	+	+	+	+	+	+	·	·	·	·	·
class B	†*-te* (sequence)	+	+	+	+	+	+	+	·	·	·	·
class B	*-temo* (assumption)	+	+	+	+	+	+	+	·	·	·	·
class B	*-nara* (assumption)	+	+	+	+	+	+	+	+	+	·	·
class B	*-tara* (assumption)	+	+	+	+	+	+	+	·	·	·	·
class B	*-ba* (assumption)	+	+	+	+	+	+	+	·	·	·	·
class B	*-noni* (reason or focus)	+	+	+	+	+	+	+	+	+	·	·
class B	*-node* (reason or focus)	+	+	+	+	+	+	+	+	+	·	·
class B	*-nagara* (contradictory)	+	+	+	+	+	+	+	·	·	·	·
class B	*-to* (assumption)	+	+	+	+	+	+	+	·	·	·	·
class B	†*-te* (other than collateral, sequence or citation)	+	+	+	+	+	+	+	·	·	·	·
class A	‡conjunctive forms of adjective)	+	·	·	·	·	·	·	·	·	·	·
class A	‡repetition of conjunctive forms	+	+	+	·	·	·	·	·	·	·	·
class A	†*-te* (collateral circumstance)	+	+	+	+	+	·	·	·	·	·	·
class A	*-tsutsu* (collateral circumstance)	+	+	+	+	+	·	·	·	·	·	·
class A	*-nagara* (collateral circumstance)	+	+	+	+	+	·	·	·	·	·	·

+ means that the constituent can exist in the clause class
· means that the constituent cannot exist in the clause class
†*-te* form is classified into 4 classes based on usages
‡conjunctive form is classified into 4 classes by the usages

References

Satoshi Ikehara. 2007. Semantic typology pattern dictionary. http://asia.shachi.org/resources/862.

Table 3: Basic statistics of the BCCWJ-DepPara (word and dependency labels)

register	samples	SUW	LUW	*Bunsetsu*	'D'	'B'	'F'	'Z'	'EOS'
PN	340	308,504	224,140	116,955	96,892 (82.8%)	1,652 (1.4%)	2,017 (1.7%)	16,394 (14.0%)	16,042
PB	83	204,050	169,730	84,733	72,340 (85.3%)	1,091 (1.2%)	1,425 (1.7%)	9,877 (11.7%)	9,678
PM	86	202,268	159,883	83,077	67,618 (81.4%)	1,187 (1.4%)	1,629 (2.0%)	12,643 (15.2%)	12,542
OW	62	197,011	129,646	68,449	59,320 (86.6%)	359 (0.5%)	2,927 (4.3%)	5,843 (8.5%)	5,825
OC	938	93,932	78,770	36,740	29,753 (81.0%)	323 (0.9%)	428 (1.2%)	6,236 (17.0%)	6,110
OY	471	92,746	75,242	38,576	29,650 (78.9%)	337 (0.9%)	1,501 (3.9%)	7,088 (18.4%)	7,059

The percentages are the number of labels { 'D', 'B', 'F', and 'Z'} / the number of *bunsetsus*.

Table 4: Basic statistics of the BCCWJ-DepPara (coordination and apposition structures)

register	Parallel			Apposition			General		
	seg	grp	seg/grp	seg	grp	seg/grp	seg	grp	seg/grp
PN	8,446	3,844	2.19	3,440	1,713	2.01	1,026	513	2.00
PB	4,640	2,060	2.25	704	352	2.00	304	152	2.00
PM	5,513	2,454	2.24	1,313	651	2.02	280	140	2.00
OW	10,709	4,613	2.32	1,326	662	2.00	656	328	2.00
OC	1,586	715	2.21	292	146	2.00	62	31	2.00
OY	1,603	682	2.35	262	131	2.00	58	29	2.00
Total	32,497	14,368	2.26	7,337	3,655	2.01	2,386	1,193	2.00

Masakazu Iwatate. 2012. *Development of Pairwise Comparison-based Japanese Dependency Parsers and Application to Corpus Annotation, Chapter 7: Joint Inference of Dependency Parsing and Coordination Analysis Using a Dual Decomposition Algorithm*. Ph.D. thesis, Graduate School of information Science, Nara Institute of Science and Technology, Japan.

Sadao Kurohashi and Makoto Nagao. 1998. Building a japanese parsed corpus while improving the parsing system. In *Proceedings of The 1st International Conference on Language Resources & Evaluation*, pages 719–724.

Kikuo Maekawa, Makoto Yamazaki, Toshinobu Ogiso, Takehiko Maruyama, Hideki Ogura, Wakako Kashino, Hanae Koiso, Masaya Yamaguchi, Makiro Tanaka, and Yasuharu Den. 2014. Balanced Corpus of Contemporary Written Japanese. *Language Resources and Evaluation*, 48:345–371.

Kikuo Maekawa. 2003. Corpus of spontaneous japanese: Its design and evaluation. In *ISCA & IEEE Workshop on Spontaneous Speech Processing and Recognition*.

Fujio Minami, 1974. 現代日本語の構造 *(Structure of Contemporary Japanese)*, pages 128–129. 大修館書店 (Taishukan publishing).

Kiyotaka Uchimoto, Ryoji Hamabe, Takehiko Maruyama, Katsuya Takanashi, Tatsuya Kawahara, and Hitoshi Isahara. 2006. Dependency-structure annotation to Corpus of Spontaneous Japanese. In *Proceedings of 5th edition of the International Conference on Language Resources and Evaluation*, pages 635–638.

SCTB: A Chinese Treebank in Scientific Domain

Chenhui Chu,[1] **Toshiaki Nakazawa,**[1] **Daisuke Kawahara**[2] and **Sadao Kurohashi**[2]
[1]Japan Science and Technology Agency
[2]Graduate School of Informatics, Kyoto University
{chu,nakazawa}@pa.jst.jp {dk,kuro}@i.kyoto-u.ac.jp

Abstract

Treebanks are curial for natural language processing (NLP). In this paper, we present our work for annotating a Chinese treebank in scientific domain (SCTB), to address the problem of the lack of Chinese treebanks in this domain. Chinese analysis and machine translation experiments conducted using this treebank indicate that the annotated treebank can significantly improve the performance on both tasks. This treebank is released to promote Chinese NLP research in scientific domain.

1 Introduction

A treebank is a text corpus consisting of usually thousands to tens of thousands of sentences annotated with linguistic knowledge such as segmentation, part-of-speech (POS) tags and syntactic structures. From the initial release of the first treebank of the Penn treebank (PTB) (Marcus et al., 1993), treebanking has remarkably promoted the research of statistical natural language processing (NLP). Inspired by the success of the English treebank, treebanks for other languages have also been constructed or under construction (Nivre et al., 2016). For Chinese, there are several existing treebanks such as the widely used Penn Chinese treebank (CTB) (Xue et al., 2005), and the Peking University (PKU) treebank (Yu et al., 2003). Chinese language processing has been significantly developed with these treebanks. For example, the F-Measures of Chinese analysis on the benchmark data set CTB version 5 (CTB5)[1] has achieved about 98% for segmentation, 94% for POS tagging (Shen et al., 2014), and 80% for syntactic parsing (Petrov and Klein, 2007).

One difficulty of statistical NLP is the domain diversity. As most treebanks such as the PTB, CTB and PKU are constructed mainly in news domain, the performance is not satisfied when analyzing sentences in other distant domains using the models trained on these treebanks. In China, the number of scientific documents has been remarkably increased. For example, the worldwide share of patent documents has increased to 30% (worldwide rank 1) in 2009,[2] and the worldwide share of scientific papers has increased to 13% on the average of 2011-2013 (worldwide rank 2) (Saka and Igami, 2015). Therefore, the needs for scientific domain text analyzing such as text mining, knowledge discovery, and translating scientific documents to other languages are increasing. However, when applying the Chinese analysis models trained on different domains to scientific domain, the F-Measures of various analysis tasks dramatically decrease to 90% for segmentation, 78% for POS tagging, and 70% for syntactic parsing (Section 3.1). This level of low accuracy analysis could significantly affect the performance of downstream applications such as text mining and machine translation (MT).

Motivated by this, we decide to construct a Chinese treebank in the scientific domain (SCTB) to promote Chinese NLP research in this domain. This paper presents the details of our treebank annotation process and the experiments conducted on the annotated treebank. The raw sentences are selected from Chinese scientific papers. Our annotation process follows that of CTB (Xue et al., 2005) with an exception of the segmentation standard. We apply a Chinese word segmentation standard based on character-level POS patterns (Shen et al., 2016), aiming to circumvent inconsistency and address data

---

[1]https://catalog.ldc.upenn.edu/LDC2005T01
[2]Statistics from Japan Patent Office.

59

Proceedings of the 12th Workshop on Asian Language Resources,
pages 59–67, Osaka, Japan, December 12 2016.

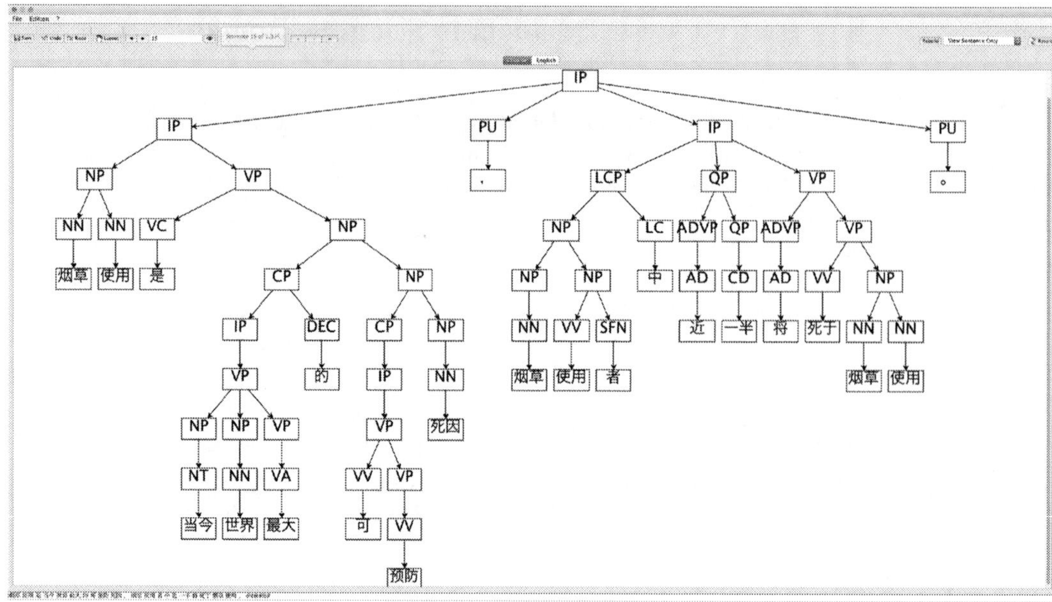

Figure 1: A screenshot of the annotation interface containing an annotation example of a Chinese sentence "烟草 (tobacco) /使用 (use) /是 (is) /当今 (nowadays) /世界 (world) /最大 (biggest) /的 ('s) /可 (can) /预防 (prevention) /死因 (cause of death) /, /烟草 (tobacco) /使用 (use) /者 (person) /中 (among) /近 (about) /一半 (half) /将 (will) /死于 (die) /烟草 (tobacco) /使用 (use) /。 " (the bottom boxes contain words, the pre-terminal boxes contain POS tags, while the upper boxes contain phrasal constituents).

sparsity of the annotated treebank. As the first version of release, we finished the annotation of 5,133 sentences (138,781 words).[3] To verify the effectiveness of the annotated SCTB, we conducted both instinct Chinese analysis experiments of segmentation, POS tagging and syntactic parsing, and extrinsic MT experiments on Chinese-to-Japanese and Chinese-to-English directions. Experimental results show that the annotated SCTB can significantly improve both Chinese analysis and MT performance.

2 Treebank Annotation

We annotate segmentation, POS tags and phrase structures for sentences in scientific domain. In this section, we describe the details for the annotation.

2.1 Raw Sentence Selection

The raw Chinese sentences for the treebank annotation are selected from the LCAS (National Science Library, Chinese Academy of Sciences) corpus provided by Japan Science and Technology Agency (JST). The LCAS corpus consists of Chinese scientific papers of various scientific subdomains. From this corpus, 780k abstracts were manually translated from Chinese to Japanese by JST (most of them also contain English translations). We randomly selected the raw sentences from the parallel part of the LCAS corpus, aiming for not only improving Chinese analysis but also multilingual NLP.

2.2 Annotation Standard

Conventional segmentation standards (Huang et al., 1996; Xia et al., 2000; Duan et al., 2003) define words based on the analysis of morphology, which could lead to two problems: inconsistency and data sparsity. For example, based on the conventional segmentation standards, both "使用 (use)" and "使用者 (user/use person)" in Figure 1 are one words, because "者 (person)" is a bound morpheme that cannot form a word itself. This leads to the inconsistent segmentation of "使用 (use)", and also makes

---

[3]http://nlp.ist.i.kyoto-u.ac.jp/EN/index.php?A%20Chinese%20Treebank%20in%20Scientific%20Domain%20%28SCTB%29

both words sparse. In this work, we adopt the Chinese word segmentation standard based on character-level POS patterns (Shen et al., 2016), which captures the grammatical roles of Chinese characters inside words. In our standard, we only treat a meaningful disyllabic string as a word if it falls into one predefined character-level POS patterns. For example, "使用 (use)" is one word as it belongs to the "verb + verb" pattern, and thus "使用者 (user/use person)" should be segmented into "使用" and "者 (person)".

Our POS standard essentially follows the one used in CTB (Xue et al., 2005). In order to tag the bound morphemes in conventional segmentation standards, we add six new tags into the tag set following (Shen et al., 2016), three for suffixes: "SFN" (nominal suffix), "SFA" (adjectival suffix), and "SFV" (verbal suffix); and three for prefixes: "PFN" (nominal prefix), "PFA" (adjectival prefix), and "PFV" (verbal prefix). For example, "者 (person)" is tagged with "SFN".

Our phrase structure annotation standard also follows that of CTB (Xue et al., 2005). For the words that should be one word according to the conventional segmentation standards, we combine them into one constituent in the phrase structure level. For example, "使用_VV (use) /者_SFN (person)" is combined into an NP (noun phrase) in Figure 1.

As we are annotating scientific texts, there are many specific expressions such as terminologies, formulas, and citations, which have not been covered by the conventional standards (Xue et al., 2005). For these, we define specific rules in particular. We plan to release the details of these rules together with our segmentation guideline along with the treebank.

2.3 Annotation Process

We used the SynTree toolkit[4] as the annotation interface. SynTree is a graphical interface for phrase structure annotation. Users can perform all the segmentation, POS tag and phrase structure annotations in this interface via dragging and editing the boxes containing words, POS tags and phrasal constituents in a bottom-up manner. We also customized the toolkit based on the feedbacks of the annotators during the annotation process. Figure 1 is a screenshot of the annotation interface.

The annotation was performed by two annotators: H and U. Annotator H had one year annotation experience, while annotator U was fresh at the beginning of the annotation. Therefore, annotator H was also responsible for training annotator U and reviewing the annotation done by annotator U. To improve the efficiency of annotation, the raw sentences were firstly processed by a baseline system described in Section 3.1. The annotators did the annotation by revising the errors in the automatic analysis results made by the baseline system using the annotation interface. The two annotators were asked to annotate different sentences, respectively. After that annotator H was asked to review and revise the sentences annotated by annotator U. We calculated the inter-annotator agreements on the sentences before and after the review/revision, and found that the agreements for segmentation, POS tagging and parsing are 98.95%, 97.78%, and 95.05%, respectively.

We have finished the annotation and review for 5,133 sentences (138,781 words) at the end of August, 2016. It took us 6 months for this annotation, and the average annotation speed was about 5 sentences/hour per person.

3 Experiments

We conducted both instinct and extrinsic experiments to verify the effectiveness of the annotated treebank. The instinct experiments were the conventional Chinese analysis tasks including segmentation, POS tagging and syntactic parsing. For the extrinsic experiments, we selected MT as an application of the Chinese analysis tasks, and conducted MT experiments on both the Chinese-to-Japanese and Chinese-to-English directions in scientific paper and patent domains, respectively.

3.1 Analysis Experiments

We conducted segmentation, POS tagging and syntactic parsing experiments. Segmentation and POS tagging experiments were conducted using the Chinese analyzing tool KyotoMorph[5] proposed by Shen

---

[4]http://syntree.github.io/index.html
[5]https://bitbucket.org/msmoshen/kyotomorph-beta

System	Precision	Recall	F-Measure
Baseline	90.99	89.97	90.48
Baseline+SCTB	94.59	94.91	94.75†

Table 1: Word segmentation results ("†" indicates that the result is significantly better than "Baseline" at $p < 0.01$).

System	Precision	Recall	F-Measure
Baseline	78.21	77.33	77.77
Baseline+SCTB	84.88	85.17	85.03†

Table 2: Joint segmentation and POS tagging results ("†" indicates that the result is significantly better than "Baseline" at $p < 0.01$).

et al. (2014). Parsing was performed by the Berkeley parser[6] (Petrov and Klein, 2007). We compared the Chinese analysis performance of the Chinese analyzers trained on the following two settings.

- Baseline: Chinese analyzers trained on CTB5 containing 18k sentences in news domain, and a previously created in-house (mainly) NLP domain treebank of 10k sentences. Note that the Chinese word segmentation of the baseline treebanks originally follows the conventional segmentation standard (Xia et al., 2000), and we manually re-annotated them based on the character-level POS patterns (Shen et al., 2016).

- Baseline+SCTB: Additionally used 4,933 sentences from the newly annotated SCTB for training the Chinese analyzers.

For testing, we used the remaining 200 sentences from the newly annotated SCTB. The significance tests were performed using the bootstrapping method (Zhang et al., 2004).

Tables 1 and 2 show the word segmentation, and the joint segmentation and POS tagging results, respectively. We can see that SCTB significantly improves both segmentation and joint segmentation and POS tagging performance by a large margin, i.e., 4.27% and 7.26% F-Measure, respectively.

Table 3 shows the parsing results. We used the Evalb toolkit[7] for the parsing accuracy calculation. As Evalb was originally designed for English, it only can evaluate the sentences that have the same segmentation as the gold data. For this reason, we showed the results based on gold segmentations in Table 3. As a reference, the parsing F-Measures from scratch for Baseline and Baseline+SCTB are 74.88% and 79.80% for 66 and 107 valid sentences (sentences that have the same segmentation as the gold data), respectively.

System	Precision	Recall	F-Measure
Baseline	67.33	72.84	69.97
Baseline+SCTB	74.82	78.89	76.80†

Table 3: Parsing results based on gold segmentations ("†" indicates that the result is significantly better than "Baseline" at $p < 0.01$).

We investigated the analyses for further understanding of the improvements. Based on our investigation, we found that most of improvements come from the domain knowledge introduced by our annotated treebank. Figure 2 shows such an example. The Baseline system incorrectly segments "骨骼亚(skeleton sub)" as one word, because it lacks the knowledge that "骨骼 (skeleton)" is a medical/biology term that should be one word. This segmentation error further propagates to POS tagging and parsing. In contrast, with the help of the scientific domain knowledge introduced by our annotated treebank, the

---

[6]https://github.com/slavpetrov/berkeleyparser
[7]http://nlp.cs.nyu.edu/evalb/

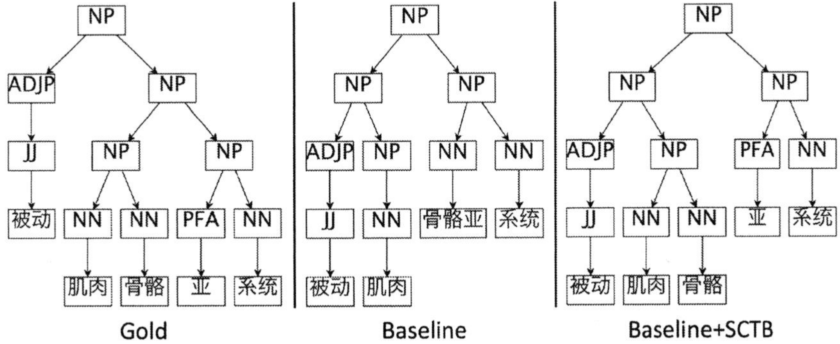

Figure 2: An improved example for Chinese analysis of a noun phrase "被动(passive) /肌肉 (muscle) / 骨骼 (skeleton) /亚(sub) /系统(system)".

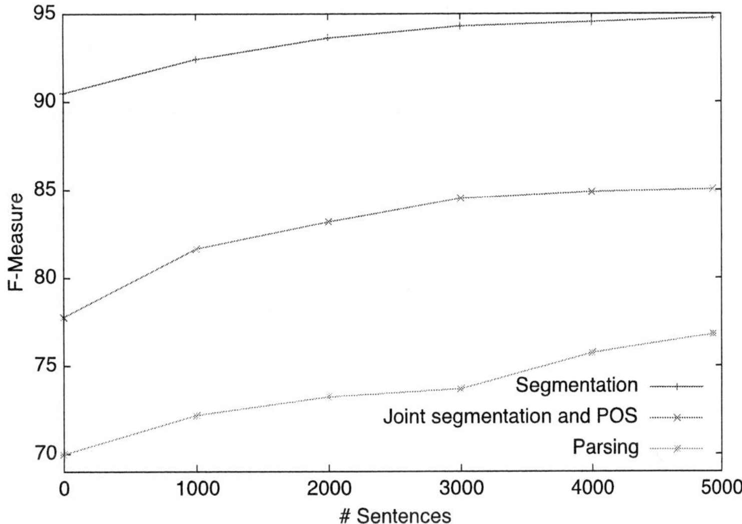

Figure 3: Chinese analysis results by adding different numbers of sentences from the newly annotated SCTB to the baseline treebanks for training the Chinese analyzers.

Baseline+SCTB system correctly segmented "骨骼 (skeleton) /亚(sub)" into two words, which also improves the POS tagging and parsing accuracy. However, the Baseline+SCTB system still fails to parse this phrase correctly, and we hope that the annotation of more sentences could be helpful for this.

To investigate the effectiveness of the treebank annotation in detail, we further conducted Chinese analysis experiments that trained the Chinese analyzers using different numbers of sentences from SCTB. In our experiments, we incrementally added 1,000 sentences to the baseline treebanks for training the analyzers. Figure 3 shows the results. We can see that for segmentation and POS tagging, the accuracy improvements slow down when more annotated sentences are used for training the analyzers; while for parsing, there is still a large potential of improvement by annotating more sentences.

3.2 MT Experiments

For Chinese-to-Japanese translation, we conducted experiments on the scientific domain MT task on the Chinese-Japanese paper excerpt corpus (ASPEC-CJ)[8] (Nakazawa et al., 2016), which is one subtask of the workshop on Asian translation (WAT)[9] (Nakazawa et al., 2015). The ASPEC-CJ task uses 672,315, 2,090, and 2,107 sentences for training, development, and testing, respectively. For Chinese-to-English translation, we conducted experiments on the Chinese-English subtask (NTCIR-CE) of the patent MT

---

[8]http://lotus.kuee.kyoto-u.ac.jp/ASPEC/
[9]http://orchid.kuee.kyoto-u.ac.jp/WAT/

System	ASPEC-CJ	NTCIR-CE
Baseline	39.12	33.19
Baseline+SCTB	40.08†	33.90†

Table 4: BLEU-4 scores for ASPEC-CJ and NTCIR-CE translation tasks ("†" indicates that the result is significantly better than "Baseline" at $p < 0.01$).

Source	环形碗状壁区段２６限定了开口２８，浸出液腔室２９位于壁２４中开口２８之下。
Reference	the annular bowl wall section 26 defines an opening 28 and a leachate chamber 29 is **located** in the wall 24 beneath the opening 28.
Baseline	annular 碗状壁区 section 26 defines opening 28, leach liquid chamber 29 in the wall 24 opening 28 below.
Baseline +SCTB	the annular bowl-shaped wall section 26 defines opening 28, leach liquid chamber 29 is **positioned** below the opening 28 in the wall 24.

Table 5: An improved MT example.

task at the NTCIR-10 workshop[10] (Goto et al., 2013). The NTCIR-CE task uses 1,000,000, 2,000, and 2,000 sentences for training, development, and testing, respectively.

We used the Moses tree-to-string MT system (Koehn et al., 2007) for all of our MT experiments. In our experiments, Chinese is in the tree format, and Japanese/English is in the string format. For Chinese, we used KyotoMorph for segmentations and the Berkeley parser for joint POS tagging and parsing. We binarized the parsing results for better translation rule extraction. We compared the MT performance of the "Baseline" and "Baseline+SCTB" settings in Section 3.1. For Japanese, we used JUMAN[11] (Kurohashi et al., 1994) for the segmentation. For English, we tokenized the sentences using a script in Moses. For the Chinese-to-Japanese MT task, we trained a 5-gram language model for Japanese, on the training data of the ASPEC-CJ corpus using the KenLM toolkit[12] with interpolated Kneser-Ney discounting. For the Chinese-to-English MT task, we trained a 5-gram language model for English, on the training data of the NTCIR-CE corpus using the same method. In all of our experiments, we used the GIZA++ toolkit[13] for word alignment; tuning was performed by minimum error rate training (Och, 2003), and it was re-run for every experiment.

Table 4 shows the translation results. The significance tests were performed using the bootstrap resampling method (Koehn, 2004). We can see that the significant improvements on Chinese analysis due to the annotated treebank, also lead to the significant MT performance improvements. Despite the language pair and slight domain difference, similar improvements are observed on both the ASPEC-CJ and NTCIR-CE MT tasks.

To further understand the reasons for the improvements, we also investigated the translation results. We found that most of the improvements are due to analysis improvements of the source sentences. Table 5 shows an improved MT example from the NTCIR-CE task. We can see that there is an out-of-vocabulary word "碗状壁区 (bowl wall section)" in the Baseline result. This is because the Baseline system incorrectly segmented "碗状壁区段 (bowl wall section)" into two words "碗状壁区 (bowl wall) /段 (section)"; while the Baseline+SCTB system correctly segmented it as "碗状 (bowl) / 壁 (wall) / 区段 (section)" leading to a correct translation. Another problem of the Baseline translation is that the word "位于 (located)" is not translated. This happens because as shown in Figure 4, the Baseline system analyzed the entire Chinese phrase after the comma as a verb phrase with the word "浸出 (leach)" as the head. In contrast, although the analysis by the Baseline+SCTB system is not fully correct, it correctly analyzed the word "位于 (located)" as the head of the following verb phrase, leading to a correct translation. Both the Baseline and Baseline+SCTB systems incorrectly translated "浸出液腔室 (leachate

[10]http://ntcir.nii.ac.jp/PatentMT-2/
[11]http://nlp.ist.i.kyoto-u.ac.jp/EN/index.php?JUMAN
[12]https://github.com/kpu/kenlm/
[13]http://code.google.com/p/giza-pp

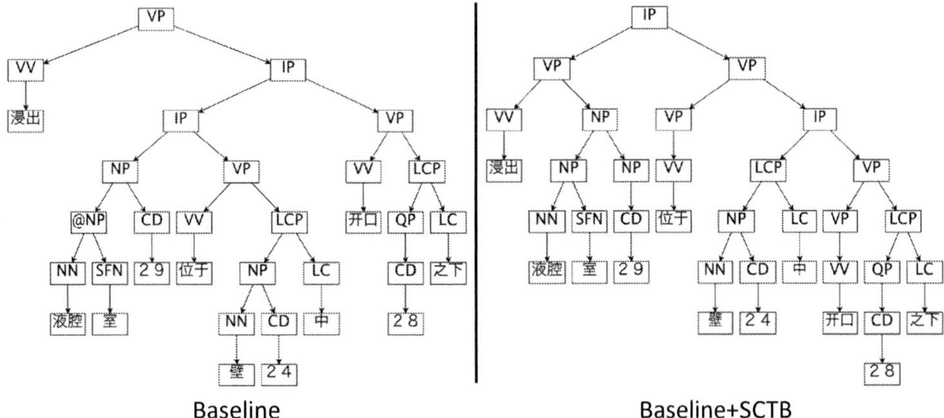

Baseline   Baseline+SCTB

Figure 4: The analysis results for the Chinese phrase after the comma of the source sentence in Table 5 "浸出 (leach) /液 (liquid) /腔室 (chamber) / 2 9 /位于 (is located) /壁 (wall) / 2 4 /中 (in) /开口 (opening) / 2 8 /之下 (beneath)".

chamber)" into "leach liquid chamber", this is due to the similar analysis results of both systems, while the correct analysis for this noun phrase should be "(NP (NP 浸出_NN 液_SFN) 腔室_NN) (leachate chamber)".

4 Related Work

Besides the widely used CTB (Xue et al., 2005), there are two other treebanks for Chinese. The Peking University (PKU) annotated a Chinese treebank, firstly only for segmentations and POS tags (Yu et al., 2003), and later also for syntax (Qiu et al., 2014). The Harbin Institute of Technologys (HIT) also annotated a treebank for dependency structures (Che et al., 2012). Besides the difference in annotation standards and syntactic structures, all the three treebanks are in news domain. CTB selected the raw sentences from People's Daily, Hong Kong newswire, Xinhua newswire etc., and PKU and HIT selected the raw sentences from People's Daily newswire. To the best of our knowledge, our treebank is the first publicly available Chinese treebank in scientific domain.

Three are two types of syntactic grammars for treebanking: phrase structures and dependency structures. We adopt the phrase structures used in CTB (Xue et al., 2005), because phrase structures can be converted to dependency structures based on predefined head rules using e.g. the Penn2Malt toolkit.[14] Treebanks with multi-view of both phrase structures and dependency structures also have been proposed (Qiu et al., 2014).

Recently, with more needs of multilingual NLP, the interests of constructing multilingual treebanks have increased. Multilingual treebanks such as the universal dependency treebank[15] (Nivre et al., 2016) and the Asian language treebank (Thu et al., 2016) are being constructed. As the raw sentences of our treebank were selected from parallel data and the translated Japanese and English sentences are available, we leave the potential to develop our treebank to a trilingual one.

5 Conclusion

In this paper, we presented the details of the annotation of SCTB: a Chinese treebank in scientific domain. Experiments conducted for Chinese analysis and MT verified the effectiveness of the annotated SCTB. As future work, firstly, we plan to annotate more sentences, and we aim to finish the annotation for 10k sentences within this year. Secondly, we also plan to annotate the Japanese and English raw sentences to further develop it to a trilingual treebank.

---

[14]http://stp.lingfil.uu.se/~nivre/research/Penn2Malt.html

[15]http://universaldependencies.org

65

Acknowledgements

This work is supported by the JST MT project "Project on Practical Implementation of Japanese to Chinese-Chinese to Japanese Machine Translation."[16] We are very appreciated for the great work of the two annotators: Ms. Fumio Hirao and Mr. Teruyasu Ueki. We thank Mr. Frederic Bergeron for his nice contribution to the annotation interface. We are also very grateful to Dr. Mo Shen for the discussion of the annotation standards.

References

Wanxiang Che, Zhenghua Li, and Ting Liu. 2012. Chinese dependency treebank 1.0. In *Linguistic Data Consortium*.

Huiming Duan, Xiaojing Bai, Baobao Chang, and Shiwen Yu. 2003. Chinese word segmentation at peking university. In *Proceedings of the Second SIGHAN Workshop on Chinese Language Processing*, pages 152–155, Sapporo, Japan, July. Association for Computational Linguistics.

Isao Goto, Ka-Po Chow, Bin Lu, Eiichiro Sumita, and Benjamin K. Tsou. 2013. Overview of the patent machine translation task at the ntcir-10 workshop. In *Proceedings of the 10th NTCIR Conference*, pages 260–286, Tokyo, Japan, June. National Institute of Informatics (NII).

Chu-Ren Huang, Keh-Jiann Chen, and Li-Li Chang. 1996. Segmentation standard for chinese natural language processing. In *Proceedings of the 16th Conference on Computational Linguistics - Volume 2*, COLING '96, pages 1045–1048, Stroudsburg, PA, USA. Association for Computational Linguistics.

Philipp Koehn, Hieu Hoang, Alexandra Birch, Chris Callison-Burch, Marcello Federico, Nicola Bertoldi, Brooke Cowan, Wade Shen, Christine Moran, Richard Zens, Chris Dyer, Ondrej Bojar, Alexandra Constantin, and Evan Herbst. 2007. Moses: Open source toolkit for statistical machine translation. In *Proceedings of the 45th Annual Meeting of the Association for Computational Linguistics Companion Volume Proceedings of the Demo and Poster Sessions*, pages 177–180, Prague, Czech Republic, June. Association for Computational Linguistics.

Philipp Koehn. 2004. Statistical significance tests for machine translation evaluation. In Dekang Lin and Dekai Wu, editors, *Proceedings of EMNLP 2004*, pages 388–395, Barcelona, Spain, July. Association for Computational Linguistics.

Sadao Kurohashi, Toshihisa Nakamura, Yuji Matsumoto, and Makoto Nagao. 1994. Improvements of Japanese morphological analyzer JUMAN. In *Proceedings of the International Workshop on Sharable Natural Language*, pages 22–28.

Mitchell P. Marcus, Mary Ann Marcinkiewicz, and Beatrice Santorini. 1993. Building a large annotated corpus of english: The penn treebank. *Computational Linguistics*, 19(2):313–330, June.

Toshiaki Nakazawa, Hideya Mino, Isao Goto, Graham Neubig, Sadao Kurohashi, and Eiichiro Sumita. 2015. Overview of the 2nd Workshop on Asian Translation. In *Proceedings of the 2nd Workshop on Asian Translation (WAT2015)*, pages 1–28, Kyoto, Japan, October.

Toshiaki Nakazawa, Manabu Yaguchi, Kiyotaka Uchimoto, Masao Utiyama, Eiichiro Sumita, Sadao Kurohashi, and Hitoshi Isahara. 2016. Aspec: Asian scientific paper excerpt corpus. In *Proceedings of the Tenth International Conference on Language Resources and Evaluation (LREC 2016)*, Paris, France, May. European Language Resources Association (ELRA).

Joakim Nivre, Marie-Catherine de Marneffe, Filip Ginter, Yoav Goldberg, Jan Hajic, Christopher D. Manning, Ryan McDonald, Slav Petrov, Sampo Pyysalo, Natalia Silveira, Reut Tsarfaty, and Daniel Zeman. 2016. Universal dependencies v1: A multilingual treebank collection. In *Proceedings of the Tenth International Conference on Language Resources and Evaluation (LREC 2016)*, pages 1659–1666, Paris, France, May. European Language Resources Association (ELRA).

Franz Josef Och. 2003. Minimum error rate training in statistical machine translation. In *Proceedings of the 41st Annual Meeting of the Association for Computational Linguistics*, pages 160–167, Sapporo, Japan, July. Association for Computational Linguistics.

---

[16]https://jipsti.jst.go.jp/jazh_zhja_mt/en.html

Slav Petrov and Dan Klein. 2007. Improved inference for unlexicalized parsing. In *Human Language Technologies 2007: The Conference of the North American Chapter of the Association for Computational Linguistics; Proceedings of the Main Conference*, pages 404–411, Rochester, New York, April. Association for Computational Linguistics.

Likun Qiu, Yue Zhang, Peng Jin, and Houfeng Wang. 2014. Multi-view chinese treebanking. In *Proceedings of COLING 2014, the 25th International Conference on Computational Linguistics: Technical Papers*, pages 257–268, Dublin, Ireland, August. Dublin City University and Association for Computational Linguistics.

Ayaka Saka and Masatsura Igami. 2015. Benchmarking scientific research 2015. pages 1–172. Ministry of Education, Culture, Sports, Science and Technology, Japan, August.

Mo Shen, Hongxiao Liu, Daisuke Kawahara, and Sadao Kurohashi. 2014. Chinese morphological analysis with character-level pos tagging. In *Proceedings of the 52nd Annual Meeting of the Association for Computational Linguistics (Volume 2: Short Papers)*, pages 253–258, Baltimore, Maryland, June. Association for Computational Linguistics.

Mo Shen, Li Wingmui, HyunJeong Choe, Chenhui Chu, Daisuke Kawahara, and Sadao Kurohashi. 2016. Consistent word segmentation, part-of-speech tagging and dependency labelling annotation for chinese language. In *Proceedings of the 26th International Conference on Computational Linguistics*, Osaka, Japan, December. Association for Computational Linguistics.

Ye Kyaw Thu, Win Pa Pa, Masao Utiyama, Andrew Finch, and Eiichiro Sumita. 2016. Introducing the asian language treebank (alt). In *Proceedings of the Tenth International Conference on Language Resources and Evaluation (LREC 2016)*, Paris, France, may. European Language Resources Association (ELRA).

Fei Xia, Martha Palmer, Nianwen Xue, Mary Ellen Okurowski, John Kovarik, Fu dong Chiou, Shizhe Huang, Tony Kroch, and Mitch Marcus. 2000. Developing guidelines and ensuring consistency for chinese text annotation. In *In Proceedings of the Second Language Resources and Evaluation Conference*.

Naiwen Xue, Fei Xia, Fu-dong Chiou, and Marta Palmer. 2005. The penn chinese treebank: Phrase structure annotation of a large corpus. *Natural Language Engineering*, 11(2):207–238, June.

Shiwen Yu, Huiming Duan, Bin Swen, and Bao-Bao Chang. 2003. Specification for corpus processing at peking university: Word segmentation, POS tagging and phonetic notation. *Journal of Chinese Language and Computing*, 13(2):121–158.

Ying Zhang, Stephan Vogel, and Alex Waibel. 2004. Interpreting bleu/nist scores: How much improvement do we need to have a better system? In *Proceedings of the Fourth International Conference on Language Resources and Evaluation (LREC-2004)*, pages 2051–2054, Lisbon, Portugal, May. European Language Resources Association (ELRA).

Big Community Data before World Wide Web Era

Tomoya Iwakura[†], Tetsuro Takahashi[†], Akihiro Ohtani[‡], Kunio Matsui[‡]
[†]Fujitsu Laboratories Ltd. [†]NIFTY Corporation
[†]{iwakura.tomoya, takahashi.tet}@jp.fujitsu.com
[‡]{ohtani.akihiro, matsui.kunio}@nifty.co.jp

Abstract

This paper introduces the NIFTY-Serve corpus, a large data archive collected from Japanese discussion forums that operated via a Bulletin Board System (BBS) between 1987 and 2006. This corpus can be used in Artificial Intelligence researches such as Natural Language Processing, Community Analysis, and so on. The NIFTY-Serve corpus differs from data on WWW in three ways; (1) essentially spam- and duplication-free because of strict data collection procedures, (2) historic user-generated data before WWW, and (3) a complete data set because the service now shut down. We also introduce some examples of use of the corpus. We plan to release this corpus to research institutes for research purpose. In order to use this corpus, please email to forum-corpus@list.nifty.co.jp.

1 Introduction

The online data on World Wide Web (WWW), such as Twitter [1], Facebook [2], and so on, are widely used for the research of Artificial Intelligence (AI). In this paper, we introduce a new corpus, NIFTY-Serve corpus, which includes a big community data before WWW.

NIFTY-Serve service was carried on from 1987 to 2006 in Japan and a big social network that had about 500 thousand users and 40 million postings. The data consists of not only texts but also movies, music files, programs, and so on. From the NIFTY-Serve data, we extracted texts by a CSV format as NIFTY-Serve corpus. In total, 27,943 text files mainly written in Japanese have been extracted. The total size of the text files is about 35 GB as of May 2014. Each text file corresponds to a bulletin board and a post of a bulletin board is a text annotated with metadata like the user who posted, the posting date, related posts, and so on. There are archives of BBS for English[34], however, to the best of our knowledge, this is the first release of a large amount of Japanese BBS data before WWW.

In this paper, we first introduce characteristics of NIFTY-Serve data in Section 2. Then, we describe NIFTY-Serve corpus in Section 3 and some of the examples of use of the NIFTY-Serve corpus in Section 4. Finally, we briefly introduce its disclosure condition in Section 5.

2 Characteristics of NIFTY-Serve Data

The NIFTY-Serve data has the following three main characteristics different from data on WWW. These characteristics make the NIFTY-Serve data worth to use for researchers.

2.1 Well Identified Users and Quality Contents

Users were required to register their credit cards or bank accounts for the use of NIFTY-Serve. In addition, in order to identify users, NIFTY-Serve sent letters to users for confirmation on a routine basis.

---

[1] https://twitter.com/
[2] https://www.facebook.com/
[3] http://www.rcat.com/fido_public/
[4] http://bbslist.textfiles.com/support/sources.html

Proceedings of the 12th Workshop on Asian Language Resources,
pages 68–72, Osaka, Japan, December 12 2016."

Figure 1: An example of a bulletin board of NIFTY-Serve.

P-ID	R-ID	NIFTY-ID	Handle ID	Post-Title	Posting-Date	Main-Content
54832	54830	ID01148299	ID01148284.handle_alpha-number_.-708377626.19930105173100	Re: By the way	960506711	Hello Mr. Smith. I have just copied the data for John. Tom

If there were letters that were not delivered to users, the accounts of the users were deleted. As a result, the users were well identified and there were essentially no user duplication and spam users.

In addition, contents of the NIFTY-Serve kept quality because the usage fee of a user was charged by how long the user connected to the NIFTY-Serve. When they posted their comments to the NIFTY-Serve, in order to avoid waste of money, users well considered what they were posting. In addition, administrators managed posts from users. As a result, NIFTY-Serve maintained better quality and there are fewer meaningless posts like just greeting that can be seen often on WWW.

2.2 Historic User Generated Data

The NIFTY-Serve service was carried on from 1987 to 2006. Therefore, the NIFTY-Serve data includes a large amount of text data written in Japanese before WWW became popular. One of the prominent examples is texts related to the Great Hanshin/Awaji Earthquake data that is an important record that includes how people acted in the disaster on online communities.

2.3 Complete Online Communities Data

NIFTY-Serve already finished its service. The complete data can be seen as a record of an online community service from beginning to end. NIFTY-Serve data includes both friendship-based communities such as Facebook and content-oriented communities such as YouTube[5] as mentioned in (Asatani et al., 2013). Therefore, we can see NIFTY-Serve as a data set that includes the whole lives of different types of online communities simultaneously.

3 Data Format

The NIFTY-Serve data includes personal information. Therefore, in addition to the original data, to reduce the risk of the leakage of the personal information as much as possible, we have prepared an anonymized corpus for the NIFTY-Serve data.

3.1 Original Data

We first introduce the original data format. Each text file corresponds to a BBS and the file name of the text file is the title of the BBS. In each text file, a post is represented by a CSV format. Figure 1 shows an example of a self-produced post. The first row indicates items of each post. The following are descriptions of the items.

- Post-ID (P-ID): A unique integer for a post.

- Response-ID (R-ID): The Post-ID of the post that is replied by a post. If Response-ID is 0, the post is not a reply to any other posts.

- NIFTY-ID: This corresponds to a user account that consists of 8 digits integer numbers beginning with "ID".

- Handle ID: The id of a user in a BBS.

- Post-Title: The title of a post.

Figure 2: A process for generating an anonymized corpus.

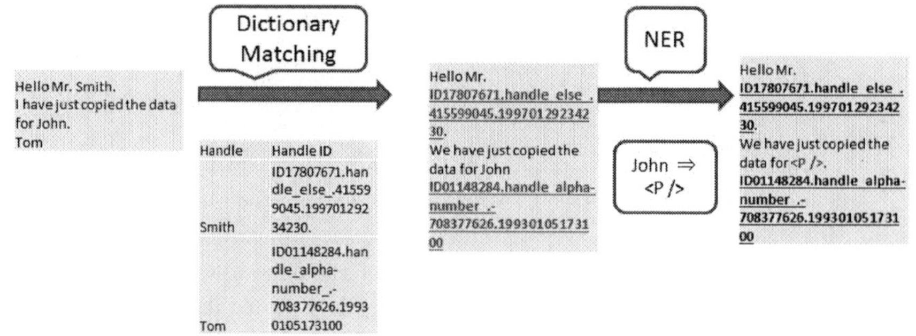

- Posting-Date: This is the date that indicates when a post was published. The format is yymmddhh-mmss, where "yy" indicates the last two digits of the dominical year, "mm" indicates a month, "dd" indicates a day, "hh" indicates hour, "mm" indicates a minute, and "ss" indicates a second.

- Main-Content: The text of a post.

3.2 Anonymized Corpus

This section introduces an anonymized version of NIFTY-Serve corpus. This corpus is mainly used for situations that users analyze as original text information as possible except sensitive personal information. In this corpus, personal names in the Main-content of each post were removed. Figure 2 shows an example of a generation of an anonymized data. First, we use a dictionary that includes pairs of Handles and "Handle ID". If there are words corresponding to handles the words are replaced with their corresponding "Handle ID".

To remove person names not included in the dictionary, we used a Japanese Named Entity (NE) recognizer (Iwakura, 2011). After identifying personal information in the text of a post, we replace the personal information by some meaningless symbols and the other words are still remained. The "... data for ⟨P/⟩. ..." in Figure 2 is an anonymized part by NER.

4 Examples of Use of NIFTY-Serve Data

This section describes four examples of the use of NIFTY-Serve data. We believe not only these examples, but also the other uses would be found by releasing this corpus.

4.1 Analysis of Changes of Word Usage

One of the examples is an analysis how use of words changes. We experimentally extracted emoticons by regular expressions. From the extraction results, we saw the following. From 1990 to 1998, a face mark "(^^)" that indicates happiness or joy was frequently used. However, around 2000, a face mark "m(_ _)m" that indicates apology or request was frequently used. This is a simple analysis, however, there may be possible to indicate something because the NIFTY-Serve data includes few meaningless information in our observation. In order to analyze real meanings of the use of face marks, one of the options is to collaborate with the other domain experts like sociologists or linguists.

4.2 Comparative Investigation of Online Communities

NIFTY-Serve data includes texts related to some historic events like disasters. One of the prominent examples is texts related to the Great Hanshin/Awaji Earthquake data. In Japan, we had the greatest earthquake, the Great East Japan Earthquake, on March 11th, 2011 since the Great Hanshin/Awaji Earthquake on January, 1995. At the Great East Japan Earthquake, services on WWW like Twitter are used for announcing information about emerging evacuation area, food support, the confirmation of the safety of disaster victims, and so on. These data are being used for researches like how users behave in such disaster (Inui et al., 2013).

To the best of our knowledge, texts in NIFTY-Serve are one of the biggest text data set related to disasters other than the earthquake on March 11th. By analyzing the both data with NLP technologies, we expect to find knowledge for the prevention of disaster.

4.3 Benchmark Data

NIFTY-Serve data includes some quality metadata and posts with such metadata can be used as benchmark data. One of the examples is an author identification task (Inoue and Yamana, 2012) by using posts annotated with user information. We think this data set is one of the most quality data for author identification tasks due to the characteristic described in Section 2.1. We expect to find the other uses by releasing this data to research communities.

4.4 Discovering Missing Data

NIFTY-Serve data also includes data other than texts such as multimedia data, programs, and so on. Therefore, we expect to discover lost multimedia data from the NIFTY-Serve data. For example, when we were converting the original NIFTY-Serve data to the NIFTY-Serve data set, we found an archive of computer viruses that is difficult to find today. We can also use the data as a source for discovering predominant multimedia data and programs before WWW became popular. Such old data discovery may help to know what happened before WWW became popular and the analysis of such data may contribute new discoveries.[6]

4.5 Online Community Analysis

NIFTY-Serve data includes a large amount of community data based on bulletin board posts. The data includes information such as when a community began and ended, how many posts and user each community had, and so on. The information would be helpful for the analysis of online communities as described in (Asatani et al., 2013). In addition, by comparing the community of NIFTY-Serve corpus with the current communities on WWW, we could find a common phenomenon shared with online communities.

5 Disclosure Condition

We cannot openly release the NIFTY-Serve corpus because of the inclusion of personal information and the condition of the contract with users. Therefore, we release this corpus for research purpose in research institutes under one of some contract types for the release of the corpus. If users make a contract with us, the users can use the NIFTY-Serve corpus by one of the formats described in Section 3. Please email to `forum-corpus@list.nifty.co.jp` for more detail of this corpus.

6 Conclusion

We have introduced the NIFTY-Serve corpus and some examples of use of the corpus. NIFTY-Serve corpus has some prominent characteristics that are different from data on WWW such as well identified users, quality contents, and so on. We also introduced examples of the use of the corpus like an analysis of the use of words. In the future, in order to contribute research communities, we plan to release this data to users by making a contract with us.

References

Kimitaka Asatani, Fujio Toriumi, Hirotada Ohashi, Mitsuteru Tashiro, and Ryuichi Suzuki. 2013. Prosperity and decline of online communities. In *PRIMA*, pages 396–404.

---

[6]Unfortunately, a worker unintentionally decompressed the archive and some machines were infected by the viruses. However, a virus software detected the viruses and killed the viruses.

Masatobu Inoue and Hayato Yamana. 2012. Authorship attribution method using n-gram part-of-speech tagger: Evaluation of robustness in topic-independence (in japanese). *DBSJ Journal*, 10(3):7–12.

Kentaro Inui, Hideto Kazawa, Graham Neubig, and Masao Utiyama. 2013. *Workshop on Language Processing and Crisis Information 2013*. IJCNLP 2013.

Tomoya Iwakura. 2011. A named entity recognition method using rules acquired from unlabeled data. In *Proc. of RANLP'11*, pages 170–177.

An Overview of BPPT's Indonesian Language Resources

**Gunarso, Hammam Riza, Elvira Nurfadhilah,
M. Teduh Uliniansyah, Agung Santosa, Lyla R. Aini**

Agency for the Assessment and Application of Technology (BPPT), Jakarta, INDONESIA

Abstract

This paper describes various Indonesian language resources that Agency for the Assessment and Application of Technology (BPPT) has developed and collected since mid 80's when we joined MMTS (Multilingual Machine Translation System), an international project coordinated by CICC-Japan to develop a machine translation system for five Asian languages (Bahasa Indonesia, Malay, Thai, Japanese, and Chinese). Since then, we have been actively doing many types of research in the field of statistical machine translation, speech recognition, and speech synthesis which requires many text and speech corpus. Most recent cooperation within ASEAN-IVO is the development of Indonesian ALT (Asian Language Treebank) has added new NLP tools.

1   Introduction

As a national language of Indonesia, Bahasa Indonesia has been used as a lingua franca in the multilingual Indonesian archipelago for centuries. Indonesia is the fourth most populous nation in the world, after China, India and the United States. Of its large population, around 255 million people, the majority speak Indonesian, making it one of the most widely spoken languages in the world.

Aside from speaking the national language, most Indonesians are fluent in any of more than 746 distinct regional languages (Amalia, 2016) such as Javanese, Sundanese and Madurese, which are commonly used at home and within the local community. Most formal education, and nearly all national media and other forms of communication, are conducted in Indonesian. Throughout the archipelago, Bahasa Indonesia has become the language that bridges the language barrier among Indonesians who have different mother-tongues.

In recent years, countries in the same region tend to establish some free trade areas such as ASEAN Economic Community (AEC), European Union (EU), and Asia-Pacific Economic Cooperation (APEC). This opens opportunities to accelerate economic growth for Indonesia. However, these efforts are hindered due to the lack ability of Indonesians in communicating with foreigners.

BPPT has started collecting language resources since 1987 as part of the development of a multilingual machine translation system in a project called "The Research and Development Cooperation Project on a Machine Translation System for Japan and its Neighbouring Countries". At the end of the project, many Indonesian language resources have been resulted, such as Indonesian basic dictionary, Indonesian grammar rule for analysis and generation system, Indonesian monolingual text corpus, and Indonesian gazetteer.

We have continued collecting language resources to improve the system which has been developed and the development of other natural language processing systems. The needs for the development of statistical machine translation with Indonesian as source language, Indonesian speech recognition and Indonesian speech synthesizer led to the development of other language resources, which are parallel corpora and speech corpora for ASR and TTS.

2   Indonesian Gazetteer

Indonesia is the world's largest island country, with more than thirteen thousand islands and has 34 provinces, of which five have Special Administrative status. Indonesia consists of hundreds of distinct

This research is funded by government research budget for BPPT fiscal year 2016 and cooperation with NICT ASEAN-IVO

Proceedings of the 12th Workshop on Asian Language Resources,
pages 73–77, Osaka, Japan, December 12 2016.

native ethnic and linguistic groups. This big country also has many districts, regencies, lakes, mounts, ports, airports, rivers, capes, bays, etc. Regarding this diversity, it needed to compile Indonesian Gazetteer as one of the language resources. Table 1 lists entries of the Indonesian Gazetteer.

No	Name Entity	Number of Data
1	Province	34
2	Regency	484
3	District	6,793
4	Lake	101
5	Mount	546
6	Airport	137
7	Harbour	295
8	Island	948
9	River	586
10	Cape	627
11	Bay	301
12	Tribe	358
13	Weapon	272
14	Art	245

Table 1: Lists entries of the Indonesian gazetteer

3   Indonesian Monolingual Corpus

Up to now, we have collected around 10.5 million sentences in an Indonesian monolingual corpus. The sentences were taken from various sources available on the internet such as national newspapers/magazines and governmental institutions (presidential speech, meeting transcriptions, trial transcriptions, etc.) by using HTTrack, a free offline browser utility (Roche et al., 2007). Table 2 lists all the corpora obtained from various sources.

Topic	Source	Number of articles	Number of sentences	Number of unique sentences	Number of words	Number of unique words
Financial	Bank of Indonesia	124	115,431	113,615	3,081,380	28,421
Various topics	DPR (House of Representative)	355	205,405	202,816	4,293,868	48,525
Law	PN (District Court)	12	39,075	38,733	662,964	17,803
Various topics	Presidential speech	16	1,268	1,266	24,695	3,502
Financial	Ministry of Finance	46	6,172	6,153	135,981	8,945
Various topics	Mail archive	3,685	68,455	56,267	1,092,195	45,323
Financial	BPK (Supreme Audit Board)	501	862,542	831,334	35,521,560	127,108
Various topics	DPD (House of Regional Representative)	755	450,270	444,836	9,902,733	72,147
Politics	KPU (National Election Commission)	1,176	23,503	16,734	399,182	19,042

Topic	Source	Number of articles	Number of sentences	Number of unique sentences	Number of words	Number of unique words
Law	Ministry of Justice and Human Rights	6,222	361,140	349,630	8,796,144	51,326
Literature	Novels	110,943	5,760,141	5,684,129	72,605,688	396,736
Various topics	National newspaper/magazine	28,795	609,728	609,275	12,484,728	111,574
Law	MK (Constitutional Court)	7,293	1,992,251	1,912,706	36,741,176	163,397
Various topics	Combination of all above	159,923	10,495,381	10,445,098	185,602,460	647,982

Table 2: Indonesian monolingual text corpus

4   Indonesian-English Parallel Corpus

No	Source	Topic	Number of sentences	Number of unique sentences
1	ASEAN MT[1]	Tourism	21,969	19,359
2	BBC	News	5,284	5,083
3	BTEC	Tourism	133,453	127,815
4	Indonesian Ministry of Finance [2]	Economics	48,778	46,400
5	PanL [3]	Economics	6,708	6,677
6	PanL	Science and Technology	10,431	10,404
7	PanL	National news	10,141	10,141
8	PanL	Sports	14,217	14,216
9	PanL	International news	9,993	9,993
10	Tatoeba[4]	Various topics	4,179	3,694
11	U-STAR[5]	Tourism	6,500	6,451
12	Warisan Indonesia	Tourism	7,517	7,161
13	Colours Magazine Garuda [6]	Tourism	10,603	10,400
14	Various expatriate blogs	Culture	33,943	33,943
15	Asian Language Treebank (ALT)[7]	WikiNews	20,000	20,000

Table 3: Indonesian-English parallel corpus

---

[1] (AseanMT, 2014)
[2] (Kemenkeu, 2015)
[3] (PanL, 2010)
[4] (Tatoeba, 2012)
[5] (Ustar, 2013)
[6] (Garuda-Indonesia, 2013)
[7] (Asian Language Treebank, ASEAN-IVO)

PTIK-BPPT collected around 311,737 sentences in an Indonesian-English parallel corpus to aid our research in statistical machine translation. The sentences were taken from various sources available on the internet such as national newspapers/magazines and governmental institutions by using HTTrack, a free offline browser utility. We hired some professional translators to check the correctness of the parallel corpus manually. Table 3 lists all parallel corpus obtained from various sources.

The Asian Language Treebank (ALT) project aims to advance the state-of-the-art Asian natural language processing (NLP) techniques through the open collaboration for developing and using ALT. The project is a joint effort of six institutes for making a parallel treebank for seven languages: English, Indonesian, Japanese, Khmer, Malay, Myanmar, and Vietnamese. In creating Indonesian - ALT, it requires tools to speed up the development. Some of these tools have been provided by the ALT project but for Indonesian we will use tools that were created from previous projects. Among them are POS Tagger, Syntax Tree Generator, Shallow Parser, word alignment, etc. Indonesian treebank resulted from this project will be utilize to enhance the exising tools and to create new tools in the field of NLP using state of the art techniques. Indonesian treebank is also expected to help the advancement of NLP researches in Indonesia.

5   Automatic Speech Recognition

To develop automatic speech recognition (ASR) system, training data in the form of speech corpus is required. The speech corpus for ASR must have a rich combination of uttered phonemes in the targeted language. And to make the ASR system speaker independent, the corpus should be created from speech recordings of many speakers with various ages and gender. Currently we have two set of speech corpus created for Indonesian ASR. The first one was made in 2010 for the joint development project with PT. INTI[7] to develop an Indonesian ASR system called PERISALAH. This speech corpus, consists of total 100,000 utterances uttered by 400 people. The utterances were coming from around 7800 unique sentences. The speakers consists of 200 adults male and 200 adults female, with the following composition: 40% Javanese, 20% Sundanese, 20% from Batak, 5% from Minang, 5% from Makassar, 5% from Maluku, and 5% from Papua, Bali and Madura. The ages of the speakers are within 20 to 50 years old. The total duration of the speech data is more than 133 hours. The average time per utterance is around 5 seconds, the longest utterance time is 22 seconds, and the shortest utterance time is 1.5 seconds. The speech data in this corpus was recorded as a single channel data with a 16KHz sampling rate and a 16-bit data size. The file format used for storing the data is WAV format. This first corpus set was already tested to create an acoustic model for Indonesian ASR with WER of around 20% using Julius[8] as the ASR engine. Since the PERISALAH corpus was created as a joint development, the ownership was a shared one, so it is not publicly available.

The second set of the corpus was created in 2013, this second corpus was planned to be made publicly available for research and education purposes. The second corpus consists of total 49,000 utterances uttered by 200 people, where each person speaks around 245 sentences. The speakers were consists of 100 male and 100 female, and the age-range were within 15 to 50 years old. Around 30% of the speakers were high-school students. The sentence used in this corpus comes from 5,000 unique sentences. The file format used to store the data is WAV with single channel recording, a 16KHz sampling rate and a 16-bit data size. The total duration of the speech data is more than 95 hours. The average time per utterance is around 6.8 seconds, the longest utterance time is 29 seconds, and the shortest utterance time is 1.0 seconds. This second corpus is planned to be released for research and education community at the end of 2016.

6   Speech Corpus for The Development of An Indonesian TTS System

For developing an Indonesian TTS system, PTIK-BPPT now uses 3 sets of speech corpus. Set 1 and 2 consists of 5,000 WAV files each, and set 3 consists of 15,645 WAV files. Table 4 describes details of the speech corpus.

Set no.	Speaker	Number of Utterances	Length (hours)	Format
1	male adult	5,000	6.56	wav, 16-bit, 16KHz
2	female adult	5,000	7.13	wav, 16-bit, 16KHz
3	male adult	15,645	40.25	wav, 16-bit, 16KHz
3	female adult	15,645	30.52	wav, 16-bit, 16KHz

Table 4: Speech TTS corpus.

The following table lists types of sentences in each speech corpus set:

Set no.	Sentence type		Sentence type			
	Number of regular sentences	Number of conversation-al sentences	Number of declarative sentences	Number of interroga-tive sen-tences	Number of imperative sentences	Number of exclamatory sentences
1	3,715	1,285	4,532	353	9	106
2	3,809	1,191	4,566	321	9	104
3	14,173	1,473	14,554	415	45	631

Table 5: Sentence types

7   Conclusion

BPPT has collected language resources to develop Indonesian-English statistical machine translation system, Indonesian ASR and text-to-speech system. The language resources will help the advancement of MT, ASR, and TTS research in Bahasa Indonesia and any NLP-related research in general. The existing data is enough for developing MT, ASR and TTS for the Bahasa Indonesia language but it needs more efforts. We have developed MT, ASR and TTS systems based on this data with adequate performance. Currently we also involved in the development of Asian Language Treebank to enrich our NLP resources. Currently all resources are for internal use only, but in the end of 2016 we are planning to release most of these resources for research and education communities under Common Criteria (CC-BY).

Reference

1. Amalia, Dora. 2016. *Lexicographic Challenges in Minority Languages of Indonesia*. Retrieved August 03, 2016 from http://compling.hss.ntu.edu.sg/events/2016-ws-wn-bahasa/pdfx/amalia.pdf

2. Asean MT. 2014. Retrieved August 03, 2016 from http://www.aseanmt.org/index.php?q=index/download

3. Garuda Indonesia. 2013. Retrieved January 15, 2014 from https://www.garuda-indonesia.com/id/en/garuda-indonesia-experience/in-flight/in-flight-entertainment/

4. PAN Localization. 2010. Retrieved September 23, 2010 from http://www.panl10n.net/

5. Roche, Xavier et al. 2007. *HTTrack Website Copier*. Retrieved May 02, 2010 from http://www.httrack.com/

6. Tatoeba. 2012. Retrieved March 15, 2012 from https://tatoeba.org/eng/

7. I-Perisalah , Retrieved August 15, 2016 from http://www.inti.co.id/index.php/id/2015-06-18-06-16-48/infrastruktur/smart-meeting

8. Lee, Akinobu, and Tatsuya Kawahara. 2009. *Recent Development of Open-source Speech Recognition Engine Julius*. Proceedings: APSIPA ASC 2009: Asia-Pacific Signal and Information Processing Association, 2009 Annual Summit and Conference, International Organizing Committee.

Creating Japanese Political Corpus
from Local Assembly Minutes of 47 Prefectures

Yasutomo Kimura
Otaru University of Commerce
kimura@res.otaru-uc.ac.jp

Keiichi Takamaru
Utsunomiya Kyowa University
takamaru@kyowa-u.ac.jp

Takuma Tanaka
Toyohashi University of Technology
t-tanaka@la.cs.tut.ac.jp

Akio Kobayashi
Toyohashi University of Technology
a-kobayashi@cs.tut.ac.jp

Hiroki Sakaji
Seikei University
hiroki_sakaji@st.seikei.ac.jp

Yuzu Uchida
Hokkai-Gakuen University
yuzu@hgu.jp

Hokuto Ototake
Fukuoka University
ototake@fukuoka-u.ac.jp

Shigeru Masuyama
Toyohashi University of Technology
masuyama@tut.jp

Abstract

This paper describes a Japanese political corpus created for interdisciplinary political research. The corpus contains the local assembly minutes of 47 prefectures from April 2011 to March 2015. This four-year period coincides with the term of office for assembly members in most autonomies. We analyze statistical data, such as the number of speakers, characters, and words, to clarify the characteristics of local assembly minutes. In addition, we identify problems associated with the different web services used by the autonomies to make the minutes available to the public.

1 Introduction

Many local autonomies in Japan provide access to various political documents on their websites. Such documents include basic urban development plans, local assembly minutes, and ordinances. The information obtained through the Internet can be used to compare the autonomies and identify the characteristics of individual autonomies. Local assembly minutes are an especially important source of such characteristics because they include various representatives' positions on policies enforced by the autonomy. Some studies that compare local assembly minutes have been conducted by political scientists (Tadashi Masuda, 2012). However, some issues arise with the analysis of local assembly minutes that should be addressed. One such issue is the different ways used to release the minutes to the public. There are 47 prefectures and several cities, towns, and villages in Japan, and local assembly minutes are made available in a variety of ways. Therefore, collecting local assembly minutes and unifying the format of the collected data for analysis on a national level is cost inefficient. In this paper, we attempt to create a corpus of local assembly minutes in Japan. This corpus realizes some research findings from NLP and sociolinguistics. Our objective is to develop a corpus that can be used for a broader range of interdisciplinary research.

We collected opinions from political scientists and economists to identify their research requirements with regard to local assembly minutes. It became clear that the scope of minutes must be controlled to conduct a strict comparative analysis. Specifically, the following requirements were identified as important: i) the periods must be identical and ii) autonomies must be classified as prefectures and other small regions such as cities, towns, and villages. For the first requirement, we collected minutes from assemblies held between April 2011 and March 2015. This four-year period is consistent with the term

Proceedings of the 12th Workshop on Asian Language Resources,
pages 78–85, Osaka, Japan, December 12 2016.

of office for assembly members' in most autonomies. To satisfy the second requirement, we collected assembly minutes from all 47 prefectures.

The objectives of this study are as follows: i) collect local assembly minutes (each of which have different formats) from all 47 prefectural assemblies, ii) obtain fundamental statistical data from the collected text data, and iii) extract political keywords using term frequency-inverse document frequency (tf-idf) weighting for a preliminary comparative analysis.

2   Collecting local assembly minutes

2.1   Outline

In this study, our primary purpose was to collect minutes of assemblies between April 2011 and March 2015 from all 47 prefectures. In the assembly minutes, all utterances are transcribed and recorded. Thus the assembly minutes will reveal policy planning and consensus building processes. As a result, assembly minutes are valuable documents for political analysis.

Local autonomies are independent, and the methods used to release assembly minutes differ, thus making the collection of assembly minutes. For example, a customized web crawler will be required for each autonomy.

The variety of text formats presents another difficulty. We need to extract assembly members' utterance from crawled web documents. Utterance attribute information, such as the speaker's name and the meeting's name and date must also be extracted. Thus, the format must be considered for each autonomy.

In the next section, we describe the procedure used to extract assembly minutes and create the corpus.

2.2   Procedure

As shown in Table 1, there are four types of primary web services used to release assembly minutes, and 42 of the 47 prefectures adopt one of these four primary web services. We prepare a web crawler for the primary four web services. However, many local autonomies have partially customized these services. We use semi-automated crawling depending on how the local autonomies release such documents. The remaining five prefectures have developed unique services, and assemblies that use such unique systems are downloaded using semi-automated crawling.

Table 1: Main Web services for providing local assembly minutes.

Name of Web service		Number of prefectures
Discuss	created by NTT-AT corporation	18
DB-Search	created by Yamato_Sokki center corporation	16
VOICES	created by Futurein corporation	6
Sophia	created by Kobe_Sogo_Sokki corporation	2
Others	Used by Iwate, Akita, Shizuoka, Wakayama and Okinawa	5

Table 2 lists the database items for the corpus. We automatically divided the raw into database items.

Below, we illustrate the method used to input text into the database after collecting the local assembly minutes. First, we designed a web crawler to automatically extract each value, such as "Year," "Month," "Day," and "Name of meeting," from a document. The following figure illustrates the extraction of "Name of meeting".

Table 2: Corpus database items.

Number	Name of item	Explanation
1	Reference number	Unique key for each utterance.
2	Name of prefectures	Name of autonomy.
3	Year	Year the meeting was held.
4	Month	Month the meeting was held.
5	Day	The day of the meeting.
6	Name of meeting	The name that includes the meeting type, volume and number.
7	Name of speaker	The name often includes a title such as "Mr.", "Pres." and "Chair."
8	Utterance	The utterance is split by either "period" or "new line mark".
9	Other	Other means outside the field of the utterance.

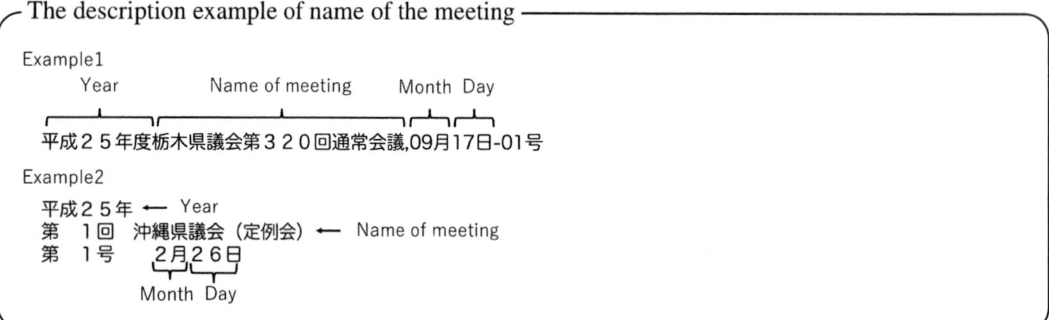

Second, we extract speakers' names and their utterances from the body text of the minutes using a post-processing program. Then, the extracted values are registered to the database.

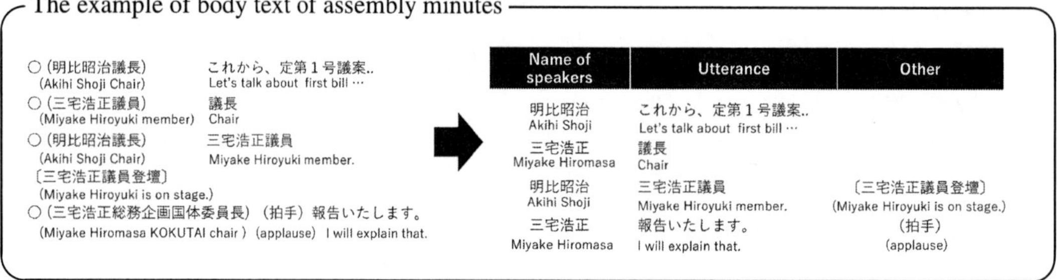

The body text of the assembly minutes does not intend to process by the program. The delimiters between speaker name and utterance differ among autonomies, with some of them having no delimiter. Some vary their delimiters arbitrarily. In such cases, we split the text manually.

3　Collecting minutes

In this section, we first clarify the characteristics of each prefecture by counting the words of the local assembly minutes. Then, we extract political keywords using the tf_idf weighting method for a preliminary study of comparative analysis.

3.1　Fundamental statistical data

Here, we show fundamental statistical data of the collected text data. Table 3 shows an overview of the minutes from the 47 prefectures. We explain two main categories in Table 3, i.e. "Prefectures" and "Speakers." The "Prefectures" column includes the web service name, the numbers of speakers, characters, words, and different words. The "Speakers" column includes the maximum number of words, minimum number of words, and the average number of words for words and characters. Hence, we explain the definition of "words" for counting. The Japanese language does not use spaces to divide sentences into words. Therefore, we must write a Japanese sentence with some space between words or grammatical units prior to counting words. If we count either the number of words or different words, the result changes according to the word division method. The results of a word division method differ depending on the employed morphological analysis tool and dictionary. In Table 3, we use MeCab(Kudo et al., 2004) in combination with the IPAdic dictionary [1].

First, we focus on the minimum and maximum number of "speakers." Speakers includes local assembly members, a governor, and someone acting on behalf of the governor. In Table 3, the minimum and maximum number of "speakers" is 61 (Akita) and 1,091 (Saitama), respectively. In contrast, according to the "Ministry of Internal Affairs and Communications" website published in March 2012[2], the minimum and maximum number of "local assembly members" is 35 (Fukui and Tottori) and 125 (Tokyo), respectively. Although speakers include a governor and someone acting on behalf of the governor, the number of "speakers" was larger than that of assembly members because speaker's names were spelled in several different ways. For example, for the "Toda" local assembly member, four different representations of the name were found.

Second, we focus on minimum and maximum number of characters. In Table 3, the minimum and maximum number of characters is 2,191,589 (Yamagata) and 19,389,614 (Nagano), respectively. In prefectures having too many characters, the collected text includes non-utterances such as "symbols," "table of contents," "description of circumstance," and "supporting data." In particular, the size of "supporting data" is the largest one among non-utterances, and it is difficult to determine whether a sentence is an utterance.

Finally, we summarize the problems associated with creating a Japanese political corpus from local assembly minutes. Using the fundamental statistical data, we could not completely extract both "Name of speakers" and "Utterances." We faced two problems: i) a speaker's name was spelled in several different ways and ii) it was difficult to determine whether a sentence is an utterance.

3.2 Extracting political keywords using tf-idf

In this section, we attempt to detect specific political keywords from each prefecture. This is a pilot political comparative analysis study.

First, utterances in the minutes are divided into words by morphological analysis. We use MeCab (ipadic-NEologd) for this analysis. The target part of speech is a noun. We exclude "noun-dependent," "noun-number," "noun-pronoun," "noun-suffix" and "noun-proper noun-person's name" forms.

Then specific political words are calculated by applying tf-idf weighting. The TF is a term's occurrence within the minutes of each prefecture divided by the number of words in the minutes. The TF of term t for document d, where d denotes minutes, is expressed as follows. The minutes contain a significant number of words; therefore, we use a logarithmic value for tf.

$$tf(t, d) = \log \frac{count(t), t \in d}{|d|}$$

A term's DF is the number of documents (i.e., prefecture minutes) containing that term divided by the total number of documents. The DF of t in N documents is expressed as follows. In this case, N becomes 47.

$$df(t, N) = |\{d_i : t \in d_i,\ i = 1..N\}|$$

The multiplied value of TF and IDF is the score of the word.

Table 4 shows the top three words obtained using tf-idf weighting. We find many political keywords spoken in the assembly. For example "HAC," the first-ranked word in Hokkaido Prefecture, is a regional airline company whose largest shareholder is the prefecture. "Daisetsu Ribaa-netto," the third word in Iwate Prefecture, is an NPO that is known to commit crimes using subsidized money. "Shimane Japanese beef cattle," the second word in Shimane prefecture, is a bland of Japanese beef cattle which is promoted by this prefecture.

---

[1] https://osdn.jp/projects/ipadic/
[2] http://www.soumu.go.jp/main_content/000151136.pdf

Table 3: Overview of collecting minutes of 47 prefectures in Japan.

| | Prefecture | Prefectures | | | | | Speakers | | | | | |
| | | Name of service | Number of speakers | Number of characters | Number of words | Number of different words | Number of words | | | Number of characters | | |
							Max	Min	Ave	Max	Min	Ave
1	Hokkaido	VOICES	202	6,690,769	4,324,553	21,410	445	2	62	270	1	38
2	Aomori	DB-Search	230	6,075,988	3,845,805	24,085	529	1	63	320	1	38
3	Iwate	Other	115	5,188,754	3,284,943	21,281	883	1	62	517	1	37
4	Miyagi	discuss	106	6,492,978	4,153,106	26,876	1,116	1	52	695	1	32
5	Akita	Other	61	3,501,499	2,268,171	20,336	545	1	61	466	1	37
6	Yamagata	discuss	102	2,191,589	1,364,855	16,071	874	1	66	501	1	39
7	Fukushima	discuss	270	3,605,556	2,248,658	18,658	1,495	1	59	884	1	35
8	Ibaraki	DB-Search	387	4,378,426	2,730,223	21,772	783	1	63	437	1	37
9	Tochigi	VOICES	150	2,563,445	1,637,756	16,311	922	1	76	554	1	46
10	Gumma	VOICES	172	5,713,837	3,520,362	24,398	1,840	1	90	1,129	1	54
11	Saitama	discuss	1,091	6,280,996	4,125,088	26,586	431	1	43	263	1	26
12	Chiba	DB-Search	172	3,392,658	2,166,942	20,951	2,578	1	52	1,527	1	31
13	Tokyo	DB-Search	408	5,746,805	3,703,744	25,896	405	1	50	234	1	30
14	Kanagawa	discuss	156	5,896,670	3,682,485	23,896	575	3	58	349	1	34
15	Niigata	discuss	900	15,885,612	9,839,042	33,855	692	1	59	424	1	35
16	Toyama	DB-Search	124	4,694,955	2,941,880	23,252	813	1	63	482	1	38
17	Ishikawa	VOICES	158	4,413,772	2,767,061	22,049	916	3	111	536	2	67
18	Fukui	DB-Search	149	4,568,260	2,954,643	24,135	590	1	52	345	1	32
19	Yamanashi	DB-Search	164	4,274,363	2,823,520	19,892	499	1	54	285	1	34
20	Nagano	VOICES	524	19,389,614	12,092,538	36,162	1,691	1	94	1,004	1	57
21	Gifu	discuss	517	6,422,363	4,032,530	26,243	653	1	60	374	1	36
22	Shizuoka	Other	239	5,376,236	3,353,750	25,556	689	1	59	530	1	35
23	Aichi	DB-Search	304	5,881,919	3,685,199	24,982	530	1	67	304	1	40
24	Mie	discuss	115	4,979,765	3,074,270	24,639	642	1	66	371	1	39
25	Shiga	VOICES	249	8,626,218	5,417,961	28,167	1,475	1	93	900	1	56
26	Kyoto	DB-Search	765	14,714,871	9,094,335	33,386	981	1	72	577	1	42
27	Osaka	discuss	536	17,318,822	10,794,849	32,611	572	1	60	347	1	35
28	Hyogo	Sophia	154	3,892,396	2,433,087	22,687	688	2	90	435	1	54
29	Nara	discuss	114	4,134,566	2,596,260	22,266	474	1	58	300	1	34
30	Wakayama	Other	102	3,427,751	2,166,894	24,731	1,212	3	54	655	2	32
31	Tottori	DB-Search	168	10,844,070	6,726,931	35,631	994	1	63	577	1	37
32	Shimane	DB-Search	122	6,010,462	3,785,152	25,948	599	1	56	353	1	34
33	Okayama	discuss	103	6,296,556	3,962,654	26,490	752	1	57	421	1	34
34	Hiroshima	DB-Search	170	3,357,629	2,125,208	18,831	580	1	62	339	1	37
35	Yamaguchi	discuss	99	4,932,992	3,133,703	23,063	559	1	60	333	1	36
36	Tokushima	discuss	86	3,812,198	2,498,206	21,113	550	1	53	319	1	33
37	Kagawa	DB-Search	388	8,752,886	5,592,540	29,344	527	1	67	326	1	41
38	Ehime	Sophia	203	4,198,966	2,593,711	22,947	798	2	90	455	1	54
39	Kochi	discuss	92	5,879,641	3,641,928	24,618	411	1	67	241	1	39
40	Fukuoka	DB-Search	177	4,948,309	3,137,731	22,890	391	1	58	246	1	35
41	Saga	DB-Search	124	5,740,329	3,680,483	22,066	487	1	59	328	1	36
42	Nagasaki	discuss	676	12,806,907	8,002,185	31,101	773	1	55	441	1	32
43	Kumamoto	discuss	116	4,700,096	2,965,285	25,752	760	1	57	461	1	34
44	Oita	discuss	183	4,595,154	2,899,446	22,475	574	1	48	327	1	29
45	Miyazaki	discuss	106	6,471,745	4,027,718	27,998	393	1	62	244	1	37
46	Kagoshima	DB-Search	151	7,266,842	4,646,583	26,674	581	1	64	349	1	39
47	Okinawa	Other	153	7,553,407	4,702,333	26,855	926	1	50	521	1	29
Total	—	—	11,853	303,889,642	191,246,307	—	—	—	—	—	—	—

There are many compound words in Japanese political words. For example "zaisei-kaikaku (fiscal reform)" comprises two nouns, i.e., "zaisei (fiscal)" and "kaikaku(reform)." Therefore, we combine continuous nouns and attempt to handle them as a single compound word. Table 5 shows the top three compound words obtained by tf-idf weighting. We find many titles of the officer, i.e. "Mr." and "Prefectural Assembly". The title of an officer is typically derived from political agendas. For example, the third words in Aomori Prefecture are "Director-General of the Tourism and International Strategy Bureau." The first words in Gunma Prefecture are "Director-General of the Transportation Infrastructure Department." The first words in Shizuoka Prefecture are "Director-General of the Transportation Infrastructure Department." From these examples, we can identify the primary political subjects in each prefecture at that time.

However, this methods has some drawbacks such as incorrect compounding. We can perform preliminary comparative analysis of political keywords using a simple tf-idf-weighting method. Further study will be required, *e.g.* statistical analysis such as corresponding analysis and machine learning methods.

4 Related work

Recently, some studies have explored document analysis, sentiment analysis, and political debates with respect to politics (Yano et al., 2009; Chambers et al., 2015; Cano-Basave et al., 2016). These studies

Table 4: Extracted political keywords without Compounding

Number	Prefecture	1	2	3
1	Hokkaido	HAC	Shigatani	Ainu culture
2	Aomori	Mutsu bay	NOVA	Towada city
3	Iwate	Uchimaru, Morioka city	Odashima	Daisetsu Ribaa-netto
4	Miyagi	Teizan canal	Sendai beef	privatization of Sendai airport
5	Akita	Kita-akita city	Ani Bear Farm	Area Nakaichi
6	Yamagata	Mogami-oguni River	Papua state	Tendo city
7	Fukushima	total inspection	South Aizu	return of the residents
8	Ibaraki	National Athletic Meet at Ibaraki	Tsuchiura city	Ushiku swamp
9	Tochigi	Tochimaru-kun	Haga district	Haga Red Cross Hospital
10	Gunma	Gunma's	Gunma Prefectural Assembly	Tomo wide-area arterial road
11	Saitama	Sasshin-no-kai	Saitama red cross hospital	members of Saitama Prefectural Assembly
12	Chiba	Lake Inba	Hokuso railway	Kujukuri
13	Tokyo	metropolitan government-owned land	an honorary citizen of Tokyo	Takaaki
14	Kanagawa	Sagami Longitudinal Expressway	KAST	Teruhiko
15	Niigata	Shibata	Shibata city	Niigata-Higashi Port
16	Toyama	members of Toyama Prefectural Assembly	kitokito	Imizu city
17	Ishikawa	Noto Satoyama Kaido	Noto Railway	Gyokusen'in
18	Fukui	Kuzuryu River	Asuwagawa Dam	Fukui Port
19	Yamanashi	Minami-Alps city	Kofu castle	Fujiyoshida city
20	Nagano	Asakawa Dam	Matsumoto Airport	NAGANO
21	Gifu	Mirai hall	Uchigatani	FC Gifu
22	Shizuoka	Granship	Yaizu fishing port	Numazu station
23	Aichi	Aichi Triennale	Linimo	Nishimikawa
24	Mie	Shinsei-Mie	AMIC	Odai town
25	Shiga	Omi Ohashi bridge	Mother Lake	Omihachiman city
26	Kyoto	Kyoto Stadium	Muko city	Nishijin Textile
27	Osaka	OTK	Neyagawa	Semboku Rapid Railway
28	Hyogo	Hometown, Hyogo	Muko River	Kobe Electric Railway
29	Nara	Nara City Hospital	Yamatotakada city	number 15, Mori-
30	Wakayama	Nisaka Yoshinobu	Obana Masahiro	Susami
31	Tottori	Lake Koyama-ike	Kurahoshi city	Wakasa town
32	Shimane	Sanko line	Shimane Japanese beef cattle	Kijima Dam
33	Okayama	Lake Kojima	Okayama marathon	Kurashiki station
34	Hiroshima	Yuzaki Hidehiko	Kaita town	members of Hiroshima Prefectural Assembly
35	Yamaguchi	Suo-oshima Island	Mitajiri-Nakanoseki Port	Shunan area
36	Tokushima	Mima city	Awa city	Miyoshi city
37	Kagawa	rare sugar	Kagawa Canal	All
38	Ehime	Mican	whole	Mikame town
39	Kochi	Kochi Junior College	Eikoku-ji Temple	Sukumo city
40	Fukuoka	Mount Hiko	Yabe River system	Okinohata River
41	Saga	Jobaru River	Ogi city	Saga Sakura Marathon
42	Nagasaki	Saikai city	Tsukumo	NERC
43	Kumamoto	Japanese brown cattle	Kumamoto urban area	Rogi Dam
44	Oita	Usa city	Hot Spring Prefecture Oita	Trinita
45	Miyazaki	Hososhima Port	Miyazaki Hospital	Toi cape
46	Kagoshima	Matsuza-	Dolphine Port	Marine Port Kagoshima
47	Okinawa	Shimojishima Airport	Nakagusuku Bay	Okinawan

used various documents as political corpora. In this section, we describe corpora that include political information.

Political document analysis has employed various document collections on the web, such as blogs (Yano et al., 2009). Probabilistic models have been proposed to generate blog posts and comments jointly within a blog site. Hassanali et al. (2010) proposed a technique to automatically tag political blog posts using support vector machines and named entity recognition. They used blog documents as a corpus. Chambers et al. (2015) modeled sentiment analysis for social sciences. They used Twitter data (over two billion tweets) as a corpus.Lerman et al. (2008) automatically predicted the impact of news on public perception of political candidates. They used daily newspaper articles as a corpus. Cano-Basave et al. (2016) used semantic frames to model argumentation in speaker discourse. Their presidential political debates corpus comprises 20 debates that took place between May 2011 and February 2012. Iyyer et al. (2014) applied a recursive neural network framework to detect political positions. They performed experiments using a dataset of Congressional debates and an original political dataset as a corpus. As mentioned above, political corpora typically comprise blogs, Twitter data, newspaper articles, and original political datasets. Therefore, a political corpus constructed from local assembly minutes is a novel and valuable source of political information.

5   Conclusion

In this paper, we described a Japanese political corpus constructed from the local assembly minutes of 47 prefectures collected over four years (April 2011 to March 2015), which represents a full term of office for assembly members in most autonomies. We collected local assembly minutes from all 47 prefectural assemblies, obtained fundamental statistical data from the collected text data, and extracted political keywords using a tf-idf weighting method.

As a result, we confirmed the following. First, we could collect 47 local assembly minutes for four years. Second, we could not completely divide the body text into "Name of speakers" and "Utterance" because the delimiter differs depending on the various autonomies. Finally, we demonstrated that the system can automatically extract political keyword using a tf-idf weighting method. We believe that this new corpus will be useful for comparative studies of local politics.

Acknowledgements

This work was supported by JSPS KAKENHI Grant Number JP16H02912.

References

Cano-Basave, Amparo Elizabeth and He, Yulan. *A Study of the Impact of Persuasive Argumentation in Political Debates*, Proceedings of NAACL-HLT, pp.1405–1413, 2016.

Chambers, N., Bowen, V., Genco, E., Tian, X., Young, E., Harihara, G., and Yang, E. *Identifying political sentiment between nation states with social media*, Proceedings of EMNLP, pp. 65–75, 2015.

Hassanali, Khairun-nisa, and Vasileios Hatzivassiloglou, *Automatic detection of tags for political blogs.*, Proceedings of the NAACL HLT 2010 Workshop on Computational Linguistics in a World of Social Media. Association for Computational Linguistics. pp. 21–22, 2010.

Iyyer, Mohit and Enns, Peter and Boyd-Graber, Jordan and Resnik, Philip. *Political ideology detection using recursive neural networks*, Proceedings of the Association for Computational Linguistics, 2014.

Kudo,Taku and Yamamoto, Kaoru and Matsumoto, Yuji, *Applying Conditional Random Fields to Japanese Morphological Analysis*, Proceedings of the 2004 Conference on Empirical Methods in Natural Language Processing (EMNLP-2004), pp.230-237, 2004.

Lerman, Kevin and Gilder, Ari and Dredze, Mark and Pereira, Fernando. Association for Computational Linguistics. *Reading the markets: Forecasting public opinion of political candidates by news analysis*, Proceedings of the 22nd International Conference on Computational Linguistics Vol. 1, pp.473–480, 2008.

Masuda, Tadashi , *Text Mining Analysis on the Minutes of Local Assemblies - A Case Study on the Takasaki City Assembly - (in Japanese)* . Takasaki City University Economics, Vol. 15, No.1, pp. 17–31, 2012.

Salton, Gerard and Buckley, Christopher, *Term-weighting approaches in automatic text retrieval*, Information processing & management Vol. 24, No 5, pp. 513–523, 1988.

Yano, Tae and Cohen, William W and Smith, Noah A. *Predicting response to political blog posts with topic models*, Proceedings of Human Language Technologies: The 2009 Annual Conference of the North American Chapter of the Association for Computational Linguistics, pp.477–485, 2009.

Table 5: Extracted political keywords with Compounding

Number	Prefecture	1	2	3
1	Hokkaido	HAC	prefectural residents' life	Tomari power plant
2	Aomori	District Administration Office	Director-General of the Department of Planning and Polices	Director-General of the Tourism and International Strategy Bureau
3	Iwate	rules of Iwate Prefectural Assembly	big earthquake and tsunami	adding
4	Miyagi	ecological life, agriculture, forestry and fisheries	the -th Miyagi Prefectural Assembly	rules of Miyagi Prefectural Assembly
5	Akita	Chairperson of the Education and Public Safety Committee	Kitaakita city	hometown Akita cheering up plan
6	Yamagata	within the committee's jurisdiction	general branch office	Yamagata prefecture general accounting supplementary budget for - fiscal year
7	Fukushima	to hand out another paper	the Superintendent of Education	a report submitted by Chairperson
8	Ibaraki	rules of Ibaraki Prefectural Assembly	Mr. Onodera, the Superintendent of Education, takes the rostrum.	Ibaraki Liberal Democratic Party Branch
9	Tochigi	Chairperson of Tochigi Prefectural Assembly	rules of Tochigi Prefectural Assembly	Tochigi Genki Plan
10	Gunma	Director-General of the Life Culture and Sports Department	Director-General of the Citizens and Cultural Affairs Department	maximum time limit for the speech
11	Saitama	proposed bills	Director-General of the Department of Crisis Management and Disaster Prevention	Manager of the Sewerage Works
12	Chiba	Hokuso Railway	Eastern Chiba Medical Center	Kita-Chiba Road
13	Tokyo	following idea	examination of a petition	to meet an objective
14	Kanagawa	emergency financial measures	Director-General of the Public Health and Welfare Bureau	Chairperson of Kanagawa Prefectural Assembly
15	Niigata	the -th proposed bill	you all	Uonuma Kikan Hospital
16	Toyama	Chairperson of Toyama Prefectural Assembly	members of Toyama Prefectural Assembly	submit something with
17	Ishikawa	Noto Satoyama Kaido	Noto Railway	Director-General of the Citizens and Cultural Affairs Bureau
18	Fukui	Energy Research & Development Centralization Plan	examination report of a petition	Yosokichi
19	Yamanashi	Chairperson of Yamanashi Prefectural Assembly	rules of Yamanashi Prefectural Assembly	- minutes speech
20	Nagano	to declare the agenda	general administrative work	to declare the schedule
21	Gifu	country Gifu	supplementing of the budget	Director-General of the Urban Architecture Department
22	Shizuoka	Director-General of the Transportation Infrastructure Department	Director-General of the Economy, Trade and Industry Department	Shizuoka Prefectural Audit Commissioners
23	Aichi	Aichi and Nagoya	priority reform program	Aichi prefecture general accounting supplementary budget for - fiscal year
24	Mie	vision of citizens power	Shinsei-Mie	Higashikisyu
25	Shiga	Director-General of the Department of Public Works and Transportation	Director-General of the Department of Lake Biwa and the Environment	Chairperson of Shiga Prefectural Assembly
26	Kyoto	festivals and events	kissing loach	management of the commission in general
27	Osaka	Osaka Prefectural Government Sakishima Building	made in Osaka	OTK
28	Hyogo	Governor Ido takes the rostrum.	Kenmin Rengo Prefectural Assembly members	Hyogo Development
29	Nara	Prefectural Nara Hospital	bills for the year	Mount Wakakusa
30	Wakayama	Mr. Yoshinobu Nisaka	Mr. Yoshinobu Nisaka, Governor	Mr. Obana Masahiro
31	Tottori	Kurayoshi city	Manga Expo	Lake Koyama-ike
32	Shimane	Minshu-Kenmin Club	Mr. Mishima, a member of a Prefectural Assembly	the agenda
33	Okayama	Director-General of the Department of Environment and Culture	Mr. Kenro	Mr. Hideki
34	Hiroshima	Mr. Hidehiko Yuzaki, Governor	bills brought up together for discussion	explainer in charge
35	Yamaguchi	involved counselor	Maguchi Industrial Strategy Promotion Plan	Industry Strategy Headquarters
36	Tokushima	full name	be unique to Tokushima	A member attends the Prefectural Assembly.
37	Kagawa	rare sugar	Mr. Keizo Hamada, Governor	Kagawa Prefectural Assembly Minutes
38	Ehime	passage and verdict	Ehime National Sports Festival	Everyone raise their hands (in agreement).
39	Kochi	opinion and bill	Director-General of the Community Welfare and Services Department	Kochi Junior College
40	Fukuoka	within the -th bill's jurisdiction	bills brought up together for discussion	Chikuho area
41	Saga	Chairperson of Saga Prefectural Assembly	Director-General of the Transport Policy Department	Director of the Health and Welfare Headquarters
42	Nagasaki	Chairperson of the committee	Mr. Magome, a committee member	Mr. Yamaguchi, Chairperson
43	Kumamoto	Chairperson of Kumamoto Prefectural Assembly	rules of Kumamoto Prefectural Assembly	Tateno Dam
44	Oita	Mr. Nonaka, the Superintendent of Education	waiting seat	beside a facing podium
45	Miyazaki	bills proposed by a member of a Prefectural Assembly	Hososhima Port	Director-General of the Citizens Policy Department
46	Kagoshima	Kagoshima	Matsuza-	order of votes
47	Okinawa	We would like to take a break.	Shimojishima Airport	Council for Promotion of Dezoning and Reutilization of Military Land in Okinawa

Selective Annotation of Sentence Parts: Identification of Relevant Sub-sentential Units

Ge Xu[1,2] , Xiaoyan Yang[1,2] and Chu-Ren Huang[3]
[1]Department of Computer Science, Minjiang University, China
[2]Fujian Provincial Key Laboratory of Information Processing and Intelligent Control,
Minjiang University, China
[3]Department of Chinese and Bilingual Studies,
The Hong Kong Polytechnic University, Hong Kong
`xuge@pku.edu.cn`, `349622662@qq.com`, `churenhuang@gmail.com`

Abstract

Many NLP tasks involve sentence-level annotation yet the relevant information is not encoded at
sentence level but at some relevant parts of the sentence. Such tasks include but are not limited to:
sentiment expression annotation, product feature annotation, and template annotation for Q&A
systems. However, annotation of the full corpus sentence by sentence is resource intensive.
In this paper, we propose an approach that iteratively extracts frequent parts of sentences for
annotating, and compresses the set of sentences after each round of annotation. Our approach
can also be used in preparing training sentences for binary classification (domain-related vs.
noise, subjectivity vs. objectivity, etc.), assuming that sentence-type annotation can be predicted
by annotation of the most relevant sub-sentences. Two experiments are performed to test our
proposal and evaluated in terms of time saved and agreement of annotation.

1 Introduction

High quality resources are essential to the performance of NLP systems and in recent information content related NLP tasks, such resources are typically constructed through annotation at sentence level. For instance, to implement opinion mining systems, sentiment/polarity/emotion expressions or lexicons are often built from a corpus of movie or product reviews; and question templates are extracted from sentence corpora for Q&A systems. The construction of these two types of resources are quite similar to construction of resources for other information content related NLP tasks, such as information quality tasks (detection of best/most help answers, hyperbole/embellishment, or lying), and speaker attitude/intention tasks (detection of metaphor/metonymy/irony/sarcasm), etc. They typically involve extraction of a set of specific expressions (words, word sequences, long-distance collocation etc.) from sentence corpora. They share the following characteristics:

- Manually annotating the corpus sentence by sentence is time-consuming, and often impractical;

- There is no prior knowledge of the number and location of expected expressions, hence the full corpus needs to be annotated;

- Information content properties must be determined at sentence (or higher) level, yet expressions marking such properties are often subsidiary units of a sentence;

- Many sentences have repeated or similar subsidiary units;

Based on the above observations, we propose in this paper a selective semi-automatic annotation schema, which aims to reduce resource requirements and improve annotation quality by utilizing human experience. Our selective annotation approach relies on a sequence mining algorithm to generate frequent patterns in sentences, and annotate patterns (as sub-sentences) instead of full sentences. Our proposed approach can find most important expressions statistically, and will annotate a pattern only once to avoid repeated annotation. Beside extracting specific expressions from the set of sentences, we can also use

Proceedings of the 12th Workshop on Asian Language Resources,
pages 86–94, Osaka, Japan, December 12 2016.

Input	lines=('caabc', 'abcb', 'cabc', 'abbca'), minSup=3
Output	('a'), 4;('a', 'b'), 4;('a', 'b', 'c'), 4;('a', 'c'), 4;('b',), 4;('b', 'c'), 4;('c',), 4;('c', 'a'), 3;('c', 'b'), 3

Table 1: Sequence mining

our approach to help construct a training corpus for a binary classifier, an related experiment in section 3 is described.

In the following sections, we will describe our approach, and two experiments are provided to show that our approach is effective in specific tasks.

2 Our Approach

2.1 Frequent Sequence Mining

Sequential pattern mining is a topic of data mining concerned with finding statistically relevant patterns between data examples where the values are delivered in a sequence (Pei et al., 2001; Yan, 2003). "Frequent" means that a sequence occurs in no less than minimum support (predefined minimum frequency) times. An example in table 1 shows the input and output of such algorithms.

In table 1, $('a','c')$, 4 means the sequence $('a','c')$ occurs 4 times in lines, and 4 is larger than minSup (minimum support), which is set to 3 in table 1. Furthermore, skip is allowed between elements of the sequence.

2.2 Algorithm

Algorithm 1 Our approach

Input:
UC(Unlabeled corpus)
MinSup(minimum support)
Initialize: YesSet,NoSet,DoubtSet,MinSupRatio
Output: YesSet,NoSet,DoubtSet
1.Breaking UC into sentences, SENS
while $True$ **do**
    2.Runing a sequence mining algorithm with MinSupRatio on SENS, the result is PATLIST.
    3.If PATLIST is empty, decrease MinSupRatio.
    4.If MinSupRatio is lower than given threshold, **break**; else goto step 2.
    5.Pruning PATLIST using YesSet, NoSet, DoubtSet.
    6.Annotating each pattern in PATLIST by the tag of Yes,No, or Doubt.
    7.Compressing SENS using YesSet, NoSet.
end while
8.return YesSet,NoSet,DoubtSet

Here are some explanations for the approach:

1. MinSup: minimum support, used for terminated sequence mining algorithm. If no patterns occurs MinSup times or more, we think manual annotation should be applied on sentences directly.

2. UC: Unlabeled corpus. For English, the corpus is naturally segmented by space; for other languages such as Chinese, word segmentation should be applied before the corpus is input.

3. MinSupRatio: It will decrease gradually to help sequence mining algorithms to find more less frequent patterns, until the $MinSupRatio * size(SENS)$ is lower than MinSup.

4. YesSet,NoSet,DoubtSet are empty initially.

2.3 Annotating Patterns

Ideally, we wish to meet only two types of patterns, namely YES patterns and NO patterns. A YES pattern is normally the thing we want to extract from a corpus. In different tasks, YES means a sentiment expression, a question template or a dish name etc. NO patterns are what we do not need.

However, the possible types of a pattern are more complicated, which are listed as follows:

1. YES means the pattern is a YES pattern.

2. YES+ means the pattern contains a YES pattern.

3. YES- means the pattern possibly is a part of a YES pattern.

4. NO means the pattern is not a YES pattern. None of its elements have relation with a YES pattern.

5. NO+ means the pattern is not a YES pattern, but some of its elements may have relation with a YES pattern.

To simplify annotation, we merge five types of patterns into three annotation options:

1. Yes(YES, YES+). Meaning that the pattern **contains** is a YES pattern or contains a YES pattern.[1].

2. No(NO). Meaning that the pattern **has nothing to do** with a YES pattern. Any word in the pattern will not be a part of a YES pattern.

3. Doubt(YES-,NO+). Meaning that the current pattern (or its part) maybe a part of a YES pattern, and want to see **longer** patterns containing the current pattern (or its part) in next rounds, then make a decision.

If a pattern is annotated, it will not be annotated again. For a No pattern, all its subsequence (skip allowed) are also No patterns; for a Yes pattern, all sequences containing it are also Yes patterns. All patterns that is annotated as "Doubt" will not be seen again by the annotator, but a longer pattern containing the "Doubt" pattern may be presented to the annotator in the later annotating.

2.4 Compressing the Set of Sentences

After finishing a round of annotation, we need to use the result of annotation to compress the set of sentences, making the set of sentences used for next round smaller. Three points should be noted.

2.4.1 Difference between YesSet and NoSet

When compressing sentences, the patterns in YesSet should be seen as a whole, which is not required for patterns in NoSet.

For example, the current YesSet is {cf} and NoSet is {ba,deh}. For the sentence "abcde"[2], after compressing by YesSet, we still have "abcdeh" since "cf" as a whole does not occur in "abcde". However, after compressing by NoSet the result is "c". The "ab" is removed by using "ba" at first, and then "de" is removed by using "deh".

Such processing is derived from how we define Yes and No for a pattern. A **Yes** pattern can not guarantee that its part is also a **Yes** pattern, but a No pattern can guarantee that its elements have no relation with YES patterns.

---

[1]Sometimes, some annotators would see YES+ patterns as more confident YES patterns. The annotation criteria is not discussed here, and we just annotate both cases Yes.

[2]One letter denotes one word.

2.4.2 Determine Valid Sentences

In compressing sentences, we must have a **predicate** to determine if a sentence is still valid for the next round of sequence mining. If a sentence is not valid after compressing, it will be discarded, thus reducing the set of sentences.

By default, if the sentence is empty after compressing, the sentence is invalid. However, in specific domains, we must define specific predicates for a valid sentence. For example, we required that length of a valid pattern should be in a specified range, or some words must occur in a valid pattern. It is also not difficult to figure out that if we are extracting relationship templates, such as a comparison between two products or part-whole relationship between two entities, a valid sentence should contain at least two members.

We leave the task-related **predicates** to be defined by users with a function prototype: *bool IsValid-Sentence(sentence)*, which can be called in compressing sentences.

2.5 The order of Annotation

After using a sequence mining algorithm to generate patterns, we have three choices on the order of annotation according to different requirements.

1. Annotating patterns in the descending order of their frequencies. This strategy guarantee will meet YES patterns before YES+ patterns, so the elements in the set of Yes patterns are of higher quality.

2. Annotating patterns in the descending order of the length of patterns. This strategy is suitable for mining long patterns. It is highly possible that we meet YES+ patterns before YES patterns, so many unrelated words are stored in YES+ patterns. However, in compressing sentences by a YES+ pattern, we require that the whole YES+ pattern occur, so these unrelated words still have a chance to be annotated as No patterns, and then remove the unrelated words in YES+ in later stage.

3. Annotating patterns in the descending order of $frequency * length$ of patterns. This strategy will compress the sentences most rapidly. As with the second strategy, it is possible that we meet YES+ patterns before.

2.6 Similarity measurement

When annotating a pattern (we call it the main pattern), to further facilitate annotating, we train a Word2Vec[3] to help finding similar patterns. Normally, most of similar patterns have the same annotating tag with the main pattern, so **one click or keystroke can annotate many patterns**. We use the default sentence similarity from the trained Word2Vec model. If the similarity between a pattern and the main pattern is larger than a given threshold, the pattern is displayed below the main pattern. In our experiments, we find that listing similar patterns when annotating the main pattern can greatly improve efficiency.

2.7 Instructions for Use

Our approach is suitable for two typical tasks:

- Extracting specific expressions from corpora. If a corpus is rich in such expression [4], our approach can help to extract such expressions efficiently. For example, given proper corpora, our approach can extract sentiment expressions, polarity shifters, dish names, or question templates etc.

- Building sentence-level training corpus for binary classification. The basic assumption is that a Yes pattern can infer that the sentence containing the pattern is also Yes. Therefore, we can annotate patterns instead of sentences, but still tag the sentences correctly.

We should pay attention when applying our approach in building the training corpus for binary classification:

---

[3]https://pypi.python.org/pypi/gensim
[4]We will not discuss how to build a corpus that is rich in a specific expression, it is highly task-related.

- In design our approach, we find that if more than two classes are considered, the annotation would become much more complicated for annotators. For classification tasks with more than two classes, we recommend to use a one-versus-rest schema or other annotation tools.

- If a Yes pattern can not infer that the sentence containing it is Yes, our approach will fail. For example, "happy" is a positive expression, but we can not infer the sentence containing "happy" is a positive sentence, because polarity shifters such as "not X", "if X"[5] may occur in the sentence, then revert or cancel the polarity.

3 Experiments

In our paper, we give two experiments for two types of tasks respectively. They are **Extracting Chinese Sentiment Expressions** and **Annotating Sentences for Binary Classification**. Because Chinese is our native language, both experiments use Chinese corpora to reduce annotation uncertainty.

3.1 Extracting Chinese Sentiment Expressions

When building a sentiment-related system, we have some general Chinese sentiment lexicons to choose, such as 1)NTU Sentiment Dictionary[6]; 2)Chinese affective lexicon ontology[7]. Furthermore, there are some work on automatically constructing task-oriented sentiment resources, such as (Choi and Cardie, 2009; Lu et al., 2011; Jijkoun et al., 2010; Cruz et al., 2011), which still needs human annotation to improve quality, and limits the coverage of the constructed resources due to the restriction of automation.

However, when constructing sentiment resources in a specified domain, the best choice should be to construct directly from the corpora, which can guarantees coverage and exploits human sentiment knowledge.

We report here how we extract Chinese sentiment expressions from a corpus. Normally, it is supposed that sentiment expressions are mainly adjectives, some of verbs (like, hate etc.) and nouns (fool, idiot etc.). However, for creating a practical system, we also must consider multi-words expressions. In Chinese, multi-words expressions may also be the words that are wrongly segmented. In this experiment, we show how to construct a list of sentiment expressions for a specific domain.

3.1.1 Experimental Setting

We set MinSupRatio=0.05 and MinSup=3. At first, we extract frequent patterns using MinSupRatio, then gradually decrease the MinSupRatio to find less frequent patterns in next rounds. When the support equals MinSup and no patterns are mined, we stop our algorithm.

3.1.2 Corpus

The domain corpus is a 88MB file about product reviews, and contain 1280000+ lines of reviews. We use the Jieba package[8] to perform word segmentation and POS tagging on the corpus.

Since we know that degree adverbs have a strong relationship with polarity expressions, and in Chinese sentiment expressions often occur after the degree adverbs, we used degree adverbs[9] to extract the word sequences after them, and we require that the length of a sequence is less than 4 or a sequence meets a punctuation. Each word sequence is stored in one line.

By using this method, we extract 76000+ word sequences from 1280000+ lines of reviews, the 76000+ word sequences is what we input into our approach, from which we want to find (frequent) sentiment expressions.

3.1.3 Experimental Results

The main statistics of annotating process is shown in table 2.

---

[5]The X in a polarity shifter denotes a sentiment expression.
[6]http://nlg18.csie.ntu.edu.tw
[7]http://ir.dlut.edu.cn/EmotionOntologyDownload.aspx
[8]github.com/fxsjy/jieba
[9]We have 17 ,10, 14 Chinese degree adverbs for adjectives, verbs, nouns respectively.

Round	MinSupRatio	SEN	PAT	ANN	time
1	0.1	76235	1	1	6
2	0.05	76232	4	5	15
3	0.025	76190	4	4	8
4	1.3×10^{-2}	76102	8	7	15
5	1.3×10^{-2}	75938	1	2	9
6	6.3×10^{-3}	75869	32	24	83
7	6.3×10^{-3}	74480	1	2	23
8	3.1×10^{-3}	74374	67	36	181
9	3.1×10^{-3}	70906	6	7	54
10	1.6×10^{-3}	70513	111	49	397
11	1.6×10^{-3}	65565	13	12	136
12	1.6×10^{-3}	65137	3	4	14
13	7.8×10^{-4}	65021	213	73	542
14	7.8×10^{-4}	58365	34	24	111
15	3.9×10^{-4}	57606	482	108	1128
16	3.9×10^{-4}	49742	123	49	361
17	3.9×10^{-4}	46957	53	29	247
18	2.0×10^{-4}	46377	847	138	2003
19	2.0×10^{-4}	38434	397	79	621
20	2.0×10^{-4}	35192	280	59	474
21	9.8×10^{-5}	32569	1526	176	3699
22	9.8×10^{-5}	25861	1182	149	2359
23		14395			

Table 2: Process of Annotating. SEN means the number of sentences; PAT means the number of patterns; ANN means the number of main patterns that are manually annotated in this round; time means how many seconds this round takes.

From table 2, we can see that the MinSupRatio is gradually decreasing for mining less frequent patterns. In 23rd round, there are 14395 sentences after iterative compressing, which mainly contain low frequent words (lower than 3) and words from "Doubt" patterns. Since the annotation already covers the frequent patterns, annotating manually the 14395 sentences becomes less urgent, and will be chosen according to practical requirement.

We totally annotated 1037 main patterns. Since at most 10 similar patterns are listed when a main pattern is displayed, we need to annotated at most 10370 patterns theoretically. However, by our experience, we only need to manually annotate 2~4 similar patterns of the 10 similar ones, since many similar patterns have the same annotation tag (Yes, No or Doubt) with the main pattern. Therefore, the number of patterns annotated manually is about 3000, which is acceptable to build a domain lexicon.

The total annotation time is 14632 seconds, which include chatting time with colleagues and some time for personal affairs. Roughly, the time used for annotating is about 12000 seconds. If a person annotates about 61000+ (76000-14395) word sequences manually, and we assume that a word sequence take 2 seconds , the total time is about 120000+ seconds, 10 times longer than our approach. So, in this experiment, our approach can **save 90% time** for extracting frequent sentiment expressions.

3.2 Annotating Sentences for Binary Classification

Let's describe the application scenario briefly.

People may want to build a Q&A robot for an online game, which take a user's question as input and return the most possible answer to the user. After analyzing the records of dialogues, we find that many questions (sentences) have no relationship with the game, such as greetings and dirty words etc., which make the Q&A robot less efficient. So we prefer to annotate a training corpus and then train a binary classifier to filter such unrelated questions.

Three annotator (X,S,W) are required to annotate sentences both **manually** and **by our approach**. We mainly check the agreement between different annotators, as well as between fully manual annotation and our approach.

Annotator	X	S	W
Manual (min.)	25	28	35
Our Approach (min.)	13	15	18
Sentences covered	879	854	867
Time saved (%)	$\approx$40%	$\approx$40%	$\approx$40%

Table 3: statistics of annotating 1000 sentences

	S	S^*	X	X^*	W	W^*
S	1.0	0.99	0.956	0.965	0.971	0.972
S^*	0.99	1.0	0.956	0.965	0.967	0.968
X	0.956	0.956	1.0	0.989	0.951	0.97
X^*	0.965	0.965	0.989	1.0	0.96	0.981
W	0.971	0.967	0.951	0.96	1.0	0.969
W^*	0.972	0.968	0.97	0.981	0.969	1.0

Table 4: Agreement of annotation. X,S,W denotes annotators X,S,W annotating sentences manually; X^*,S^*,W^* denote annotators X,S,W annotating sentences by our approach

3.2.1 Data

The data are users' questions collected from the game dialogues. To control the time used for manually annotating, we randomly selected 1000 sentences from the database of the user's questions.

3.2.2 Annotators

Annotator X is the first author, with NLP background, who designed the experiment and is familiar with domain of the corpus.**Annotator S** is a programmer who is quite familiar with the corpus, and read a lot of related corpus before this annotating. **Annotator W** is a person with medical science background and never plays online games or uses Q&A systems for games, who is introduced about the corpus and given some instructions on how to annotate by the first author for several minutes.

3.2.3 Experimental Results

Some statistics of the annotating process are shown in table 3.

Using our approach, we can cover 850~880 sentences by annotating frequent patterns, and the rest 120~150 sentences mainly contain words of low-frequency and still need manual annotation.

Averagely, 40% time are saved for those sentences annotated by our approach. If there are more sentences, the time saved by our approach is supposed to increase.

During the annotating, the significant difference between W and other two annotators is that W took a long time to annotate short patterns which are often single Chinese characters due to wrong word segmentation. Annotator W tended to annotate more "Doubt" patterns because she lacked domain knowledge, which causes more long patterns in the later rounds annotated. From such observation, it can be seen that our approach has a higher requirement for domain knowledge, which is the cost for high speed.

3.2.4 Agreement Analysis

At first, for each annotator, the agreement between manual annotation and our approach is 0.99,0.989 and 0.969 for S, X, W respectively in table 4. As introduced in section 3.2.2, annotators S and X both have domain knowledge for the annotating, so when patterns are short, they can use the domain knowledge to help annotating, and make their annotation using our approach more consistent with the fully manual annotation. For annotator W, due to lack of domain knowledge, many short patterns are annotated as No.

(a) Manually Annotation

	S	X	W
S	1.0	0.956	0.971
X	0.956	1.0	0.951
W	0.971	0.951	1.0

(b) Our Approach

	S^*	X^*	W^*
S^*	1.0	0.965	0.968
X^*	0.965	1.0	0.981
W^*	0.968	0.981	1.0

Table 5: Agreement of annotation

In fact, such No patterns help to infer a sentence as Yes when the sentence is shown to annotator W as a whole.

Agreement between different annotators using manual annotation are shown in table 4(a), and agreement between different annotators using our approach are shown in table 4(b). We are happy to see that the average agreement using our approach is a bit higher than agreement using manual annotation, which may suggest that our approach can provide more consistent annotation among different annotators. Furthermore, the agreement between manual annotation and our approach is averagely higher than the agreement between different annotators, which also suggests that our approach will not harm the annotation quality while accelerating the annotation.

4   Conclusion and Future work

In this paper, to extract a set of specific expressions from corpora, we propose an approach that iteratively uses sequence mining algorithms to extract frequent parts of sentences for annotating. The approach can also be used in constructing training corpus for a binary classification under specific condition.

The approach has the following merits:

1. Our approach can greatly save human labor when extracting specific expressions from corpora. In an experiment on extracting sentiment expressions (see section 3.1), our approach can save 90% time.

2. In constructing training corpus for a binary classification, our approach can also save human labor. Furthermore, our approach annotate a pattern only once and can reduce the inconsistent annotation, especially when the annotator is tired after long time annotating. Agreement statistics support our analysis.

We have used our approach to extracting sentiment expressions from a domain reviews, Chinese polarity shifters from the corpus of product reviews, dish names from the corpus of food reviews; we also have used our approach to construct training corpus for a classifier to detect if a text has relationship with Internet games, and removed noise texts for a recognition system of flowers.

In the future, we would use our approach in extracting patterns of some binary relationship such as part-whole, hyponymy etc., and also relationship across sentences may be considered.

Acknowledgements

This research is supported by National Natural Science Foundation of China (No.61300156, No.61300152) and Fujian Provincial Department of Education (JAT160387).

5

References

Y. Choi and C. Cardie. 2009. **Adapting a polarity lexicon using integer linear programming for domain-specific sentiment classification. In** *In Proceedings of the Conference on Empirical Methods in Natural Language Processing (EMNLP).*

Fermín L. Cruz, José A. Troyano, F. Javier Ortega, and Fernando Enríquez. 2011. **Automatic expansion of feature-level opinion lexicons. In** *In Proceedings of the 2nd Workshop on Computational Approaches to Subjectivity and Sentiment Analysis (WASSA 2.011) (June 2011),.*

Valentin Jijkoun, Maarten de Rijke, and Wouter Weerkamp. 2010. **Generating focused topic-specific sentiment lexicons. In** *In Proceedings of the 48th Annual Meeting of the Association for Computational Linguistics.*

Yue Lu, Malu Castellanos, and Umeshwar Dayal Chengxiang Zhai. 2011. Automatic construction of a context-aware sentiment lexicon : An optimization approach. In *www2011*.

J. Pei, J. Han, Mortazavi-Asl B, H. Pinto, Q. Chen, U. Dayal, and Hsu M-C. 2001. Prefixspan: mining sequential patterns efficiently by prefix-projected pattern growth. In *In: Proceeding of the 2001 international conference on data engineering (ICDE?01), Heidelberg, Germany, pp 215?224.*

J.and Afshar R. Yan, X.and Han. 2003. Clospan: Mining closed sequential patterns in large databases. In *Proceedings of the 3rd SIAM International Conference on Data Mining. San Francisco, CA.*

The Kyutech corpus and topic segmentation using a combined method

Takashi Yamamura, Kazutaka Shimada and Shintaro Kawahara
Department of Artificial Intelligence, Kyushu Institute of Technology
680-4 Kawazu Iizuka Fukuoka Japan
{t_yamamura, shimada}@pluto.ai.kyutech.ac.jp

Abstract

Summarization of multi-party conversation is one of the important tasks in natural language processing. In this paper, we explain a Japanese corpus and a topic segmentation task. To the best of our knowledge, the corpus is the first Japanese corpus annotated for summarization tasks and freely available to anyone. We call it "the Kyutech corpus." The task of the corpus is a decision-making task with four participants and it contains utterances with time information, topic segmentation and reference summaries. As a case study for the corpus, we describe a method combined with LCSeg and TopicTiling for a topic segmentation task. We discuss the effectiveness and the problems of the combined method through the experiment with the Kyutech corpus.

1   Introduction

In collaborative work, people share information, discuss it, and then make decisions through multi-party conversations, such as meetings. Therefore, understanding such conversations and meetings is one of the most important tasks in natural language processing. Conversation summarization is useful to understand the content of conversations for both participants and non-participants. Many researchers have studied meeting and conversation summarization (Banerjee et al., 2015; Mehdad et al., 2014; Oya et al., 2014).

For the summarization tasks, corpora are very important to analyze characteristics of conversations and to construct a method for summary generation. There are some corpora in English, such as the AMI corpus (Carletta, 2007) and the ICSI corpus (Janin et al., 2003). In contrast, there is no corpus for conversation summarization tasks in Japanese. In this study, we construct a Japanese conversation corpus about a decision-making task with four participants. We call it "the Kyutech corpus." To the best of our knowledge, the Kyutech corpus is the first Japanese corpus annotated for summarization tasks and freely available to anyone[1].

The final goal of our study is to generate a summary from a multi-party conversation. Topic segmentation has often been used as the first process in summarization (Banerjee et al., 2015; Oya et al., 2014). In a similar way, we apply topic segmentation to the Kyutech corpus. In this paper, we combine two different text segmentation methods; LCSeg (Galley et al., 2003) and TopicTiling (Riedl and Biemann, 2012). We evaluate the effectiveness of the methods on the Kyutech corpus.

The contributions of this paper are as follows:

- We open the Kyutech corpus, a freely available Japanese conversation corpus for a decision-making task, on the web. This is the first Japanese corpus for summarization.

- As a case study, we examine a combined method based on LCSeg and TopicTiling for topic segmentation with the Kyutech corpus. This is the first step of our conversation summarization.

[1]http://www.pluto.ai.kyutech.ac.jp/~shimada/resources.html

Proceedings of the 12th Workshop on Asian Language Resources,
pages 95–104, Osaka, Japan, December 12 2016.

2 Related work

The AMI (Carletta, 2007) and the ICSI (Janin et al., 2003) are very famous meeting corpora and contain numerous annotations, such as dialogue acts and summaries. These corpora are useful and freely available. In addition, they contain a variety of resources, such as speech information in the AMI and ICSI and Powerpoint slides in the AMI corpus. In this paper, we, however, focus on Japanese corpora. Some discussion and conversation corpora in Japanese have been collected on the basis of different task settings; a chat corpus for a detection task of dialogue breakdown (Higashinaka and Funakoshi, 2014) and a multi-modal corpus for three discussion tasks, such as travel planning for foreign friends (Nihei et al., 2014). On the other hand, our task is summarization and our corpus is annotated for the task. The current version contains topic tags of each utterance and reference summaries. In addition, the corpus is freely available to anyone.

For the topic segmentation, some methods have been proposed. The methods were generally based on lexical cohesion for the topic segmentation. TextTiling proposed by (Hearst, 1994) is one of the most famous approaches using a cosine similarity in word vector space. Galley et al. (2003) have proposed a topic segmentation method, LCSeg. It is also a domain-independent discourse segmentation method based on lexical cohesion. It considered the more sophisticated notion of lexical chains as compared with TextTiling. Eisenstein and Barzilay (2008) have proposed an unsupervised approach to topic segmentation based on lexical cohesion modeled by a Bayesian framework. Banerjee et al. (2015) reported that LCSeg tended to outperform the Bayesian segmentation in the summarization. Therefore, we employ LCSeg as a segmentation method. Riedl and Biemann (2012) have proposed a topic segmentation method using the Latent Dirichlet Allocation (LDA) topic model. It was not based on words, but on the topic IDs assigned by the Bayesian Inference method of LDA. Since the topic model alleviated the problem of the sparsity of word vectors, it led to the improvement of the segmentation accuracy. TopicTiling is essentially different from LCSeg because of the use of the topic model. Therefore, we also employ TopicTiling as another method for the topic segmentation. Since the characteristics of the two methods are different, they have a potential to improve the accuracy by a complementary style. Therefore, in this paper, we combine the two methods with a weight factor.

3 Kyutech corpus

In this section, we explain the Kyutech corpus and the annotation for summarization.

3.1 Task

The Kyutech corpus contains multi-party conversations with four participants. The conversations are a decision-making task. The participants pretend managers of a virtual shopping mall in a virtual city, and then determine a new restaurant from three candidates, as an alternative to a closed restaurant. Before the discussion, the participants read a 10-pages document including information about the three candidates, the closed restaurant and the existing restaurants in the mall, the city information, statistics information about the shopping mall, and so on. Figure 1 is a part of the document for the discussion[2].

The environment of the discussion is shown in Figure 2. The participants are seated around a 1.8m $\times$ 1.8m table in a meeting room. We record the discussion by using a four-direction camera[3] and a video camera. They read the document for 10 minutes, then discuss the candidates for 20 minutes and finally determine one restaurant as a new restaurant opening. We prepared four scenarios with different settings, e.g., different candidates. The participants for each discussion were selected from 20 students consisting of 16 males and 4 females. The current Kyutech corpus consists of nine conversations. After discussion, the participants answer a questionnaire about the satisfaction for the decision, and so on.

3.2 Annotation

We transcribe and annotate the conversations. We annotate topic tags for each utterance and generate summaries for each conversation. The working time for the topic annotation was two hours on average

---

[2]The original document is written in Japanese because the corpus is Japanese. This is English translation of the document.
[3]KingJim MR360. http://www.kingjim.co.jp/sp/mr360/

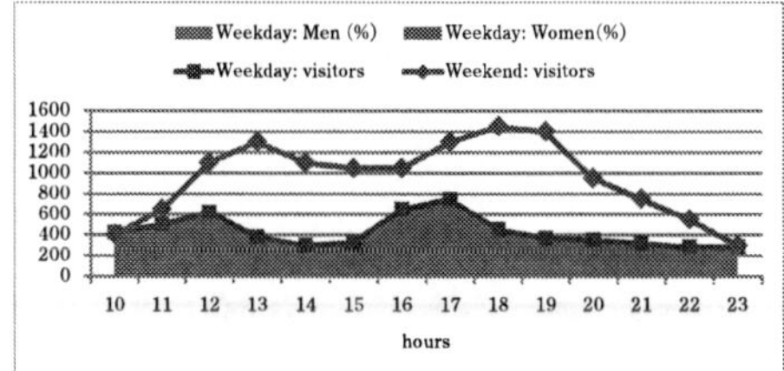

The restaurant "Japanese WAYA" in the shopping mall UBC was closed.
Please select one restaurant from three candidates on the basis of the following information.

Name	Taiwan Noodles	Chinese Shisen	Ramen Fu-Jin
Menu	Beef noodles: ¥ 880 Zhajiangmian: ¥ 980	Mabo tofu: ¥ 720 Chukadon: ¥ 900	Ramen: ¥ 700 Dumpling: ¥ 200
Price range	¥ 800 - ¥ 1,200	¥ 900 - ¥ 1,500	¥ 700 - ¥ 1,000
Seats	25	25	30
business hours	11:00 - 23:00	11:00 - 23:00	11:00 - 23:00
Information	A famous local noodle restaurant in this area. Strong smell but good taste.	A famous Chinese chain restaurant. There are 300 restaurants in Japan.	A popular Ramen noodle restaurant in Japan. There is no same restaurant in the U city.
Reviews	· This is unique taste! (20's male) · The smell of the soup is too strong (30's male)	· Good price. (20's female) · I need more big-portion (30's male)	· Good and plain taste. (20's female) · The set menu is really great. (30's male)

* Information about UBC mall

UBC mall consists of a supermarket, 60 specialty stores, a game arcade, a movie theater and seven restaurants. It is located in U city of Z prefecture. The main target is residents in U city and X city which is located near U city. There are some office buildings near UBC mall. The graphs show the statistics about visitors.

* Information about U city

The U city is the 4th city on population in Z prefecture (150,000 people and 50,000 family units). The population of Z prefecture is about three million. The population of B city, the prefectural capital of Z, is about one million. The distance between U city and B city is about 30 km. R town is located between the cities. There is one university in U city. The U city confronts the serious concerns of rapid aging and very low birth rate.

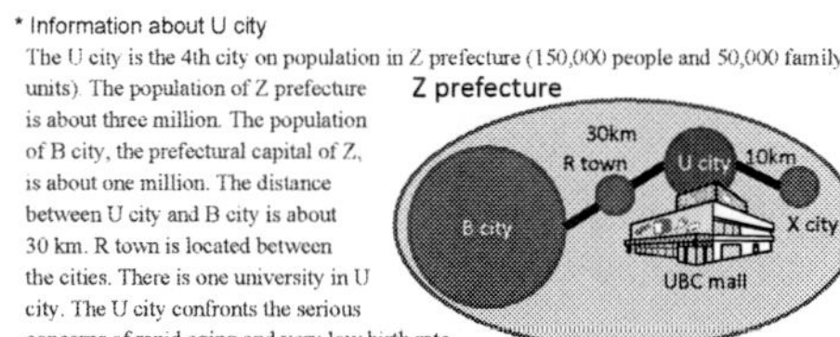

Figure 1: A part of a document in the decision-making task.

Figure 2: The discussion environment.

Tag	Description
(F) tag	Filler
(D) tag	Falter and Repair
(Q) tag	Question: based on the intonation
(?) tag	Low confidence by inaudibleness
(L) tag	Whispering voice and Monologue
<laugh>	Laughing

Table 1: Tags in transcription.

for one conversation. Besides, the time for the summary generation by an annotator was 30 minutes on average for one conversation. In this sub-section, we explain the way for the corpus construction and report the results.

3.2.1 Transcription

We transcribed the conversations by using ELAN[4]. The transcription rules were based on the construction manual of Corpus of Spontaneous Japanese (CSJ) by (National Institute for Japanese Language and Linguistics, 2006). More properly, we separated utterances by 0.2-sec interval on the basis of the manual and annotated some tags shown in Table 1. As a result, the corpus consists of 4509 utterances.

Each utterance is not always sentence-level because it depends on the 0.2-sec interval rule. Other researchers that want to use this corpus might need sentence-level segmentation for their purpose. Therefore, we added another tags, +, / and *, to the end of each utterance for sentence-level identification[5]. Here "+" denotes that the current utterance links to the next utterance. "/" denotes the actual end of a sentence. "*" has an intermediate meaning between + and /.

---

[4]https://tla.mpi.nl/tools/tla-tools/elan/
[5]This is just a subjective annotation for other users. Note that we do not use this annotation in the latter part of this paper, namely topic segmentation.

Topic	Description
CandX	Topic about the candidate 1
CandY	Topic about the candidate 2
CandZ	Topic about the candidate 3
CandS	Topic about the candidates
Closed	Topic about the closed restaurant
Exist1	Topic about the existing restaurant 1
Exist2	Topic about the existing restaurant 2
Exist3	Topic about the existing restaurant 3
Exist4	Topic about the existing restaurant 4
Exist5	Topic about the existing restaurant 5
Exist6	Topic about the existing restaurant 6
Exists	Topic about the existing restaurants
ClEx	Topic about the existing restaurants and the closed restaurant
Mall	Topic about the shopping mall
OtherMall	Topic about other shopping malls

Topic	Description
Location	Topic about the positional relation among restaurants
Area	Topic about areas and cities
People	Topic about the target customers
Price	Topic about the price
Menu	Topic about the menu
Atomos	Topic about the atmosphere
Time	Topic about the business hours
Seat	Topic about the number of seats
Sell	Topic about the sales
Access	Topic about the access to the shopping mall
Meeting	Topic about the proceedings and final decision
Chat	Chats that not related to the task
Vague	Others and unknown

Table 2: Topic tags in the Kyutech corpus.

An example

A: ahh, in this condition +
A: which one is suitable (Q) /
C: I think the ramen is better /
B: me too /

In this example, the first and the second utterances by the participant A are connected by the tag +. The process is as follows:

Step1: The worker of the transcription subjectively judges whether the end of each utterance should be + or /.

Step2: After that, we check the worker's results with some conditions. If a condition is satisfied, replace + with /. The following is a condition.

Condition: the next utterance begins with "conjunction", "filter" or "adverb".

Step3: Replace + with ∗ if we subjectively judge that the current utterance links to the next one although the condition in **Step2** is not satisfied.

3.2.2 Topic annotation

There are a wide variety of tags that should be annotated to utterances; e.g., communicative functions such as INFORM and REQUEST. Here we focus on a summarization task. In general, topic segmentation has an important role as the first step in the meeting summarization (Banerjee et al., 2015; Oya et al., 2014). Therefore, we manually annotated the topics of each utterance in the Kyutech corpus, as the first annotation[6].

First, we examined the conversations in the Kyutech corpus by four annotators including the authors. We repeated this process twice, and then created a topic tag set consisting of 28 tags. Table 2 shows the tag names and the descriptions.

Next, six annotators who included persons not related to this study annotated topic tags to each utterance, on the basis of the tag set. We applied two annotators into one conversation and the annotation was independently executed. In this process, each annotator annotated at least one tag to one utterance as the main tag of the utterance. In addition, we allowed adding the second-tag if an annotator wanted to add it. The annotators checked the document in Section 3.1 during the annotation process and considered the context in the conversation to select suitable topic tags. Although we allowed creating a new tag if an annotator wanted to create it, no new tags were generated in this process. After the annotation with two

---

[6]Currently we are also developing the corpus with communicative functions

	Annotator1		Annotator2		Final tags			Utternace
	Main	Addition	Main	Addition	Main	Addition1	Addition2	
D	Closed	Sell	Closed		Closed	Sell		the closed restaurant was (D not profitable) unprofitable /
A	Closed	Sell	Closed		Closed	Sell		yes /
A	Closed	Sell	Sell		Closed	Sell		if unprofitable restaurant must be closed, profitability is +
D	Closed	Sell	Sell		Closed	Sell		<笑> /
A	Closed	Sell	Sell		Closed	Sell		the most important thing, isn't it /
D	Closed	Sell	Sell		Closed	Sell		<笑> /
A	Exist4	Sell	Exist4	Sell	Exist4	Sell		so, in terms of the existing and profitable restaurant, "FamilyPlate" made the biggest sale in the restaurants +
D	Exist4	Sell	Exist4		Exist4	Sell		(L uhn) /
A	Exist4	Sell	Meeting		Exist4	Sell		and the restaurant is ... +
A	Exist4	Sell	Meeting		Exist4	Sell		the reason, what is the reason (Q) /
D	Exist4	Menu	People		Exist4	Menu		many menus and branches (? maybe) /
C	Exist4	People	People		Exist4	Menu	People	in addition +
C	Exist4	People	People		Exist4	Menu	People	families +
C	Exist4	People	People		Exist4	Menu	People	visit in the restaurant, the document says, many menus +
A	Exist4	People	People		Exist4	Menu	People	Unnnn /
A	Exist4	People	People		Exist4	Menu	People	(?) families are /
C	Exist4	People	People		Exist4	Menu	People	might contribute to getting customers /
D	Exist4	People	People		Exist4	Menu	People	Ah /
D	People		People		People	Mall		the document says low buying motivation on holidays, for couples and families/

Figure 3: Topic tags by two annotators and final tags with utterances.

annotators, we computed an agreement between tags of the annotators. The agreement score was based on a partial match scheme (AS_p) as follows:

$$AS_p(A_1, A_2) = \frac{\sum_{i \in U} PM_i(A_1, A_2)}{U_N} \tag{1}$$

where PM_i is the partial match scheme between tag sets of annotators, A_1 and A_2, for an utterance i. In other words, PM_i is true if a tag of an annotator for an utterance is the same as at least one tag of another annotator. For example, $PM_i(A_1, A_2)$ is 1 in the case that $A_1 = \{CandX, People\}$ and $A_2 = \{People\}$ for an utterance i. U is the set of utterances and U_N is the number of utterances, namely 4509. The agreement score AS_p was 0.879.

After that, we checked the tags of two annotators in each conversation. Here we extended the number of tags for one utterance; 2 to 3, namely one main tag and two additional tags. We discussed each tag from annotators, and then determined the final tags of each utterance. After the discussion and the determination of the final tags[7], we also computed an agreement score of them. Here the agreement score was also based on a partial match scheme between the final tag that the authors created (F) and the tag set from two annotators (A_{all}). For example, assume $F = \{People\}$, $A_1 = \{People, Mall\}$ and $A_2 = \{Mall, Menu\}$. Here A_{all} is $\{People, Mall, Menu\}$ and A_{all} contains $F = \{People\}$. Therefore, $PM_i(F, A_{all})$ in this situation is 1. The partial agreement score between the final tags and the tags by two annotators, namely $AS_p(F, A_{all})$, was 0.965. Thus, we obtained a corpus with the high agreement topic tag set. Figure 3 shows an example of the annotation result. In the Kyutech corpus, assuming that the main tag sequence is one topic, one topic sequence usually consists of approximately 10 utterances.

3.2.3 Reference summary

Next, each annotator generated a summary of the conversation. The size of a summary is from 250 characters to 500 characters[8]. The summary generation complied with the guideline of abstractive hand summaries of the AMI corpus[9]. Based on the guideline, the generation carried out after the process in

---

[7]The working time for the final tag determination was approximately two hours for each conversation.

[8]The number of words was approximately 150 content words on average. The number of unique words was 80 words on average.

[9]http://groups.inf.ed.ac.uk/ami/corpus/guidelines.shtml

> At the beginning of the discussion, a targeted customer segment and various menus were the important
> evaluation points to obtain the high sales for the new restaurant because the closed restaurant was almost
> unprofitable. From the viewpoints, "The Ramen Kaibutsu" was rejected in the early stage of the discus-
> sion because the main target of the restaurant differs from the target that they want and the restaurant
> probably acquires limited customers. After that, they discussed the advantages and disadvantages of the
> remaining candidates, "The Tsukemen Fujin" and "BonoPasta". The advantages of "BonoPasta" were .....

Figure 4: The abstractive summary in the Kyutech corpus.

Section 3.2.2. Each annotator received the following message for the summary generation: "Write a summary that is understandable for somebody who was not present during the meeting."

We obtained two abstractive summaries from two annotators for one conversation. We computed an agreement rate between the two summaries by using ROUGE-N (Lin and Hovy, 2003). ROUGE-N is an n-gram recall between a reference summary and a system summary and widely used in automatic evaluation of summaries. ROUGE-N is computed as follows:

$$ROUGE\text{-}N(S, R) \;\; = \;\; \frac{\sum_{e \in n\text{-}gram(S)} Count_{match}(e)}{\sum_{e \in n\text{-}gram(R)} Count(e)} \tag{2}$$

where n stands for the length of the n-gram, e and $Count_{match}(e)$ is the maximum number of n-grams co-occurring in a system summary and a reference summary. We used ROUGE-1 in this paper. The ROUGE-1 between the two summaries was 0.527 on average; one is a summary from an annotator as a reference summary and the other is a summary from the other annotator as a system summary. In general, the score, 0.527, is qualitatively reasonable in summarization tasks although it is difficult to evaluate whether the score is quantitatively adequate. In a similar way to the topic annotation, we generated a summary from the two summaries of annotators. For generating the third summary, we scanned not only the two summaries but also the transcription of each conversation. Thus, the third summary we made is sort of a consensus summary of two annotators. Figure 4 shows an example of the consensus summary. The ROUGE-1 between each consensus summary and two annotators' summaries was 0.564. We also regard each consensus summary and each annotator's summary as a reference summary and a system summary, respectively, in the ROUGE calculation. The ROUGE score of consensus summaries was higher than that between two annotators' summaries (0.564 vs. 0.527). This result shows that the third summaries are appropriate as consensus summaries.

4 Topic segmentation

In this section, we explain topic segmentation for the Kyutech corpus. There are two types of methods for topic segmentation; supervised and unsupervised methods. In this paper, we focus on unsupervised methods. We describe three topic segmentation methods, LCSeg, TopicTiling and the combined method, and then evaluate the methods on the Kyutech corpus, as a case study.

4.1 LCSeg

LCSeg is an unsupervised cohesion-based technique proposed by (Galley et al., 2003) to topic modeling for meeting transcripts. We compute the $tfidf$ score for LCSeg.

$$tfidf(R_i) \;\; = \;\; freq(t_i) \cdot log(\frac{L}{L_i}) \tag{3}$$

where R_i denotes a repetition score of a term t_i. $freq(t_i)$ is the frequency of t_i in a chain. L_i and L are the respective length and the length of the text, respectively. Then, we compute a lexical cohesion by using the cosine similarity at the transition between two windows. For the calculation, LCSeg uses lexical chains that overlap with the two windows. The similarity cos_L between windows (A and B) is

ConvID	Utterances	Segments
Conv1	505	52
Conv2	637	77
Conv3	324	33
Conv4	502	36
Conv5	566	48
Conv6	487	51
Conv7	284	31
Conv8	445	42
Conv9 (dev)	759	48

Table 3: The number of utterances and segments of each conversation in the Kyutech corpus.

computed with

$$cos_L(A, B) = \frac{\sum_i w_{i,A} \cdot w_{i,B}}{\sqrt{\sum_i w_{i,A}^2 \sum_i w_{i,B}^2}} \tag{4}$$

where

$$w_{i,\Gamma} = \begin{cases} tfidf(R_i) & if\ R_i\ overlaps\ \Gamma \in \{A, B\} \\ 0 & otherwise \end{cases}$$

4.2 TopicTiling

TopicTiling is a text segmentation method with the Latent Dirichlet Allocation (LDA) topic model (Riedl and Biemann, 2012). It uses topic IDs obtained from the LDA inference method, instead of words. The method first estimates a topic distribution from the Kyutech corpus. Then, it generates a vector space based on topic IDs in the LDA model. The calculation of the similarity is similar to LCSeg. The similarity cos_T between windows (A and B) is also computed as follows:

$$cos_T(A, B) = \frac{\sum_n tp_{n,A} \cdot tp_{n,B}}{\sqrt{\sum_n tp_{n,A}^2 \sum_n tp_{n,B}^2}} \tag{5}$$

where tp denotes the probabilistic distribution from LDA.

4.3 Combined method

Since the characteristics of the two methods are different, they have a potential to improve the accuracy by a complementary style. Therefore, in this paper, we combine the two methods with a weight factor wf. The similarity cos_C between windows (A and B) is computed as follows:

$$cos_C(A, B) = wf \times cos_L(A, B) + (1 - wf) \times cos_T(A, B) \tag{6}$$

The weight factor wf is a trade-off parameter.

4.4 Experiment for topic segmentation

We evaluated these methods with the Kyutech corpus. The details of the Kyutech corpus are shown in Table 3. In the experiment, we used the main tags as the topic sequence. In other words, a changing point of the main tags is a border of two topics, e.g., the 7th utterance in Figure 3.

We used one conversation (Conv9) as the development data for the method. Hence we evaluated the methods with eight conversations without Conv9. In the experiment, we compared two weight factors $wf = 0.3$ and $wf = 0.7$. For the LDA, we compared three types of the number of topics, 10, 20 and 30. Parameters on LCSeg, such as the window size, were based on (Galley et al., 2003).

Method	Comp	Partial
LCseg	0.195	0.396
Topic(10)	0.142	0.394
Topic(20)	0.148	0.345
Topic(30)	0.100	0.299
Comb(10,0.3)	0.155	0.401
Comb(10,0.7)	0.182	0.399
Comb(20,0.3)	0.168	0.367
Comb(20,0.7)	0.184	0.391
Comb(30,0.3)	0.132	0.308
Comb(30,0.7)	0.172	0.362

Table 4: The F-measure on complete match and partial match.

We evaluated these methods with two criteria; complete matching and partial matching that were used in (Tajima, 2013). We computed the F-measure from the recall and precision rates for the complete and partial matching. The values are computed as follows:

$$p_{comp} = \frac{|B_r \cap B_h|}{[B_h]}, \; r_{comp} = \frac{|(B_r \cap B_h)|}{|B_r|} \tag{7}$$

where B_r is the set of the sentence IDs before each topic change. B_h is the set of the outputs from each method.

$$p_{part} = \frac{|B'_r \cap B_h|}{[B_h]}, \; r_{part} = \frac{|(B_r \cap B'_h)|}{|B_r|} \tag{8}$$

where $B'_r = \bigcup_{i \in B_r} i-1, i, i+1$ and $B'_h = \bigcup_{i \in B_h} i-1, i, i+1$. The F-measure is the harmonic mean between the recall and precision rates.

Table 4 shows the experimental result about the complete match and the partial match. Topic and Comb are the methods with TopicTiling and the combined methods, respectively. Topic(β) in the table denotes the number of topics in LDA and $\beta = \{10, 20, 30\}$. β and wf in Comb(β, wf) denote the number of topics and the value of the weight factor ($wf \in \{0.3, 0.7\}$). For the complete matching, LCSeg produced the best performance. For the partial matching, Comb(10,0.3) obtained the highest F-measure value although there is no dramatic improvement as compared with the single methods, LCSeg and TopicTiling. TopicTiling-based methods were low accuracy on the whole. This is one reason that the combined methods did not improve the accuracy. The size of the Kyutech corpus is not always sufficient for the statistical methods, as compared with the AMI corpus. For the TopicTiling-based methods, we need a larger dataset. Moreover, the values on the F-measure were not high (0.401 even on the partial match scheme). Galley et al. (2003) reported that a feature-based segmentation method outperformed LCSeg. Applying a supervised method into our task leads to the improvement of the accuracy of the topic segmentation. In general, machine learning methods need a large dataset to generate a strong classifier. Therefore, scaling up the Kyutech corpus is the most important future work.

5 Discussion and Conclusions

In this paper, we explained the Kyutech corpus and a topic segmentation task for the corpus as the first step of multi-party conversation summarization. The Kyutech corpus consists of conversations about a decision-making task with four participants. The corpus contained utterances with time information, topic annotation and reference summaries.

For the topic annotation, we prepared 28 topic tags, and generated the annotated corpus in the two steps; (1) annotation by two annotators and (2) final judgment of each tag by three annotators. The partial agreement score AS_p between annotators was 0.879. In addition, the AS_p between final tags that the authors created and tag sets from two annotators was 0.965. In a similar way, we generated three summaries; two summaries by annotators and a consensus summary of the two summaries. The ROUGE-1 score among them was 0.564 on average. To the best of our knowledge, the Kyutech corpus is the first Japanese corpus annotated for summarization tasks and freely available to anyone.

As a case study of the corpus, we evaluated some topic segmentation methods. We compared LCSeg, TopicTiling and a combined method on the Kyutech corpus. However, there is no dramatic improvement of the accuracy. One reason was that TopicTiling was not effective in our experiment. It was caused by the size of the Kyutech corpus. Therefore, scaling up the Kyutech corpus is the most important future work.

The Kyutech corpus contains the topic tags and summaries. On the other hand, the AMI corpus contains numerous annotations, such as extractive summaries and dialogue-acts. Our topic tags focused on semantic contents of each utterance because of our purpose, namely summarization. However, communicative functions (Bunt, 2000), such as `INFORM` and `Auto-Feedback`, are also an important role as a conversation corpus. We are currently developing the Kyutech corpus with communicative functions, and then are going to open the new corpus in the next phase. In addition, hierarchical topic tag definition, such as (Ohtake et al., 2009), might be appropriate for our summarization task because each utterance often contained some topic tags. Other annotation to the Kyutech corpus is also future work. In addition, an extension of the Kyutech corpus to a multi-modal corpus with audio-visual data, such as (Sanchez-Cortes et al., 2013) and (Nihei et al., 2014), is important future work. In this paper, we just dealt with a topic segmentation task. However, the main purpose is to summarize a multi-party conversation. Abstractive summarization using the segmented topics is also the important future work.

Acknowledgments

This work was supported by JSPS KAKENHI Grant Number 26730176. A part of this work was carried out during the second author's stay at the University of British Columbia. We would like to express our gratitude to Giuseppe Carenini and Raymond T. Ng.

References

Siddhartha Banerjee, Prasenjit Mitra, and Kazunari Sugiyama. 2015. Generating abstractive summaries from meeting transcripts. In *Proceedings of ACM Symposium on Document Engineering (DocEng '15)*, pages 51–60.

Harry Bunt, 2000. *Abduction, Belief and Context in Dialogue: Studies in computational pragmatics*, chapter Dialogue pragmatics and context specification, pages 81–150. John Benjamins Publishing Company.

Jean Carletta. 2007. Unleashing the killer corpus: experiences in creating the multi-everything AMI meeting corpus. *Language Resources and Evaluation*, 41(2):181–190.

Jacob Eisenstein and Regina Barzilay. 2008. Bayesian unsupervised topic segmentation. In *Proceedings of the Conference on Empirical Methods in Natural Language Processing (EMNLP2008)*, pages 334–343.

Michel Galley, Kathleen McKeown, Eric Fosler-Lussier, and Hongyan Jing. 2003. Discourse segmentation of multi-party conversation. In *Proceedings of the 41st Annual Meeting on Association for Computational Linguistics (ACL 2003)*, pages 562–569.

Marti A. Hearst. 1994. Multi-paragraph segmentation of expository text. In *Proceeding of the 32nd Annual Meeting on Association for Computational Linguistics (ACL 1994)*, pages 9–16.

Ryuichiro Higashinaka and Kotaro Funakoshi. 2014. Chat dialogue collection and dialogue breakdown annotation in the dialogue task of project next nlp (in Japanese). In *JSAI, SIG-SLUD-B402-08*, pages 45–50.

Adam Janin, Don Baron, Jane Edwards, Dan Ellis, David Gelbart, Nelson Morgan, Barbara Peskin, Thilo Pfau, Elizabeth Shriberg, Andreas Stolcke, and Chuck Wooters. 2003. The ICSI meeting corpus. In *Proceedings of the IEEE ICASSP*, pages 364–367.

Chin-Yew Lin and Eduard Hovy. 2003. Automatic evaluation of summaries using n-gram co-occurrence statistics. In *Proceedings of NAACL '03 Proceedings of the 2003 Conference of the North American Chapter of the Association for Computational Linguistics on Human Language*, pages 71–78.

Yashar Mehdad, Giuseppe Carenini, and Raymond T. Ng. 2014. Abstractive summarization of spoken and written conversations based on phrasal queries. In *Proceedings of the 52nd Annual Meeting of the Association for Computational Linguistics*, pages 1220–1230.

Fumio Nihei, Yukiko I. Nakano, Yuki Hayashi, Hung-Hsuan Hung, and Shogo Okada. 2014. Predicting influential statements in group discussions using speech and head motion information. In *Proceedings of the 16th International Conference on Multimodal Interaction*, ICMI '14, pages 136–143.

Kiyonori Ohtake, Teruhisa Misu, Chiori Hori, Hideki Kashioka, and Satoshi Nakamura. 2009. Annotating dialogue acts to construct dialogue systems for consulting. In *Proceedings of the 7th Workshop on Asian Language Resources*, pages 32–39.

Tatsuro Oya, Yashar Mehdad, Giuseppe Carenini, and Raymond Ng. 2014. A template-based abstractive meeting summarization: Leveraging summary and source text relationships. In *Proceedings of INLG 2014*, pages 45–53.

Martin Riedl and Chris Biemann. 2012. Topictiling: A text segmentation algorithm based on LDA. In *Proceedings of the 50th Annual Meeting on Association for Computational Linguistics (ACL 2012)*, pages 37–42.

Dairazalia Sanchez-Cortes, Oya Aran, Dinesh Babu Jayagopi, Marianne Schmid Mast, and Daniel Gatica-Perez. 2013. Emergent leaders through looking and speaking: from audio-visual data to multimodal recognition. *Journal on Multimodal User Interfaces*, 7(1):39–53.

Yasuhiro Tajima. 2013. Performance comparison between different language models on a text segmentation problem via hmm (in Japanese). *Information Processing Society of Japan. Transactions on mathematical modeling and its applications*, 6(1):38–46.

National Institute for Japanese Language and Linguistics. 2006. Construction manual of Corpus of Spontaneous Japanese (CSJ) (in Japanese).

Automatic Evaluation of Commonsense Knowledge
for Refining Japanese ConceptNet

Seiya Shudo and **Rafal Rzepka** and **Kenji Araki**
Graduate School of Information and Technology, Hokkaido University
Sapporo, Kita-ku, Kita 14 Nishi 9, 060-0814, Japan
`{shudo,rzepka,araki}@ist.hokudai.ac.jp`

Abstract

In this paper we present two methods for automatic common sense knowledge evaluation for Japanese entries in ConceptNet ontology. Our proposed methods utilize text-mining approach, which is inspired by related research for evaluation of generality on natural sentences using commercial search engines and simpler input: one with relation clue words and WordNet synonyms, and one without. Both methods were tested with a blog corpus. The system based on our proposed methods reached relatively high precision score for three relations (*MadeOf, UsedFor, AtLocation*). We analyze errors and discuss problems of common sense evaluation, both manual and automatic and propose ideas for further improvements.

1 Introduction

The lack of commonsense knowledge has been one of main problems for creating human level intelligent systems and for improving their tasks as natural language understanding, computer vision, or robot manipulation.

Researchers have tackled with this deficiency usually taking one of the following three approaches. One is to hire knowledge specialists to enter the knowledge manually and CyC (Lenat, 1995) is the most widely known project of this kind. Second is to use crowdsourcing. In Open Mind Common Sense project (OMCS) (Singh et al., 2002), non-specialists input phrases or words manually, which generates knowledge in relatively short time. For making the input process less monotonous, researchers also use Games With A Purpose (GWAPs), for instance *Nāja-to nazo nazo*[1] (Riddles with Nadya)[2] for acquiring Japanese commonsense knowledge. Third approach is to use text-mining techniques. KNEXT (Schubert, 2002), NELL[3] or WebChild (Tandon et al., 2014) are famous projects for acquiring commonsense knowledge automatically.

Last two approaches are immune to quality problems. For example, knowledge acquired through Nadya interface reached 58% precision (Nakahara and Yamada, 2011), and NELL system reached 74% precision (Carlson et al., 2010). This is because public contributors input and source Web texts tend to be noisy. Therefore, acquired knowledge should be evaluated, but there is no gold standard method for estimating whether acquired knowledge is commonsensical or not. Usually, manual evaluation by specialists or by crowdsourcing (Gordon et al., 2010) is used. However, this is costly and time-consuming, and even specialists have different opinions on concepts' usualness. Another method is to evaluate automatically acquired knowledge by utilizing it in some tasks. For example, there is a research using IQ tests (Ohlsson et al., 2012) for commonsense knowledge level estimation, but it does not help improving or refining quality of existing or newly acquired concepts.

In this paper, we present automatic evaluation system for commonsense knowledge. Our approach is to use frequency of phrase occurrences in a Web corpus. There is a previous research using Internet resources and Japanese WordNet (Bond et al., 2009) for evaluating generality of natural sentences from

---

[1]Original Japanese words are represented in italic throughout the paper.
[2]`http://nadya.jp/`
[3]`http://rtw.ml.cmu.edu/rtw/`

105

Proceedings of the 12th Workshop on Asian Language Resources,
pages 105–112, Osaka, Japan, December 12 2016.

OMCS (Rzepka et al., 2011). In that research, frequency of occurrence in Yahoo Japan search engine[4] search results snippets are used to determine thresholds for eliminating noise and verb conjugation is used to increase number of hits. Our approach for evaluating commonsense knowledge is similar but we aim at higher precision without using commercial search engines. Currently access to commercial engines is limited even for a researchers so we decide to introduce methods that can be used also with relatively smaller, self-made (crawled), corpora. Our research can also improve crowdsourcing methods, because it can decrease costs or be less time-consuming if distinctly wrong entries are automatically filtered out. Last but not least, we work on concepts and relations while in previous research only simple word pairs (e.g. "to throw" + "a ball") were used.

Our contributions presented in this paper can be summarized as follows:

- We evaluate Japanese commonsense knowledge from ConceptNet (Speer and Havasi, 2012) (explained in the next section) by using phrase occurrences in a blog corpus.

- We apply proposed methods to three relation types to investigate their flexibility.

- We analyze evaluation errors, discuss problems of our methods and propose their expansion for increasing efficiency of automatic evaluation.

2 Japanese ConceptNet

ConceptNet is a semantic network-like ontology allowing to process commonsense knowledge. It is created from other sources as hand-crafted OMCS or GlobalMind (Chung, 2006), JMdict[5], Wiktionary[6] and so on. In ConceptNet, there are two ways of representation. First is a graph structure where nodes show concepts, and their relations such as "IsA" or "PartOf". One set of two concepts and their relation is called an assertion. This is represented by $Relation(Concept1, Concept2)$ abbreviated from now as (C_1, R, C_2). Another way of representation is a natural sentence, and there are entries in various languages as English, Chinese, German, Korean, Portuguese and also Japanese. In Japanese Concept-Net concept terms are in Japanese, but relations are in English (the same is true for all non-English languages). For this research we used latest version 5.4[7]. Japanese ConceptNet contains 1.08 million assertions in total, but more than 80% of them belong to "TranslationOf" relation, therefore we treated them as irrelevant to the commonness evaluation task.

For this research we chose three relations for the first series of trials: "MadeOf" (1008 assertions), "UsedFor" (2414 assertions), and "AtLocation" (13213 assertions). Main reason for choosing these relations is that they can be distinctly associated with physical objects, while e.g. "RelatedTo" relation (98.6 thousands assertions) is very often semantically vague and needs different approach for evaluating its correctness.

3 System Overview

In this section we present an outline of our system for automatic commonness estimation of ConceptNet assertions (see Figure 1). In the first step, our system searches a blog corpus (Ptaszynski et al., 2012) for left C_1 and right C_2 concepts, and then parses snippets of search results and concepts using morphological analyzer MeCab[8]. Without this process, if an assertion shows that one concept includes the other concept such as (C_1) *karē* (curry), (R) "MadeOf", and (C_2) *karēko* (curry powder), (C_2) *karēko* end up also matching as (C_1) *karē*.

Concepts can be represented in multiple morphemes including not only nouns but also verbs, adjectives or particles. If there are compound nouns in a concept, system treats them as one noun. In the next step, our system checks whether each sentence contains a relation clue word or not. We manually selected

---

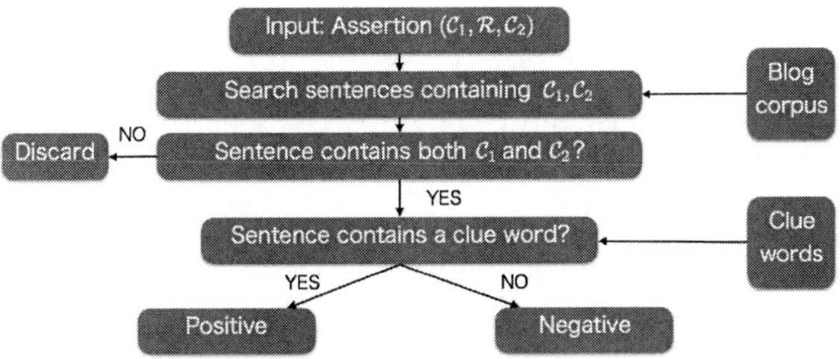

Figure 1: Overview of our system for evaluating assertion by using a blog corpus and clue words.

clue words in Japanese semantically related to a given relation (R) for retrieving their co-occurrences with concepts.

For evaluating "MadeOf" assertion, we used *tsukuru* (to make). For "UsedFor" assertion, we chose *tsukau* (to use). Because these basic verbs do not ensure sufficient number of hits, we added their synonyms from Japanese WordNet (Bond et al., 2009). It is a lexical database consisting of synsets which are represented in nouns, verbs, adjectives, and adverbs. One word can be linked to multiple meanings and even more synonyms. For instance, *tsukuru* (to make) has 21 synsets which provide 111 synonyms in total. Some of them are rare or semantically far from the basic clue verb. For this reason we chose only 10 synonyms with the following procedure. First, we extracted synonyms used in two or more synsets linked to a given clue word (relation verb), and then selected 10 synonyms with the highest frequency in the blog corpus. To increase hit number even further, we conjugated all verbs, which gave up to 7 forms depending on the verb type. For instance, except basic *tsukau* (to use) following forms were also used as queries: *tsukawa-, tsukao-, tsukae-, tsukat-, tsukai-*.

To investigate differences between precision and recall we introduced two separate methods with different matching conditions. In order to evaluate an assertion, the most natural approach would be to match C_1, R, and C_2 in one sentence, e.g. "butter (C_1) is **made** (R) from milk (C_2)". Therefore, in our first proposed method all these three elements must occur at least once in one sentence (we call it a "All Elements" method). Because this method is expected to achieve rather low recall, we also proposed a second method requiring only C_1 and C_2 to co-occur in one sentence ("Concepts Only" method). For "AtLocation" relation we selected two clue verbs with connotations of existence: "*aru*" for animate and "*iru*" for inanimate nouns. Although both verbs are widely used, "*aru*" and "*iru*" cause significant amount of noise because they are also used as auxiliary verbs, e.g. *tabete-**iru*** (eating). Therefore, for "AtLocation" assertions we altered the second method used for "MadeOf" or "UsedFor" by replacing relations R with place-indicating particles: "C_2 - *ni* C_1" and "C_2 - *de* C_1". *Ni* and *de* convey a preposition function similar to "in" or "at" in English.

4   Experiments and Results

To confirm the efficiency of our proposed system in automatic evaluating commonness of a concept, we performed series of experiments. From ConceptNet 5.4 we randomly selected 100 assertions for each of the three relations under investigation. To create the correct data set, 10 annotators (one female student, 8 male students, one male worker, all in their 20's) evaluated 300 assertions presented in Japanese sentences. We needed to manually create these using a fixed template, because there were many cases where ConceptNet did not contain a natural sentence in Japanese, and the way of expression was not united. For instance, in case of (C_1) *banira* (vanilla), (R) "MadeOf", and (C_2) *gyūnyū* (milk), we inserted all elements into following template: "*Banira-wa gyūnyū-kara tsukurareru*" (vanilla is made from milk). As we treated unarguably common facts starting zero point with growing peculiarity of assertinos, annotators evaluated commonness of such sentences using 10 points scale (from 1 to 10, where 1 is common sense, and 10 is non-common sense). We treated the results labelled 1-5 as usual (commonsensical,

Table 1: Possible False / True relations between human and automatic evaluation.

	System Positive	System Negative
Questionnaire True	TP	TN
Questionnaire False	FP	FN

$$Accuracy = \frac{TP + FN}{TP + TN + FP + FN} \quad (1)$$

$$Precision = \frac{TP}{TP + FP} \quad (2)$$

$$Recall = \frac{TP}{TP + TN} \quad (3)$$

$$F - score = \frac{2 \times Precision \times Recall}{Precision + Recall} \quad (4)$$

Figure 2: Equation for calculating f-score.

correct), and 6-10 as unusual (not commonsensical, incorrect).

In Table 1 and Figure 2, we show possible combinations of relations between human annotators and system agreement, and f-score calculation equation. Experiments results showed that our proposed methods achieved high precision for each type of relation (see Tables 2, 3, and 4). These results also proved that the proposed text-mining approach can be used to evaluate relational commonsense knowledge without commercial search engines and thresholds manipulation.

5 Error Analysis

We analysed errors of "All Elements" method (C_1, R, C_2) by reading source sentences which caused incorrect commonness estimations and by comparing system's results with human annotations. It appears that annotators' evaluation scores differ significantly: only three assertions out from 300 were the same (all three judged them as false). For example, *Kogata reizōko-niwa hoteru-ga aru* (There is a hotel in a small refrigerator) and *Tokyo-niwa Fujisan-ga aru* (There is Mt. Fuji in Tokyo) were evaluated as explicitly incorrect. Very small number of agreed evaluations shows clearly the difficulty with making an evaluation system for commonsense knowledge due to discrepancies in human annotators opinions.

Below, we present examples explaining reasons for erroneous automatic evaluations. There are some

Table 2: Evaluation results for "MadeOf" relations ("All Elements" and "Concepts Only" methods).

MadeOf	Accuracy	Precision	Recall	F-score
All Elements Method (C_1, R, C_2)	0.450	0.780	0.410	0.538
Concepts Only Method (C_1, C_2)	0.640	**0.792**	0.730	0.760

Table 3: Evaluation results for "UsedFor" relations ("All Elements" and "Concepts Only" methods).

UsedFor	Accuracy	Precision	Recall	F-score
All Elements Method (C_1, R, C_2)	0.530	**1.00**	0.413	0.584
Concepts Only Method (C_1, C_2)	0.650	0.868	0.662	0.735

Table 4: Evaluation results for "AtLocation" relations ("All Elements" and "Concepts Only" methods).

AtLocation	Accuracy	Precision	Recall	F-score
All Elements Method (C_1, R, C_2)	0.500	**0.615**	0.285	0.390
Concepts Only Method (C_1, C_2)	0.550	0.582	0.696	0.634

cases where, an assertion was judged as non-commonsense knowledge but sentences in the corpus suggested otherwise. For instance, (C_1) *furaipan* (frying pan), (R) "MadeOf", and (C_2) *arumi* (aluminum) elements were discovered in the sentence *Wagaya-wa moppara daisō-de utteiru saisho-kara arumi-no furaipan-to setto-ni natteiru-node tukutte-masu* (In my house we always make it because it is in a set with an aluminum frying pan sold by Daisō). The system matched "make" as "we make" (meaning "to cook"), but it should be related to "aluminum frying pan" (meaning "frying pan made of aluminum").

Another problem arises from the fact that some concepts in ConceptNet are not written in simple, commonsensical manner or are simply strange. For example, for (R) "MadeOf" we have (C_1) *aisatsu* (greeting) and (C_2) *genshō-kara yomitorareru imi* (meaning that can be read from a phenomenon). The reason is that in knowledge gathering systems like Nadya or GlobalMind some contributors try to be original. It is difficult to remove all inappropriate assertions by knowledge providers, so they end up remaining in the database. Annotators judged the given assertion above as non-commonsense knowledge. However, in some cases such as (C_1) *esukarēta* (escalator), (R) "UsedFor", and (C_2) *ue-ni agattari oritari suru* (to go up and down) or (C_1) *henken* (prejudice), (R) "MadeOf", and (C_2) *taishō-ni tai-suru jōhō-no ketsujo* (information shortage of object information) were judged as common sense. From these results we can conclude that contributors provided semantically correct knowledge, although their input was unorthodox on the lexical level.

Evaluation also seems to depend on how the assertion was presented in the questionnaire. For assertions like (C_1) *eiga* (movie), (R) "UsedFor", and (C_2) *kanshō-suru* (to watch), it would be more natural to say *eiga-wo kanshō-suru* (to watch a movie) than *kanshō-suru-niwa eiga-wo tsukau* (for watching a movie is used) which we created to keep all forms consistent. *Kanshō-suru* (to watch) implicitly indicates *tsukau* (to use), therefore it is difficult to create a natural sentence in such cases without allowing synonyms or more specific verbs.

Different problems were caused by the fact that the proposed system did not use part of speech information during the matching processing. This led to ambiguity which is visible in an example of the following assertion: (C_1) *sutorēto* (undiluted), (R) "MadeOf", and (C_2) *arukōru* (alcohol). *Sutorēto* has two meanings: "directly"/ "frankly" and "undiluted". While it was correctly evaluated as uncommon by majority of evaluators, the system labelled "alcohol is made of straight" as common. This is because the following corpus sentence was retrieved and used for matching: *Shōsei-mo kyō byōin-no kensa-de, shinitaku-nai nara, kyō-kara arukōru-wo tate-to storēto-ni iwaremashita* (At the hospital, I was also **told straight** that if I do not want to die, I should give up **alcohol**). *Shōsei-mo* means "I also", while written with the same Chinese character as *sei-mo* it can be read *umo* which is one of conjugated forms of *umu* (to give birth) used as a clue word and lack of morphological recognition caused system to incorrectly assume that "straight can be born from alcohol". There was another example for the assertion (C_1) *tōri* (street), (R) "AtLocation", and (C_2) *kuruma* (car). The assertion suggests "street" (*tōri*) can be found at a "car" (*kuruma*), so the concepts (C_1) and (C_2) were naturally negated by the human subjects (cars can be found on the streets, not the opposite). However, the system evaluated the assertion as common, because noun *tōri* was incorrectly matched as a verb which is one of conjugated forms of *tōru* (to pass). This error was caused by the following corpus sentence: *kono-mae, chikaku-wo kuruma de tōri mashita.* (recently, **I passed** near by **car**). Above examples show that although it significantly increases the processing time, part of speech information should be added in future.

Another obvious problem is the insufficient corpus size. Even if an assertion represents common sense, it does not always exist in the corpus. We also found problems related not only to concepts (C_1, C_2) but also to relations (R), which co-occur with different objects or subjects in the corpus. For instance, for assertion (C_1) *nattō* (fermented soybeans), (R) "MadeOf", and (C_2) *tōfu* (bean curd), following sentence was retrieved from the corpus: *O-tōfu-mo nattō-mo daisuki-nanode, kondo tsukutte-mimasu* (I'll try to make fermented soybeans and tofu because I love them). Both concepts can be made but there is no relation indicating what is made with what.

6 Discussion and Additional Tests

Considering "All Elements" method, when compared to "MadeOf" and "UsedFor" relations, "AtLocation" reached lower f-score. This is because for "MadeOf" and "UsedFor" assertions we used verbs (and their synonyms) with wide meaning like "*tsukuru*" (to make) and "*tsukau*" (to use), but we did not find their appropriate equivalents for "AtLocation". As presented earlier, we replaced $\mathcal{R}$ with place-indicating particles and added them to concepts: "C_2-*de* C_1" and "C_2-*ni* C_1". However this method did not bring satisfying results (see end of the sections)

For "MadeOf" and "UsedFor" relations f-score is higher for "Concepts Only" than for "All Elements" method due to the higher recall. Taking "UsedFor" relation as example, 53 assertions agreed with human annotators in "All Elements" method, but 12 more correct ones were retrieved when "Concepts Only" method was used. For "MadeOf" relation, our intuition was that retrievals would also be more precise when "All Elements" method is used it was impossible to retrieve correct relations as: (C_1) *shōmei kigu* (lighting equipment), ($\mathcal{R}$) "MadeOf" and (C_2) *garasu* (glass), (C_1) *makura* (pillow), ($\mathcal{R}$) "MadeOf" and (C_2) *menka* (cotton), (C_2) *borushichi* (borscht), ($\mathcal{R}$) "MadeOf" and (C_2) *gyūniku* (beef). However, only in this case precision was lower for $\mathcal{R}$ (C_1, C_2) retrievals (see Table 2).

To improve recall, using only two elements in one sentence is better. However we believe that if the task is to decrease number of assertions for human evaluation, precision is more important. Insufficient corpus and too few appropriate clue words seem to be two main remaining problems. The former is relatively easier to solve by further extension of web-crawling process. On the other hand, the latter is difficult because a concept often depends on context and there is no universal clue word to cover all cases. For example, (C_1) *memo* (note), ($\mathcal{R}$) "UsedFor", and (C_2), *monooboe* (memorizing) did not occur in the corpus together as (C_1, $\mathcal{R}$, C_2), but when we checked (C_1, C_2), the following sentence was found: *Monooboe-no ii hito-hodo memo-wo toru* (The faster learner the more notes he takes). Theoretically we could utilize the verb *toru* (to take) as "UsedFor" clue word for finding other assertions, but this would cause substantial amount of noise because the semantic scope of "to take" is too wide. (C_1) *ōbun* (oven), ($\mathcal{R}$) "UsedFor", and (C_2) *pan-wo yaku* (to bake a bread), did not occur in any sentence. Similarly, in *Haitte sugu, me-no mae-niwa pan-wo yaku obun* (Soon after you enter, in front of you, there will be an oven for baking bread), it would be better to use *yaku* (to bake) instead of *tsukau* (to use).

As shown in the previous section, annotators' evaluation scores differ largely, therefore it is difficult to unambiguously determine if a given evaluation is commonsensical or not. In order to see if the system can be more precise, we repeated evaluation with removed clearly doubtful assertions which were judged from 4 - 7 (see Table 5, 6, 7). Results indicate that with this restriction in "All Elements" method can reach higher precision for all three relations and that "All Elements" achieved higher precision than "Concepts only" method. Consequently, as shown in Table 2, we managed to confirm that the reason why precision of "All Elements" method was lower than in the case of "Concepts Only" method is that annotators' evaluations were highly inconsistent.

To see if we can improve f-score without losing precision, we used separate C-$\mathcal{R}$ pairs for retrieval. For "MadeOf" and "UsedFor" relations, our system counted (C_1, $\mathcal{R}$) and (C_2, $\mathcal{R}$) in the corpus. For ($\mathcal{R}$) "AtLocation", we set *iku* (to go), *kuru* (to come), and *hataraku* (to work) as $\mathcal{R}$ relations, and this method shows capability to improve f-score of the automatic evaluation of assertions. If both expressions (C_1, $\mathcal{R}$) and (C_2, $\mathcal{R}$) occur in the corpus separately, it increases possibility that a given assertion is commonsensical. The results (see Table 8) show that For ($\mathcal{R}$)"MadeOf" and ($\mathcal{R}$) "UsedFor", f-score is higher than for "All Elements" method, but it did not reach the level of "Concepts Only" method. However, for ($\mathcal{R}$) "AtLocation", f-score is relatively higher than other two methods. This shows that whether C_2 stands for place or not plays an important role in evaluating assertions.

7 Conclusion and Future Work

Commonsense knowledge evaluation task is harder than commonsense knowledge acquisition, because for the latter you can acquire relatively high quality as errors look like a small fraction of all retrievals and there is a tendency for ignoring them. However, for evaluation task, more precise judgement is needed

Table 5: Evaluation results for "MadeOf" relations ("All Elements" and "Concepts Only" methods) without doubtful assertions.

MadeOf	Accuracy	Precision	Recall	F-score
All Elements Method (C_1, R, C_2)	0.464	**0.870**	0.426	0.571
Concepts Only Method (C_1, C_2)	0.679	0.837	0.766	0.800

Table 6: Evaluation results for "UsedFor" relations ("All Elements" and "Concepts Only" methods) without doubtful assertions.

UsedFor	Accuracy	Precision	Recall	F-score
All Elements Method (C_1, R, C_2)	0.479	**1.00**	0.390	0.561
Concepts Only Method (C_1, C_2)	0.667	0.903	0.682	0.778

Table 7: Evaluation results for "AtLocation" relations ("All Elements" and "Concepts Only" methods) without doubtful assertions.

UsedFor	Accuracy	Precision	Recall	F-score
All Elements Method (C_1, R, C_2)	0.547	**0.765**	0.342	0.473
Concepts Only Method (C_1, C_2)	0.594	0.630	0.763	0.690

Table 8: Evaluation results for each relations when (C_1, R) and (C_2, R) were used.

Relation Method	Accuracy	Precision	Recall	F-score
MadeOf (C_1, R) and (C_2, R)	0.620	0.786	0.705	0.743
UsedFor (C_1, R) and (C_2, R)	0.550	0.872	0.513	0.646
AtLocation (C_2, R)	0.590	0.619	0.696	0.650

to deal not only with those errors from acquisition systems but also with often wrong input from human annotators.

In this paper we present a new text-mining approach for automatic commonsense knowledge evaluation. "All Elements" method using both concepts and their relation achieved precision of over 70% on average for the three following ConceptNet relations: "MadeOf" (78.0%), "UsedFor" (100.0%) and "AtLocation" (61.5%). We described how different concepts and relation combinations can be utilized and showed their strengths and weaknesses. From the error analysis we revealed main problems which are database contributors originality, the insufficient corpus size, discrepancies in evaluators' opinions, and setting proper clue words. Especially the first problem shows that it is often hard to evaluate concepts stored in their current form. To solve it, instead of using a concept as it is, its more frequently used synonymic concepts should be utilized. For example, in the case of assertion (C_1) *shōmei kigu* (lighting equipment), (R) "MadeOf", and (C_2) *garasu* (glass), our system could search for "lamp" instead of the "lighting equipment" (there were 11 hits instead of 0 when we tried this for "All Elements" method). In near future, we plan to increase the number of annotators, because commonsense knowledge differs depending on subjects and their particular experiences. We will also experiment with different clue words for higher recall without losing precision.

Our methods are also planned to be utilized in commonsense knowledge acquisition system as its self-evaluation module. We are also going to test our idea in different languages used in ConceptNet.

References

Francis Bond, Hitoshi Isahara, Sanae Fujita, Kiyotaka Uchimoto, Takayuki Kuribayashi, and Kyoko Kanzaki. 2009. Enhancing the Japanese WordNet. In *Proceedings of the 7th workshop on Asian language resources*, pages 1–8. Association for Computational Linguistics.

Andrew Carlson, Justin Betteridge, Bryan Kisiel, Burr Settles, Estevam R Hruschka Jr, and Tom M Mitchell. 2010. Toward and architecture for Never-Ending Language Learning. In *AAAI*, volume 5, page 3.

Hyemin Chung. 2006. *GlobalMind- -Bridging the Gap Between Different Cultures and Languages with Common-sense Computing*. Ph.D. thesis, Massachusetts Institute of Technology.

Jonathan Gordon, Benjamin Van Durme, and Lenhart K Schubert. 2010. Evaluation of commonsense knowledge with Mechanical Turk. In *Proceedings of the NAACL HLT 2010 Workshop on Creating Speech and Language Data with Amazon's Mechanical Turk*, pages 159–162. Association for Computational Linguistics.

Douglas B Lenat. 1995. Cyc: A large-scale investment in knowledge infrastructure. *Communications of the ACM*, 38(11):33–38.

Kazuhiro Nakahara and Shigeo Yamada. 2011. Development and evaluation of a Web-based game for common-sense knowledge acquisition in Japan (in Japanese). *Unisys Technology Review*, (107):295–305.

Stellan Ohlsson, Robert H Sloan, György Turán, Daniel Uber, and Aaron Urasky. 2012. An approach to evaluate AI commonsense reasoning systems. In *FLAIRS Conference*, pages 371–374.

Michal Ptaszynski, Pawel Dybala, Rafal Rzepka, Kenji Araki, and Yoshio Momouchi. 2012. Annotating affective information on 5.5 billion word corpus of Japanese blogs. In *Proceedings of The 18th Annual Meeting of The Association for Natural Language Processing (NLP*.

Rafal Rzepka, Koichi Muramoto, and Kenji Araki. 2011. Generality evaluation of automatically generated knowl-edge for the Japanese ConceptNet. In *Australasian Joint Conference on Artificial Intelligence*, pages 648–657. Springer.

Lenhart Schubert. 2002. Can we derive general world knowledge from texts? In *Proceedings of the second in-ternational conference on Human Language Technology Research*, pages 94–97. Morgan Kaufmann Publishers Inc.

Push Singh, Thomas Lin, Erik T Mueller, Grace Lim, Travell Perkins, and Wan Li Zhu. 2002. Open Mind Com-mon Sense: Knowledge acquisition from the general public. In *OTM Confederated International Conferences "On the Move to Meaningful Internet Systems"*, pages 1223–1237. Springer.

Robert Speer and Catherine Havasi. 2012. Representing General Relational Knowledge in ConceptNet 5. In *LREC*, pages 3679–3686.

Niket Tandon, Gerard de Melo, Fabian Suchanek, and Gerhard Weikum. 2014. WebChild: harvesting and orga-nizing commonsense knowledge from the Web. In *Proceedings of the 7th ACM international conference on Web search and data mining*, pages 523–532. ACM.

SAMER: A Semi-Automatically Created Lexical Resource for Arabic Verbal Multiword Expressions Tokens Paradigm and their Morphosyntactic Features

Mohamed Al-Badrashiny, Abdelati Hawwari, Mahmoud Ghoneim, and Mona Diab
Department of Computer Science, The George Washington University
{badrashiny,abhawwari,mghoneim,mtdiab}@gwu.edu

Abstract

Although *MWE* are relatively morphologically and syntactically fixed expressions, several types of flexibility can be observed in *MWE*, verbal *MWE* in particular. Identifying the degree of morphological and syntactic flexibility of *MWE* is very important for many Lexicographic and NLP tasks. Adding *MWE* variants/tokens to a dictionary resource requires characterizing the flexibility among other morphosyntactic features. Carrying out the task manually faces several challenges since it is a very laborious task time and effort wise, as well as it will suffer from coverage limitation. The problem is exacerbated in rich morphological languages where the average word in Arabic could have 12 possible inflection forms. Accordingly, in this paper we introduce a semi-automatic Arabic multiwords expressions resource (SAMER). We propose an automated method that identifies the morphological and syntactic flexibility of Arabic Verbal Multiword Expressions (*AVMWE*). All observed morphological variants and syntactic pattern alternations of an *AVMWE* are automatically acquired using large scale corpora. We look for three morphosyntactic aspects of *AVMWE* types investigating derivational and inflectional variations and syntactic templates, namely: 1) inflectional variation (inflectional paradigm) and calculating degree of flexibility; 2) derivational productivity; and 3) identifying and classifying the different syntactic types. We build a comprehensive list of *AVMWE*. Every token in the *AVMWE* list is lemmatized and tagged with POS information. We then search Arabic Gigaword and All ATBs for all possible flexible matches. For each *AVMWE* type we generate: a) a statistically ranked list of *MWE*-lexeme inflections and syntactic pattern alternations; b) An abstract syntactic template; and c) The most frequent form. Our technique is validated using a Golden *MWE* annotated list. The results shows that the quality of the generated resource is 80.04%.

1 Introduction

Multiword expressions (*MWE*) are complex lexemes that contain at least two words reflecting a single concept. They can be morphologically and syntactically fixed expressions but also we note that they can exhibit flexibility especially in verbal *MWE*. Such morphosyntactic flexibility increases difficulties in computational processing of *MWE* as they are harder to detect. Characterizing the internal structure of *MWE* is considered very important for many natural language processing tasks such as syntactic parsing and applications such as machine translation (Ghoneim and Diab, 2013; Carpuat and Diab, 2010). In lexicography, entries for *MWE* in a lexicon should provide a description of the syntactic behavior of the *MWE* constructions, such as syntactic peculiarities and morphosyntactic constraints (Calzolari et al., 2002). Automatically identifying the syntactic patterns and listing/detecting their possible variations would help in lexicographic representation of *MWE*, as the manual annotation of *MWE* variants suffer from many disadvantages such as time and effort consuming, subjectivity and limited coverage.

The problem is exacerbated for morphologically rich languages, where an average word could have up to 12 morphological analyses such as the case for the Arabic language which is highly inflectional.

Proceedings of the 12th Workshop on Asian Language Resources,
pages 113–122, Osaka, Japan, December 12 2016.

Several challenges are encountered in automatic identification and parsing of *MWE* in Arabic especially verbal ones, because of their highly morphosyntactic flexibility.

This paper focuses on the Arabic verbal *MWE*(*AVMWE*) in Modern Standard Arabic (MSA). We broadly consider a *MWE* as a verbal one if it contains at least one verb in its elements. We focus exclusively on the flexibility of the elements existing in the *AVMWE* and their syntactic alternatives. Lexical flexibility (word/word) is meant to be outside the scope of this paper (Ex. *rajaE bixuf~ayo Hunayon*[1] Vs. *EAd bixuf~ayo Hunayon* where both expressions mean **return empty handed**).

From a theoretical point of view, we identify four components, for each *AVMWE* as shown in Table 1. The verbal components are any verb within a *MWE*. Elements are the non-verbal components such as noun, adjective or particle. The syntactic variable is a slot that reflects the syntactic function in a *MWE* without being itself a part of the construction, and the gaps are some inserted modifiers that might occur between *MWE* elements (Hawwari et al., 2014).

	Verbal component	Gap	Syntactic variable	Element-1	Element-2	Element-3	Syntactic variable
BW	>aEoTaY	>amosi	(FulAnN)	AlDawo'	Al>axoDar	li-	(FulAnK)
En-Gloss	gave	yesterday	(somebody)	the-light	the-green	to	(something/somebody)
En-translation	(somebody) gave the green light to (somebody/something)						

Table 1: Example for the entities we are considering within a *MWE*

The main objective of our work is to automatically acquire all observed morphological variants and syntactic pattern alternations of a *MWE* using large scale corpora, using an empirical method to identify the morphological and syntactic flexibility of *AVMWE*.

2   Related Work

A considerable amount of literature has been published on the morphosyntactic characteristics of *MWE* . These studies focused on various morphological aspects, within different contexts on different languages. Gurrutxaga and Alegria (2012) and Baldwin et al. (2003) applied latent semantic analysis to build a model of multiword expression decomposability. This model measures the similarity between a multiword expression and its elements words, and considers the constructions with higher similarities are greater decomposability.

Diab and Bhutada (2009) present a supervised learning approach to classify the idiomaticity of the Verb-Noun Constructions (VNC) depending on context in running text.

Savary (2008) presents a comparative survey of eleven lexical representation approaches to the inflectional aspects in *MWE* in different languages, including English, French, Polish Serbian German, Turkish and Basque.

Al-Haj et al. (2013) applied to Modern Hebrew an architecture for lexical representation of MWEs. The goal was to integrate system that can morphologically process Hebrew multiword expressions of various types, in spite of the complexity of Hebrew morphology and orthography.

Zaninello and Nissim (2010) present three electronic lexical resources for Italian *MWE*. They created a series of example corpora and a database of *MWE* modeled around morphosyntactic patterns.

Nissim and Zaninello (2013) employed variation patterns to deal with morphological variation in order to create a lexicon and a repository of variation patterns for *MWE* in morphologically-rich Romance languages.

Al-Sabbagh et al. (2013) describe the construction of a lexicon of Arabic Modal Multiword Expressions and a repository for their variation patterns. They used an unsupervised approach to build a lexicon for Arabic Modal Multiword Expressions and a repository for their variation patterns. The lexicon contains 10,664 entries of MSA and Egyptian modal *MWE* and collocation, linked to the repository.

The closest work to ours is that of (Hawwari et al., 2012). They created a list of different types of Arabic *MWE* collected from various dictionaries which were manually annotated and grouped based on their syntactic type. The main goal was to tag a large scale corpus of Arabic text using a pattern-

---

[1] We use Buckwalter transliteration encoding for Arabic: http://www.qamus.org/transliteration.htm

matching algorithm and automatically annotated to enrich and syntactically classify the given *MWE* list. Their work didn't approach the derivational or lexical aspects.

To the best of our knowledge, to date, none of the previous addressed the systematic investigation of morphosyntactic features and derivational productivity of *AVMWE* and their syntactic properties.

3 Linguistic Background

This section gives a brief overview of the linguistic background of the verbal inflectional and derivational system in Modern Standard Arabic.

3.1 Arabic Verbal MWE (AVMWE)

The verbal *MWE* is a *MWE* that includes a verb or more within its word elements. *AVMWE* could be classified, according to their lexical nature, into three types:

- Verbal Idioms: We mean by verbal Idiom any idiomatic expression that has a verb within its components. An example of verbal idiom is as follows: *taraka (fulAnN) Al-jamala bi-maA Hamala*[2]. [**(someone) left every thing behind**]

- Light verb (support verb): a light verb construction is consisting of: a) a verb that is semantically light, and b) a noun or verbal-noun carries the core meaning of the construction. *>axa* (fulAnN) Al-v >ora* [**(someone take a revenge**]

- Verb Particle construction: An expression includes a verb and a particle that they have together a meaning. (this construction includes phrasal verbs): *ragiba (fulAnN) fi* [**wish for**]

A *MWE* is considered flexible when it has more than one accepted inflected or syntactic form. Flexibility can be applied to inflectional, derivational, syntactic and lexical aspects of a MWE. We roughly distinguish between flexibility and idiomaticity as follows: flexibility affects the morphosyntactic properties, and idiomaticity is more related to the compositionality and semantic content of an *MWE*.

Inflection is a morphological subfield that belongs to single words encoding its inflectional categories (number, gender, person, case, tense, voice, mood, aspect) using several affixes to represent the morphosyntactic variation. Inflectional flexibility of an *MWE* is a sum of the inflectional flexibility of its elements.

A *MWE* token instance includes every possible inflectional variation form of the *MWE* type that can occur in a corpus. On the other hand, a *MWE* type is the canonical (citation) form that is used to be the basic form representing all the possible tokens of a *MWE* lexeme. Lexicographers chose the simplest form to be a canonical form serving as a head word or citation form for a lexical entry. By an *MWE* lexeme we refer to all the possible inflectional forms that are observed for the *MWE* in a corpus.

3.2 Inflectional Categories

The Arabic verb has the following inflectional categories:

- Tense: perfective, imperfective, imperative

- Voice: active, passive

- Mood: indicative (*marofuwE*), subjunctive (*manoSuwb*), jussive (*majozuwm*)

However, verb subject inflects for person (first, second, third person), gender (masculine, feminine), number (singular, dual, plural) and syntactic case (nominative (*marofuwE*), accusative (*manoSuwb*), genitive (*majoruwr*)).

AVMWE vary in their inflectional flexibility degree. One group is fixed, for example *Had~ivo wa-lA Haraj* (**speak freely**), second group has a degree of flexibility as *>aTolaq (fulAnN) sAqyohi li-AlryiH* (**ran away**), the verb *>aTolaq* is fully flexible for any affixes (*>aTlaqA, >aTlaquw, >aTlaqato*, etc).

---

[2]We use Buckwalter transliteration scheme to represent Arabic in Romanized script throughout the paper. http://www.qamus.org/transliteration.htm

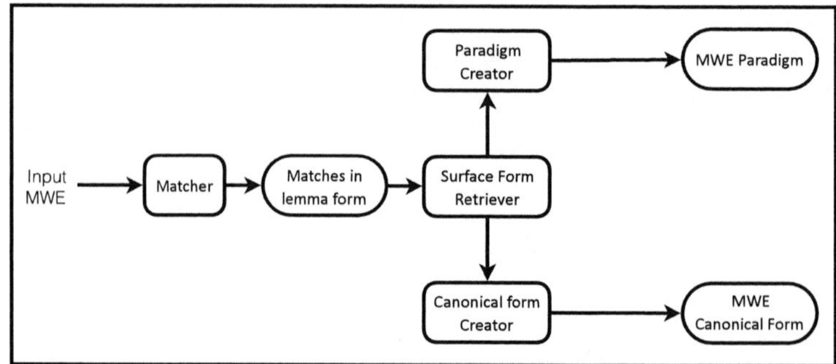

Figure 1: MWE paradigm and canonical form finder pipeline: MPD.

3.3 Derivational Productivity

Derivation is a very productive and regular word-formation mechanism in the Arabic language. Unlike inflection, derivation belongs to the lexicon and is completely syntax independent. As *AVMWE* vary in productivity, some allow verbal derivations, for example *fAza bi-qaSabi Alsaboqi* (**he came first/he is the winner**) allows the derived nominal *MWE fA}izN bi-qaSabi Alsaboqi*, where the verb *fAza* is derivationally related to the noun *fA}izN*. On the other hand, there are many *AVMWE* that are fixed derivationally as they do not exhibit derivational productivity for example *>aSobaH ha$iymaF ta*oruw-hu AlriyAHu* (**vanish**).

3.4 Syntactic flexibility

As it is a Verb Phrase (VP), *AVMWE* is governed by VP grammatical rules and operations such as word order, agreement, government. Syntactic flexibility for an *MWE* occurs in texts in different configurations. Some of *AVMWE* have some degree of syntactic flexibility, which appears in word order variability for a given *MWE* (VSO: *balag Alsayolu AlzubaY* (**it reached the limits**), SVO: *Alsayolu balag AlzubaY*). Although word order in Arabic is relatively free, the word-order flexibility in *AVMWE* occurs rarely, because the *AVMWE* phrases are more rigid than ordinary phrases syntactically. An example for the syntactic fixed *AVMWE* is *AixotalaTa AlHAbilu biAln~Abili* (**it became a mess**).

4 Approach

We introduce an automatic approach for building a morphosyntactic lexicon for Arabic verbal *MWE* starting from a gold seed list. We use a manually created list of Arabic verbal *MWE* and try to find all possible matches with any morphological variations in a large dataset in a process of *MWE* Paradigm detection (MPD). After that we create the morphosyntactic feature vector of each match and calculate the level of flexibility of each *MWE*.

Figure 1 illustrates the different components of the MPD system. For each new *MWE* expression in seed list, the "Matcher" component replaces each word in the input *MWE* with its lemma to find all possible inflections for the *MWE* during the matching process. Since deverbals such as verbal nouns, past participle active, and past participle passive inherit the semantic and syntactic structures from their verbs they are derived from, the "Matcher" component adds the derivatives of each verb in the input *MWE* as possible matching candidates in addition to its lemma. Technically these are derivational variants. That way, we can find all possible forms of the input *MWE* during the matching process. For example, if the input is the *MWE* "*fAz biqaSabi Alsaboqi* meaning **he is the winner**", it will be matched with "*fAzuw biqaSabi Alsaboqi* meaning **the winning**" and "*fA}izN biqaSabi Alsaboqi* meaning **the winner**", reflecting inflectional variation with *fAz* being observed as *fAzuw* in the former, and derivational variation with *fAz* being observed as *fA}izN* in the latter.

The "Matcher" looks up the new form of the MWE (i.e. the lemma form with the different verb derivatives candidates) in large preprocessed datasets that are described in section 5.2 below while enabling any possibility of gapping between the words (Ex. *fAz Alwalad biqaSabi Alsaboqi* **the boy is the winner**) or word ordering (Ex. *waqaEa fiy HaySa bayoSa*. Or *fiy HaySa bayoSa waqaEa* **got confused**).

The preprocessed datasets have a one-to-one mapping between the input surface form of each sentence and its corresponding lemma form. Thus, the "Surface Form Retriever" component uses that to find the original surface form of each sentence retrieved by the "Matcher" component. The "Paradigm Creator" component generates a unique list of all surface form sentences retrieved by the "Surface Form Retriever" component to create a list of all possible morphological variations of the input *MWE*. To make the list as generic as possible, we replace each word that is not part of the MWE with its POS tag. The "Canonical Form Creator" after that uses the full list of sentences created by the the "Surface Form Retriever" component and finds the most frequent matched form of the input *MWE*

For each word in the matched *MWE*, we create a morphosyntactic feature vector of nine elements that are being extracted from the POS tags of the matched *MWE*.The first element is the POS. Three elements (aspect, voice, mood) are only for verbs, while nominals have the following attributes (case, state), and (person, number, gender) apply to all words. In addition to that, we try to identify the candidate subject and object for each match as follows:

- Subject: The candidate subject is identified as the pronoun attached to the verb if it is explicitly mentioned in the pos of the verb, otherwise it is the first nominative nominal after the verb;

- Object: The candidate object is identified as the pronoun attached to the verb if it is explicitly mentioned in the pos of the verb. Otherwise it is the first accusative nominal after the verb.

5 Experimental Setup

5.1 Datasets

We use different types of datasets to evaluate our approach for creating the *MWE* token paradigm resource.

Corpora used for the resource creation:

- *ATB*: The Arabic Treebanks.   The selected *ATBs* represent three different genres: Newswire;[3] Broadcast News;[4] and, Weblogs;[5]

- *Gigawords*: The Arabic Gigaword fourth edition;[6]

- *AVMWE*: Is a list of more about 4000 verbal *MWE* semi automatically extracted from two traditional Arabic Monolingual Dictionaries;

- *Verbs-to-Derivatives*: Is a list of 10k MSA verbs and their possible derivations. It is developed to help our system recognize the derivational relations between verbs and their nominal counterparts (Active participle, passive participle and Gerund) (Hawwari et al., 2013).

Evaluation Datasets:

- *DevDB*: 2000 randomly selected lines from the *ATB* and *Gigawords* used for system tuning;

- *TstDB*: 2000 randomly selected lines from the *ATB* and *Gigawords* used for system evaluation.

Both *DevDB* and *TstDB* are manually annotated. Each line is annotated with a presence/absence tag indicating whether an *MWE* from the *AVMWE* list or not. If a line is annotated as having an *MWE*, all of the elements of this *MWE* are annotated and the number of gaps between each two elements is identified. Table 2 shows the annotation distribution of both datasets

---

[3] ATB-P1-V4.1(LDC2010T13),ATB-P2-V3.1 (LDC2011T09) and ATB-P3-V3.2 (LDC2010T08)

[4] ATB-P5-V1.0 (LDC2009E72), ATB-P7-V1.0 (LDC2009E114), ATB-P10-V1.0 (LDC2010E22) and ATB-P12-V2.0 (LDC2011E17)

[5] ATB6-v1.0(LDC2009E108) and ATB11-v2.0(LDC2011E16)

[6] LDC2009T30

	Has-MWE	No-MWE
DevDB	42.85%	57.15%
TstDB	45.55%	54.45%

Table 2: *MWE* Annotation distribution across the evaluation datasets.

5.2 Data Preparation

To enable matching based on Lemma and POS, we processed the *ATB* and *Gigawords* into a a series of tuples with the following elements: "Token-Lemma-POS". For *ATB*, we extracted this format from the gold analysis in the integrated files. For *Gigawords*, we used *MADAMIRA* toolkit (Pasha et al., 2014) for tokenization, lemmatization and POS tagging. The selected tokenization scheme is ATB-tokenization and the POS tag-set is *ATB* full tag-set. The *AVMWE* was also processed using *MADAMIRA* to guarantee consistency in the matching process. *MADAMIRA* provides a list of possible analyses per word with the most probably one selected as the candidate analysis. Due to short context, the accuracy of the selected analysis by *MADAMIRA* wasn't high. Accordingly, we post-processed the list of possible analyses per word and selected the most probable analysis that matches the gold assigned coarse-grained POS.

6 Paradigm Detection Evaluation

We used the processed *AVMWE* list as the input gold *MWE* list to our paradigm detection system MPD. Also, *Verbs-to-Derivatives* is used to help the matching algorithm to match the derivatives of each verb in the input multi words expressions as well.

Table 3 shows the results of running the paradigm detector on *DevDB* with different schemes (i.e. different gapping sizes and with and without enabling word reordering). We report the results as the F-score of correctly tagging an *MWE* in *DevDB*, the F-score of correctly tagging the sentences that do not have *MWE*, and the weighted average F-score of both of them for all schemes. The results shows that the best weighted Average F-score is 80.61% when we allow a maximum gap size of 2 between the *MWE* constituent words and without enabling the word order to be varied.

By running the best setup on the *TstDB*, we found that the weighted average F-score is 80.04%

| | with-words-reordering | | | without-words-reordering | | |
Max-Gap-Size	MWE tagging	No-MWE tagging	Avg-Fscore	MWE tagging	No-MWE tagging	Avg-Fscore
0	66.62%	81.75%	75.27%	65.80%	81.75%	74.92%
1	75.14%	82.34%	79.25%	73.81%	83.29%	79.23%
2	77.40%	80.39%	79.11%	77.09%	83.25%	**80.61%**
4	73.87%	70.30%	71.83%	76.20%	79.89%	78.31%
8	68.39%	52.53%	59.33%	73.42%	74.07%	73.79%
16	63.15%	26.02%	41.93%	69.94%	66.24%	67.83%
32	60.64%	5.93%	29.37%	68.04%	61.45%	64.27%
65	60.08%	0.70%	26.14%	67.82%	60.67%	63.73%
any	59.99%	0.00%	25.71%	67.82%	60.67%	63.73%

Table 3: F-score of correctly tagging the *MWE* in *DevDB* and the F-score of correctly tagging the sentences that do not have *MWE* with different experimental setups.

6.1 Error Analysis

Type	%
gap	31.23%
order	20.15%
pp-attachment	20.15%
polysemous	17.88%
MADAMIRA	6.55%
literal	3.53%
Eval-err	0.25%
Syn-function	0.25%

Table 4: Paradigm detector error analysis

Table 4 shows the error distribution of the paradigm detector on the *TstDB*. We can see that limiting the maximum gapping size to two and disabling word reordering while matching are the main sources of errors. Together they are responsible for 51.38% of the errors, which suggests that the gap size and word reordering should be more flexible. We should have some smarter way to decide the gapping size and words reordering status per *MWE* type; not by generalizing them on all types. For example *"ya>oxu* bi+ Eayon AlAiEotibAr* means **considers**" did not match with *"ta>oxu* mA TuriH fiy mu&otamar AlmanAmap bi+ Eayon Aljid~iyap wa+ AlAiEotibAr"* because of the gapping size restriction. And *"ba*al jahodi +h* means **did his effort**" did not match with *"Aljuhuwd Altiy tabo*ulul +hA"* because the word reordering is disabled.

Another challenging problem responsible for 20.15% of the errors is the verb particle construction; where a certain verb when attached to a certain preposition, they act like an *MWE*. This issue is that while matching, it is hard to know if a certain preposition should be attached to the target verb or another one. This leads to false identification for the match if the decision of the attachment was not correct. Ex: *"yajib EalaY +h* means **he should be**" incorrectly matched with *"yajib >n yaEoqid EalaY >roDihi* **he has to held on his land**" because *EalaY* is considered attached to *"yajib"* while it is actually attached to *yaEoqid* as it assumed a gapping of two words, while it should have attached the particle to the low, second and closest verb *yaEoqid*.

Polysemy is also a hard problem. It is responsible for 17.88% of the errors. Errors due polysemy occur when words in the input *MWE* type have more than one meaning. But since the matching process only takes the lemma and POS into account and word senses are not part of the matching, the paradigm detector could tag some cases as valid matches. Ex:*"Hayovu kAn* meaning **wherever**" is incorrectly matched with *"Hayovu kAn AlAibonu yaloEab* meaning **because the sone was playing**". The issue came from the word *Hayovu* that means **where** or **because**.

The morphological analyzer and POS tagger (*MADAMIRA*) is the source of 6.55% of the errors. When *MADAMIRA* incorrectly analyzes some words, some wrong matches occur. Ex: *"*ahabat riyHu +hu* means **has been forgotten**" did not match with *"*ahabot riyHi +hu"* because *MADAMIRA* analyzed the word *"*ahabat* means **gone**" as *"*ahabot* means **I went**"

3.53% of the errors are due to the *MWE* being idiomatic in some contexts and literal in others. Ex. *"tajAwaz Huduwd +hu"* meaning "**Exceeded his limits**" incorrectly matched *"tatajAwaz AlHuduwd AljugorAfiy~ap"* meaning "**Transcended the geographic boundaries**"

The remaining 0.5% errors are due to some minor issues: 0.25% errors are due to manual annotation errors, while the other 0.25% errors are due to fact that the matched morphological variant from the input *MWE* has a different syntactic function than the input *MWE*. Ex. *"HAwal EabavAF"* meaning "**Tried in vain**" is incorrectly matched with *"yHAwl AlEbv"* meaning "**Attempted to tamper with**". This is because the word *"EabavAF"* which is an adverb is a derivation of the noun *"AlEbv"* which plays the role of an object in this verb noun construction.

7 SAMER

To build the proposed Arabic *MWE* resource, we ran the paradigm detector on the *ATB* and *Gigawords* using the best configuration we found. The system found 732335 matches for 1884 *MWE* out of the 4000

MWE in the input *AVMWE* list.

The automatically created resource is reflected in the following five tables:

- All matches table: Contains the 732335 matches that are automatically detected by the paradigm detector and pointers to their original locations in the *ATB* and *Gigawords*;

- Flexibility table: This table has the 1884 rows representing the types of *MWE* that the paradigm detector found matches for. The columns represent the words of the *MWE* where the value of each cell shows the number of different forms that this element matched with. For example if a certain cell has the number "5", this means that its corresponding word matched with five different unique morphological variants;

- MWE-Lexeme table: This table shows the different morphological forms of each word in each *MWE* and their probabilities that are identified by the paradigm detector;

- Sorted-Grouped-tokens table: Shows the probability of all matches of each *MWE* in a descending order. So, if there is a *MWE* that has 10 matches, we calculate the unique form for each of them and find the probability of each unique value. The number of grouped types of all matches is 38408;

- MWE-Types table: this table has1884 rows; one row for each *MWE* type. The columns show number of matches, the most frequent token with its probability, and the union of the morphosyntactic features of each word across all tokens of each *MWE* type. Example: if the union of the gender of the second word across all matches of *MWE* number i is {M,F}; this means that the second word of the *MWE* number i has a flexibility to change the gender between masculine or feminine.

7.1 Statistical Analyses

The number of the *MWE* types in our automatically created resource is 1884. They consist of 1901 unique verbal words and 3104 unique non-verbal words. Each type of the 1884 *MWE* has an average fan out of 20 different forms due to the morphological or inflectional changes the *MWE* words.

The results show that 15.5% of the *MWE* types do not allow any gaps between the constituent words (No-Gaps), while 52.1% of the *MWE* types allow gapping between all the constituent words (Full-Gaps) and the remaining 32.4% of the types allow gapping only between some of the constituent words (Part-Gaps).
Examples:

- No-Gaps: "*dub~ira bi+ layolK* meaning **conspired**" matched with "*dub~ira bi+ layolK*"

- Full-Gaps: "*ka\$af AlqinAE Ean* meaning **unveiled** " matched using one gap between the first two words with "*ka\$af b +h AlqnAE En* meaning **unveiled using it**" and using one gap between the second two words with "*tk\$f AlqnAE AlzA}f En* meaning **unveiled the fake thing**"

- Part-Gaps: "*ka\$~ar Ean >anoyAbi +h* meaning **express anger**" matched using one gap between the first two words with "*tuka\$~ir turokiyA Ean >anoyAbi +hA* meaning **Turkey expressed its anger**"

We found that 15.7% of the *MWE* types are fixed. They do not have any morphological or inflectional variations in all matched instances (Ex: *lA yaxoTuro bi+ bAlK* meaning **it will never come to your mind**). But the other 84.4% have a higher degree of flexibility that they can match with instances with different morphological or inflectional variations (Ex: *HAla duwna* that means **"prevented"** has a match with *tHwl duwna*). 4.7% of the matched verbal *MWE* types have matches with the derivatives of the verbal part (Ex: *kAl bi+ mikoyAlayon* meaning **"injustice"** is matched with *Alkyl bi+ mikoyAlayon*). Furthermore, the results show that non-verbal components of the *MWE* type have more tendency to stay fixed than the verbal parts. Since 51.7% of the non-verbal components stay fixed in all matched instances while only 17.7% of the verbs stay fixed.

Tables 5 and 6 show the morphosyntactic feature flexibility distribution for the non-verbal components and the verbal ones respectively across all *MWE* matches. The tables show that the mood is the most rigid feature (76.4% of the *MWE* types have fixed mood) while gender is the most flexible feature (87.08% of the *MWE* types have different values of the gender within the matched cases).

Feature	Fixed	Flexible
gender	87.08%	12.92%
number	85.18%	14.82%
case	56.28%	43.72%
state	63.66%	36.34%

Table 5: Morphosyntactic feature flexibility of the non-verbal components of all *MWE* types

Feature	Fixed	Flexible
aspect	27.7%	72.3%
voice	82.9%	17.1%
mood	23.6%	76.4%

Table 6: Morphosyntactic feature flexibility of the verbal components of all *MWE* types

8 Conclusion

We introduced an automatically built *MWE* resource that covers all the morphological variations of a list of *AVMWE* in the basic form. Each morphological variant is accompanied with all of its instances in the *ATB* and Arabic *Gigawords*. Furthermore, for each word in the *MWE*, we added a morphosyntactic feature vector of nine elements {pos, aspect, voice, mood, person, gender, number, case, state)}. We validated our approach constructing an automatic *MWE* paradigm detector in running text. Our system yielded an weighted average f-score of 80.61% on a dev set, and 80.04% on an unseen test data. The error analysis shows that there is no generalized maximum gapping size, and enabling or disabling word reordering decisions should not be generalized on all *MWE* in the input list. Instead, more sophisticated techniques are required to find the best decisions for each case.

References

Hassan Al-Haj, Alon Itai, and Shuly Wintner. 2013. Lexical representation of multiword expressions in morphologically-complex languages. *International Journal of Lexicography*, page ect036.

Rania Al-Sabbagh, Jana Diesner, and Roxana Girju. 2013. Using the semantic-syntactic interface for reliable arabic modality annotation. In *Proceedings of the Sixth International Joint Conference on Natural Language Processing*, pages 410–418, Nagoya, Japan, October. Asian Federation of Natural Language Processing.

Timothy Baldwin, Colin Bannard, Takaaki Tanaka, and Dominic Widdows. 2003. An empirical model of multiword expression decomposability. In *Proceedings of the ACL 2003 Workshop on Multiword Expressions: Analysis, Acquisition and Treatment - Volume 18*, MWE '03, pages 89–96, Stroudsburg, PA, USA. Association for Computational Linguistics.

Nicoletta Calzolari, Charles J Fillmore, Ralph Grishman, Nancy Ide, Alessandro Lenci, Catherine MacLeod, and Antonio Zampolli. 2002. Towards best practice for multiword expressions in computational lexicons. In *LREC*.

Marine Carpuat and Mona Diab. 2010. Task-based evaluation of multiword expressions: A pilot study in statistical machine translation. In *Human Language Technologies: The 2010 Annual Conference of the North American Chapter of the Association for Computational Linguistics*, HLT '10, pages 242–245, Stroudsburg, PA, USA. Association for Computational Linguistics.

Mona T. Diab and Pravin Bhutada. 2009. Verb noun construction mwe token supervised classification. In *Proceedings of the Workshop on Multiword Expressions: Identification, Interpretation, Disambiguation and Applications*, MWE '09, pages 17–22, Stroudsburg, PA, USA. Association for Computational Linguistics.

Mahmoud Ghoneim and Mona T Diab. 2013. Multiword expressions in the context of statistical machine translation. In *IJCNLP*, pages 1181–1187.

Antton Gurrutxaga and Iaki Alegria. 2012. Measuring the compositionality of nv expressions in basque by means of distributional similarity techniques. In Nicoletta Calzolari (Conference Chair), Khalid Choukri, Thierry Declerck, Mehmet U?ur Do?an, Bente Maegaard, Joseph Mariani, Asuncion Moreno, Jan Odijk, and Stelios Piperidis, editors, *Proceedings of the Eight International Conference on Language Resources and Evaluation (LREC'12)*, Istanbul, Turkey, may. European Language Resources Association (ELRA).

Abdelati Hawwari, Kfir Bar, and Mona Diab. 2012. Building an arabic multiword expressions repository. *Proc. of the 50th ACL*, pages 24–29.

Abdelati Hawwari, Wajdi Zaghouani, Tim O'Gorman, Ahmed Badran, and Mona Diab. 2013. Building a lexical semantic resource for arabic morphological patterns. In *Communications, Signal Processing, and their Applications (ICCSPA), 2013 1st International Conference on*, pages 1–6, Feb.

Abdelati Hawwari, Mohammed Attia, and Mona Diab. 2014. A framework for the classification and annotation of multiword expressions in dialectal arabic. *ANLP 2014*, page 48.

Malvina Nissim and Andrea Zaninello. 2013. Modeling the internal variability of multiword expressions through a pattern-based method. *ACM Transactions on Speech and Language Processing (TSLP)*, 10(2):7.

Arfath Pasha, Mohamed Al-Badrashiny, Mona Diab, Ahmed El Kholy, Ramy Eskander, Nizar Habash, Manoj Pooleery, Owen Rambow, and Ryan M. Roth. 2014. MADAMIRA: A Fast, Comprehensive Tool for Morphological Analysis and Disambiguation of Arabic. In *Proceedings of LREC*, Reykjavik, Iceland.

Agata Savary. 2008. Computational Inflection of Multi-Word Units, a contrastive study of lexical approaches. *Linguistic Issues in Language Technology*, 1(2):1–53.

Andrea Zaninello and Malvina Nissim. 2010. Creation of lexical resources for a characterisation of multiword expressions in italian. In Nicoletta Calzolari (Conference Chair), Khalid Choukri, Bente Maegaard, Joseph Mariani, Jan Odijk, Stelios Piperidis, Mike Rosner, and Daniel Tapias, editors, *Proceedings of the Seventh International Conference on Language Resources and Evaluation (LREC'10)*, Valletta, Malta, may. European Language Resources Association (ELRA).

Sentiment Analysis for Low Resource Languages:
A Study on Informal Indonesian Tweets

Tuan Anh Le, David Moeljadi
Division of Linguistics and Multilingual Studies
Nanyang Technological University
Singapore
{H130030,D001}@ntu.edu.sg

Yasuhide Miura, Tomoko Ohkuma
Fuji Xerox Co., Ltd.
6-1, Minatomirai, Nishi-ku,
Yokohama-shi, Kanagawa
{Yasuhide.Miura,
ohkuma.tomoko}@fujixerox.co.jp

Abstract

This paper describes our attempt to build a sentiment analysis system for Indonesian tweets. With this system, we can study and identify sentiments and opinions in a text or document computationally. We used four thousand manually labeled tweets collected in February and March 2016 to build the model. Because of the variety of content in tweets, we analyze tweets into eight groups in total, including pos(itive), neg(ative), and neu(tral). Finally, we obtained 73.2% accuracy with Long Short Term Memory (LSTM) without normalizer.

1   Introduction

Millions of internet users send, post, and share text messages every day via various platforms, such as online social networking service (Twitter, Facebook, etc.), instant messaging service (WhatsApp, Telegram, etc.), online blogs, and forums. One of them, Twitter, has become popular among computational linguistics and social science researchers since it supports a policy of open data access and provides a means of getting vast amounts of linguistic, network, and other forms of data from actual human behavior with relatively little effort. Researchers can use Twitter's Application Programming Interface (API) to get the tweets in text data using particular search terms for their research, such as sentiment analysis.

At Twitter,[1] users can sign up for free, choose a 'handle' or user name, get a profile, post 'tweets' or short messages of 140 characters maximum with '@' symbols followed by other user-handles if they want their tweets to appear on the other users' profiles, and add '#' symbols for topic indicators. Unlike Facebook, Twitter users broadcast their messages to anyone who chooses to "follow" them as a broadcast medium and the 140-character limit forces users to be brief and makes it easy for anyone reading and reviewing tweets.

Carley et al. (2015) notes that since its launch in 2006, Twitter has grown to 284 million monthly active users who send about 500 million tweets per day, 80% of which are from mobile devices (as of 2014). Indonesia was ranked as the fifth most tweeting country in 2014. The number of users is increasing and it is predicted that there will be 22.8 million users in 2019.[2] The capital city of Indonesia, Jakarta, is the worlds most active Twitter city,[3] ahead of Tokyo and London.[4] Therefore, tweets data can be a good source for research on Indonesian sentiment analysis.

One of the basic tasks for sentiment analysis is polarity classification, i.e. determining whether a given text expresses positive, negative, or neutral sentiment. Much research has been done to address the problem of sentiment analysis on Indonesian tweets. Aliandu (2013) conducted research on Indonesian tweet classification into three labels: positive, negative, and neutral, using emoticons for collecting sentiment-bearing tweets as proposed by Pak and Paroubek (2010). The conclusion is that Support Vector Machine

[1] twitter.com

[2] http://www.emarketer.com/Article/Southeast-Asia-Has-Among-Highest-Social-Network-Usage-World/1013275

[3] http://blogs.wsj.com/digits/2015/09/02/twitter-looks-to-indonesia-to-boost-growth/

[4] https://www.techinasia.com/indonesia-social-jakarta-infographic

Proceedings of the 12th Workshop on Asian Language Resources,
pages 123–131, Osaka, Japan, December 12 2016.

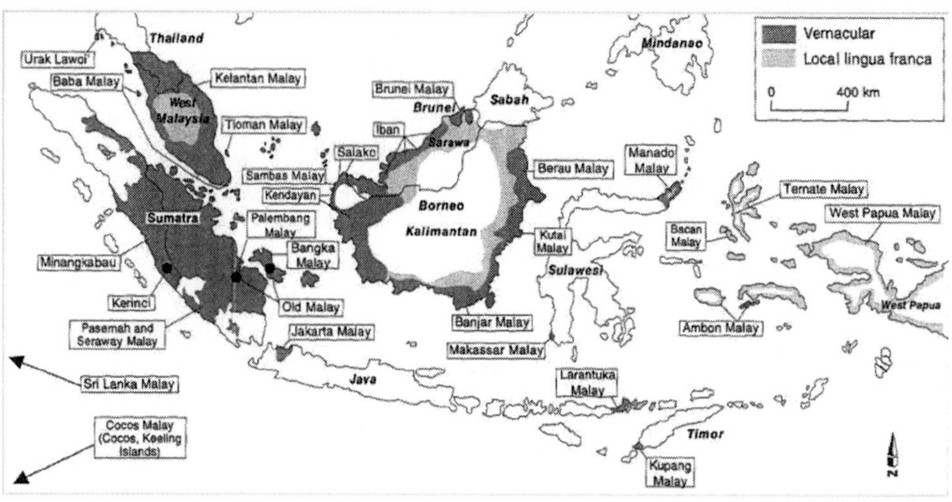

Figure 1: Malay dialects (Adelaar, 2010, p. 203)

(SVM) method (77.57% accuracy for TF-IDF and 77.79% for term frequency) was slightly better than Naive Bayes method (75.86% accuracy for TF-IDF and 77.45% for term frequency). Wicaksono et al. (2014) performed opinion tweet extraction and tweet polarity classification by automatically building a set of labeled seed corpus using opinion lexicon based technique and clustering based technique and obtaining more training instances from a huge set of unlabeled tweets by employing a classifier model. Their experiment shows that their method outperforms the baseline system which merely uses emoticons as the features for automatically building the sentiment corpus (81.13% accuracy with Naive Bayes and 86.82% accuracy with Maximum Entropy).

2   Indonesian language

Indonesian (ISO 639-3: ind), called *bahasa Indonesia* (lit. "the language of Indonesia") by its speakers, is a Western Malayo-Polynesian language of the Austronesian language family. Within this subgroup, it belongs to the Malayic branch with Standard Malay in Malaysia and other Malay varieties (Lewis, 2009) (see Figure 1). It is spoken mainly in the Republic of Indonesia as the sole official and national language and as the common language for hundreds of ethnic groups living there (Alwi et al., 2014, pp. 1-2). In Indonesia it is spoken by around 43 million people as their first language and by more than 156 million people as their second language (2010 census data). The lexical similarity is over 80% with Standard Malay (Lewis, 2009). It is written in Latin script.

Morphologically, Indonesian is a mildly agglutinative language, compared to Finnish or Turkish where the morpheme-per-word ratio is higher (Larasati et al., 2011). It has a rich affixation system, including a variety of prefixes, suffixes, circumfixes, and reduplication. Most of the affixes are derivational.

The diglossic nature of the Indonesian language exists from the very beginning of the historical record when it is called Old Malay around the seventh century A.D. to the present day (Paauw, 2009, p. 3). While much attention has been paid to the development and cultivation of the standard "High" variety of Indonesian, little attention has been particularly paid to describing and standardizing the "Low" variety of Indonesian. Sneddon (2006, pp. 4-6) calls this variety "Colloquial Jakartan Indonesian" and states that it is the prestige variety of colloquial Indonesian in Jakarta, the capital city of Indonesia, and is becoming the standard informal style. Paauw (2009, p. 40) mentions that Colloquial Jakartan Indonesian is a variety which has only been recognized as a separate variety recently. Historically, it developed from the Low Malay varieties spoken in Java by Chinese immigrant communities, which have been termed "Java Malay". It has also been influenced by the Betawi language of Jakarta, a Low Malay variety which is thought to have been spoken in the Jakarta region for over one thousand years.

In addition to this "Low" variety, the more than 500 regional languages spoken in various places in

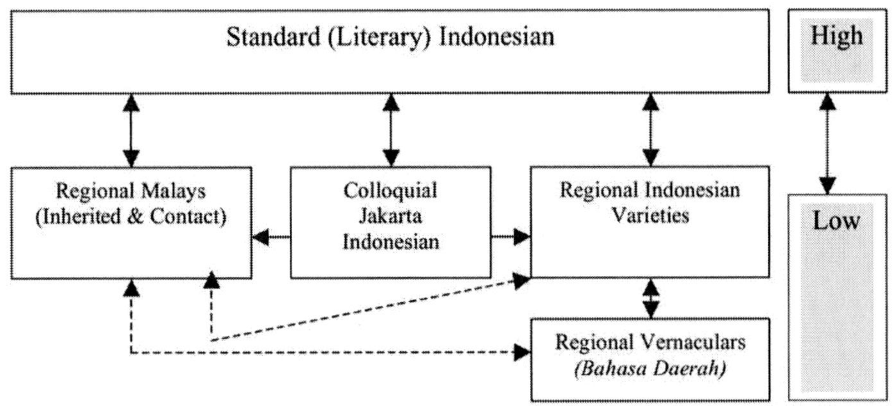

Figure 2: Diglossic situation in Indonesia (Paauw, 2009, p. 16)

Feature	Example
Abbreviation	*yg* (*yang* "REL"), *bsk* (*besok* "tomorrow"), *bw* (*bawa* "bring"), …
Interjection	*bhahaha* (*haha* "ha-ha"), *wkwk* (*haha* "ha-ha"), *yahhh* (*ya* "well"), …
Foreign word	ht (hot topic), Korean *nuna* "sister", Japanese *ggrks* (*gugurekasu* "google it, you trash"), …
Blending	*gamon* (*gagal* move on "fail to move on"), *ganchar* (*ganti* character "change the character"), *wotalay* (*wotaku alay* "exaggerative fan"), …
Emoji	☺, ☹, ●, …
Emoticon	:) , :(, ;v , …

Table 1: Features in Indonesian tweets

Indonesia add to the complexity of the sociolinguistic situation in Indonesia. The "High" variety of Indonesian is used in the context of education, religion, mass media, and government activities. The "Low" variety of Indonesian is used for everyday communication between Indonesians. The regional vernaculars (*bahasa daerah*) are used for communication at home with family and friends in the community. In some areas, Indonesian coexists with yet another regional lingua franca, which is often a Malay variety. For example, in the city of Kalabahi of Alor Island, locals speak Indonesian, Kupang Malay, and one of the local languages such as Abui in different contexts. This complex situation is well described in Paauw (2009) and shown in Figure 2.

3 Linguistic analysis of Indonesian tweets

Tweets in Indonesian reflect the diglossic nature of the Indonesian language, as mentioned in Section 2. In addition to the "High" and "Low" registers in spoken Indonesian, many informal features in contemporary written text appear, such as abbreviations, interjections, foreign words (sometimes abbreviated), blending of Indonesian and foreign words, emoji, and emoticons, as shown in Table 1. Interesting phenomena, such as word play, also appear, as shown in Table 2.

Type	Example	Note
Abbreviation	*semangka* "watermelon"	abbreviated from *semangat, kawan!* "do your best, my friend!"
Reversed word	*kuda* "horse"	reversed syllabically from *daku* "I"
	kuy	reversed letter by letter from *yuk* "let's"
Others	*udang* "shrimp"	made from informal word *udah* "already"

Table 2: Word play in Indonesian tweets

Below is an example of a tweet in Indonesian with some features mentioned above.

> @username @username makasih kk tfb yg paling hitz buat doa2nya :) amin yaallah aminnnn . Sukses juga buat band nya yahhh!

makasih "thanks" and *buat* "for" are low register words. *kk*, *tfb*, and *yg* are abbreviations of *kakak* "brother", True Friend Band, and *yang* "REL" respectively. *hitz* and *band* are English words. Reduplication is represented as number two "2" in *doa2nya* "the prayers". Repetition of letters appears in a word *aminnnn* "amen" and a discourse particle *yahhh*. A space is inserted between the word *band* and enclitic =*nya* "DEF" but a particle *ya* and the word *allah* "God" are written without a space in between. Also, there is one emoticon :).

If the tweet above is translated into standard, high register Indonesian, it would be as follows.

> @username @username terima kasih, kakak TFB yang paling hit, untuk doa-doanya :) amin, ya Allah, amin . Sukses juga untuk band-nya, ya!

Translated into English: "thank you, the most popular TFB brothers, for the prayers :) amen, o God, amen. Success for the band, too!".

4 Sentiment Analysis Approach

The problem with sentimental information is that it is often vague and mixed. There may be more than one opinion or sentiment in a tweet. For example "I like this product but I do not like the price". To simplify the problem, we assume there is only one major sentiment in any given tweet. This sentiment must be either negative (NEG), positive (POS) or neutral (NEU). With this assumption, we transformed the sentiment analysis task into a single-label text classification problem.

We want to automate the sentiment analysis task as much as possible. To do that we use supervised machine learning approach. First, we prepare labeled tweet data set. Each data entry in the data set is a pair of tweet (textual data) and corresponding label. Next, we transform this data set into a suitable format to train the classifier model. After the model is trained, it can assign label to new tweets automatically.

4.1 Data Collection

From February to March 2016, we collected 900 thousands Indonesian tweets from Twitter Public Streams[5] using Python script and Tweepy package.[6] The script listens to Twitter's public stream and download any tweet with language code equals to 'id'. We also downloaded and processed 1,694 Emoji definitions for normalization as well as 61,374,640 Indonesian tokens from Wikipedia for building word2vec model (Mikolov et al., 2013).

4.2 Data labeling

We decided to add five more labels to categorize the tweets better. In total, we made eight labels (POS for positive, NEG for negative, NEU for neutral, FOR for foreign, RET for retweet, ADV for advertisement, INF for information, and XXX for others) for classifying Indonesian tweets, as shown in Table 3. Because of resource limitations, we chose 4,000 tweets as data and labeled them manually using the eight labels. Tweets written in languages such as English, Standard Malay, regional Malays, regional Indonesian varieties, and regional vernaculars such as Javanese and Sundanese are given FOR label. We only used tweets written in Standard Indonesian and Colloquial Jakarta Indonesian for POS, NEG, and NEU labels. Tweets containing news, tips, and quotations are given INF label. We found difficulties in labeling because of the absence of context, ambiguity, and new slangs.

Out of 4,000 tweets, we got about 25% or 1,005 tweets having sentiments (positive, negative, or neutral). More than half of them (569 tweets) are neutral, the rest of them have positive or negative sentiments with roughly the same number, as shown in Figure 3.

---

[5]https://dev.twitter.com/streaming/public
[6]http://www.tweepy.org/

Label	Type	Example
POS	Positive	*Seger banget ini buat mata...*
		"This is very fresh for eyes..."
NEG	Negative	*Lo gak tau apa-apa tntang gue ! Jadi jangan sok ngatur !!*
		"You know nothing about me! So don't control me!!"
NEU	Neutral	*cara daftar teman ahok gimana ya*
		"how to register for teman ahok?"
RET	Retweet	*RT @username: Menarik nih!*
		"This is interesting!"
INF	Article title	*Tips Merawat Layar Ponsel Xiaomi* https://xxx
		"Tips for Caring for Xiaomi Mobile Phone Screen"
	Date and time	*@username Selasa, 01 Maret 2016 Pukul 12:33 [Indonesia]*
		"Tuesday, 1 March 2016 12:33"
	Quote	*waktu memang bukan dokter yang baik ..., tapi dia adalah guru terbaik ...*
		"time is indeed not a good doctor ..., but it is the best teacher ..."
	Story	*(cont.) duduk di kursi taman ... sambil memegang ponselnya ... (cont.)*
		"sitting on a bench ... holding his phone ..."
FOR	Foreign language	Polisi Yaua Majambazi Watatu....Baada ya Kupekuliwa Walikutwa...
ADV	Advertisement	DELL Desktop C2D 2.66GHz-CPU 3Gb-RAM... https://xxx...
XXX	Others	EEEEEEHEHEHEHE TIRURITUTURURURURUTURURUTUT

Table 3: Eight labels used in labeling tweets and examples of tweets

Label	Type	Number
POS	Positive	221
NEG	Negative	215
NEU	Neutral	569
RET	Retweet	1176
INF	Information	837
FOR	Foreign language	483
ADV	Advertisement	272
XXX	Others	227
Total		4000

Figure 3: Manual tweets labeling with eight labels, their numbers, and percentage

Action	Example	
	Before	**After**
Remove page links	*Suaranya mantep* https://xxx…	*Suaranya mantep*
Remove user names	@username *asek dah :**	*asek dah :**
Add spaces between emoji	*terlalu semangat*☺☺☺	*terlalu semangat* ☺ ☺ ☺

Table 4: Adjustments before tokenization

Action	Pattern	Example	
		Before	**After**
Remove *nya* or *ny*	ABC*nya* → ABC	*doa2nya*	*doa2*
	ABC*ny* → ABC	*ujanny*	*ujan*
Remove reduplication with hyphen (-) or 2	ABC-ABC → ABC	*ular-ular*	*ular*
	ABC2 → ABC	*doa2*	*doa*
Remove reduplicated letters	AABBBCC → ABC	*mannaaaa*	*mana*
Make several groups of same two letters to two groups	ABABABA → ABAB	*hahahahah*	*haha*

Table 5: Normalizing tweets

4.3 Feature Design

Machine learning algorithms do not work directly on textual data. In order to use machine learning algorithm, we have to convert textual data into numerical format. First, we split tweets into tokens and normalize them (replacing informal words, etc.). We then use the word2vec representation to represent tokens. If the token can be found in word2vec model (i.e. we have vector representation for a word), we will use word2vec vector to represent the token. However, if we cannot find the word, we will use a zero vector instead. The input then will be a vector of $n * m$ dimensions where n is the maximum number of words in a tweet and m is the dimension of a word vector. In this system, we assumed that the longest tweet may has up to 72 words and we used a 200 dimensions word2vec model. Therefore the input will be 72 x 200 = 14400 dimensions.

4.4 Normalizer

We used the default word tokenizer from NLTK 3 (Python) and normalized the tweets. In order to get only the tweet, we removed page links which begin with `https` and user names which begin with '@' symbols. We did not remove the topic indicators which begin with '#' symbols because they can be a feature for the supervised machine learning algorithm. Since emojis are important for sentiment analysis, we added spaces between emojis to make them easier to tokenize. Table 4 summarizes these adjustments. Afterwards, we used NLTK (Bird et al., 2009) word tokenizer to tokenize the tweets.

After tokenizing the tweets, we removed the enclitic *nya* "DEF" and its orthographic variant *ny* and made reduplicated words, letters, and syllables into its non-reduplicated counterparts as shown in Table 5. Since there are many informal words and orthographic variants in tweets as mentioned in Section 3, we compiled a list of 376 frequent informal words in tweets and their corresponding formal, standard Indonesian words. Since most informal words are written in their short forms, we also listed down the full forms, in addition to the corresponding formal words, as shown in Table 6. Some informal words, such as *peje* or *pajak jadian*, do not have a corresponding word or compound in formal Indonesian and thus we translated them into many words. In addition, since tweets use various emojis which are essential for sentiment analysis, we made a file which contains a list of emojis and their English equivalents. One emoji may have two or more equivalents, for example ↘ has two equivalents: "arrow lower right" and "south east arrow".

For each tokenized word, we checked whether it is listed in the informal word list. If yes, it is changed to its formal counterpart and tokenized. If it is in emoji list, each word in each English definition of the emoji is translated into Indonesian word(s) using WordNet in NLTK (Bird et al., 2009). If the English word is in Princeton WordNet and has Indonesian translation(s), it is translated into Indonesian. Thus,

128

Informal word	Full form	Standard Indonesian word	Meaning
acc	account	*akun*	"account"
blg	*bilang*	*berkata*	"say"
mager	*malas gerak*	*malas bergerak*	"lazy to move"
peje	*pajak jadian* (lit. "dating tax")	*uang traktir teman saat resmi berpacaran*	"money to treat friends for food after someone is officially in a relationship"

Table 6: Some examples of informal Indonesian words and the corresponding formal words

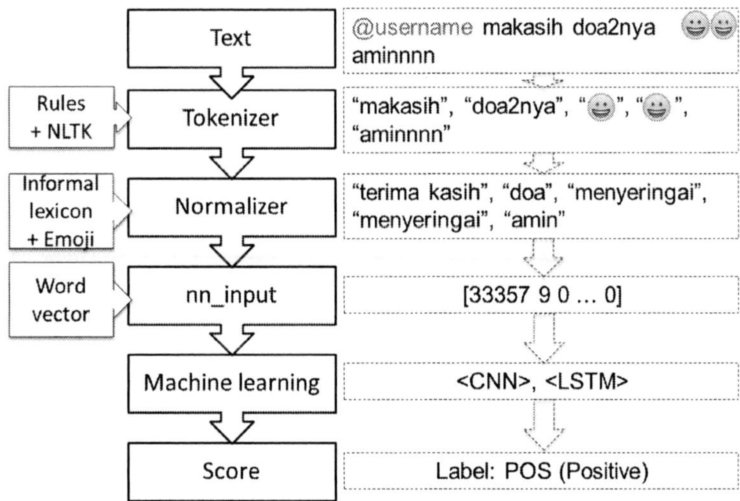

Figure 4: Summary of our system architecture with examples

we get a list of formal Indonesian words from each tweet which is used for the next step.

4.5 Text and word2vec

We downloaded Indonesian Wikipedia data and use Python to convert it into text format. We then use word2vec tool[7] to train the word2vec model. Each word in this model is represented by a vector of 200 dimensions.

4.6 Machine learning

We used Python and Theano package[8] to build the classification model. The input is 72 dimensions × 200 dimensions per word. The output is 8 dimensions (labels). We experimented with two algorithms, i.e. Convolutional Neural Network (CNN) and LSTM.

As the data set that we could prepare was small, we used k-fold cross-validation method with k=10. We split the data set into 10 groups and test the model 10 times. Each time we use one group for testing and the other 9 groups for training. We take the average of the accuracy as the final accuracy for each method.

5 Results and evaluation

Having conducted our sentiment analysis with CNN and LSTM, we obtained the results as shown in Table 7. The best accuracy we got was 73.22% using LSTM without normalizer. We have not conducted LSTM with normalizer, but looking at the results for CNN, it seems that the normalizer we made at

---

[7] https://code.google.com/archive/p/word2vec/
[8] http://deeplearning.net/software/theano/

	Matched	Sentences	Accuracy	STD
CNN without normalizer	3,440	4,920	69.92%	1.87
CNN with normalizer	2,898	4,428	65.45%	2.12
LSTM without normalizer	3,440	4,428	73.22%	1.39

Table 7: Results of sentiment analysis with CNN and LSTM

the present stage does not make the accuracy higher. The reason is perhaps because it covers very few informal words.

5.1 Discussion

We developed a sentiment analysis system and it has good accuracy according to our test set. In our opinion, it has yet to be practical enough for many real-life applications.

However, this system proved to be useful in aiding us to generate labeled data much faster. We noticed that by using the output of the system as the starting point, our annotator can annotate much faster compare to manual labeling. This finding can be helpful for generating data for low resource languages such as Indonesian.

6   Conclusions and future works

We have built a system architecture which includes tokenizer, normalizer, CNN and LSTM. The result is that we obtained 73.2% accuracy with LSTM without normalizer. The model can be used as a baseline to build a more complex state-of-the arts neural networks model in Indonesian. Since the result of the current model is comparable to results in English and Japanese, some known cross-lingual extensions using a multilingual resource are possible future directions of the model. We plan to put more efforts in building a dictionary for informal words because the normalizer contains very few informal words. We believe that this can make the accuracy higher and it is maybe better to perform an error analysis of the normalization rules. We used only emojis in our system, in the future we will use emoticons, too.

In addition, we plan to use Indonesian SentiWordnet Barasa[9] which was built based on SentiWord-Net[10] (Baccianella et al., 2010) and Wordnet Bahasa (Bond et al., 2014). We will focus more on the constructions or sentence structures in Indonesian. Franky et al. (2015) present a few things to note related to the words and sentence structures, such as word sense disambiguation and multi-word expressions. They also list some features for sentiment prediction, such as negation words and question words. In order to do this, we will use an Indonesian POS Tagger (Rashel et al., 2014). In the future, we plan to employ a computational grammar for Indonesian, such as Indonesian Resource Grammar (INDRA) (Moeljadi et al., 2015), to obtain higher accuracy and better results.

Acknowledgements

Thanks to Francis Bond for his support and precious advice.

References

Alexander Adelaar. 2010. Structural Diversity in The Malayic Subgroup. In *The Austronesian languages of Asia and Madagascar*, pages 202–226. Routledge Language Family Series, London and New York.

Paulina Aliandu. 2013. Sentiment analysis on Indonesian tweet. In *The Proceedings of International Conferences of Information, Communication, Technology, and Systems*, pages 203–208.

Hasan Alwi, Soenjono Dardjowidjojo, Hans Lapoliwa, and Anton M. Moeliono. 2014. *Tata Bahasa Baku Bahasa Indonesia*. Balai Pustaka, Jakarta, 3 edition.

---

[9] https://github.com/neocl/barasa
[10] http://sentiwordnet.isti.cnr.it/

Stefano Baccianella, Andrea Esuli, and Fabrizio Sebastiani. 2010. Sentiwordnet 3.0: An enhanced lexical resource for sentiment analysis and opinion mining. In Nicoletta Calzolari (Conference Chair), Khalid Choukri, Bente Maegaard, Joseph Mariani, Jan Odijk, Stelios Piperidis, Mike Rosner, and Daniel Tapias, editors, *Proceedings of the Seventh International Conference on Language Resources and Evaluation (LREC'10)*, Valletta, Malta, may. European Language Resources Association (ELRA).

Steven Bird, Edward Loper, and Ewan Klein. 2009. *Natural Language Processing with Python*. O'Reilly Media Inc.

Francis Bond, Lian Tze Lim, Enya Kong Tang, and Hammam Riza. 2014. The combined wordnet bahasa. *NUSA: Linguistic studies of languages in and around Indonesia*, 57:83–100.

Kathleen M. Carley, Momin Malik, Mike Kowalchuk, Jrgen Pfeffer, and Peter Landwehr. 2015. Twitter usage in Indonesia. Technical report, Institute for Software Research, School of Computer Science, Carnegie Mellon University, Pittsburgh, December.

Franky, Ondřej Bojar, and Kateřina Veselovská. 2015. Resources for Indonesian Sentiment Analysis. In *The Prague Bulletin of Mathematical Linguistics 103*, pages 21–41, Prague. Charles University in Prague, Faculty of Mathematics and Physics, Institute of Formal and Applied Linguistics.

Septina Dian Larasati, Vladislav Kubo, and Daniel Zeman. 2011. Indonesian Morphology Tool (MorphInd): Towards an Indonesian Corpus. *Springer CCIS proceedings of the Workshop on Systems and Frameworks for Computational Morphology*, pages 119–129, August.

M. Paul Lewis. 2009. *Ethnologue: Languages of the World*. SIL International, Dallas, Texas, 16 edition.

Tomas Mikolov, Ilya Sutskever, Kai Chen, Greg S Corrado, and Jeff Dean. 2013. Distributed representations of words and phrases and their compositionality. In C. J. C. Burges, L. Bottou, M. Welling, Z. Ghahramani, and K. Q. Weinberger, editors, *Advances in Neural Information Processing Systems 26*, pages 3111–3119. Curran Associates, Inc.

David Moeljadi, Francis Bond, and Sanghoun Song. 2015. Building an HPSG-based Indonesian Resource Grammar (INDRA). In *Proceedings of the GEAF Workshop, ACL 2015*, pages 9–16.

Scott H. Paauw. 2009. *The Malay contact varieties of Eastern Indonesia: A typological comparison*. PhD dissertation, State University of New York at Buffalo.

Alexander Pak and Patrick Paroubek. 2010. Twitter as a corpus for sentiment analysis and opinion mining. In Nicoletta Calzolari (Conference Chair), Khalid Choukri, Bente Maegaard, Joseph Mariani, Jan Odijk, Stelios Piperidis, Mike Rosner, and Daniel Tapias, editors, *Proceedings of the Seventh International Conference on Language Resources and Evaluation (LREC'10)*, Valletta, Malta, may. European Language Resources Association (ELRA).

Fam Rashel, Andry Luthfi, Arawinda Dinakaramani, and Ruli Manurung. 2014. Building an Indonesian Rule-Based Part-of-Speech Tagger. Kuching.

James Neil Sneddon. 2006. *Colloquial Jakartan Indonesian*. Pacific Linguistics, Canberra.

Alfan Farizki Wicaksono, Clara Vania, Bayu Distiawan, and Mirna Adriani. 2014. Automatically building a corpus for sentiment analysis on Indonesian tweets. In *Proceedings of the 28th Pacific Asia Conference on Language, Information, and Computation*, pages 185–194, Phuket,Thailand, December. Department of Linguistics, Chulalongkorn University.

Author Index